———————)( )(———————

For those who not only dream of a gentle and compassionate world
But make the commitment to realize that dream
This book is dedicated to you…

———————)( )(———————

Acknowledgments

I wish to express my love and gratitude to my dearly departed friend Jean, who first introduced me to vegetarianism many years ago; to my best friends Gretchen, Heather and Angela, whose work for animal rights and welfare continues to inspire me daily; to Kathryn Hill, my social media manager and Gentle Chef Forum administrator on Facebook; to the other Gentle Chef Forum moderators on Facebook: Sandra Pope Hays, Melissa Keller, Nancy Boisselle Stein, Martina Moore and Jason Friedman; and to all of my readers for their continuing support and encouragement.

"The word "veganism" denotes a philosophy and way of living which seeks to exclude - as far as is possible and practical - all forms of exploitation and cruelty to animals for food, clothing or any other purpose; and by extension, promotes the development and use of animal-free alternatives for the benefit of animals, humans and the environment. In dietary terms it denotes the practice of dispensing with all products derived wholly or partly from animals." ...The Vegan Society

Compassion (derived from Latin and meaning: "to suffer together with") is a profound human virtue and emotion prompted by the pain of other living beings and is ranked as one of the greatest virtues in numerous philosophies and spiritual traditions. More vigorous than empathy, the feeling of compassion commonly gives rise to an active desire to alleviate another's suffering.

Sentience implies the ability to experience pleasure and pain. As vegans, we believe that all sentient beings are entitled, at the very least, to the right not to be subjected to unnecessary suffering.

This understanding of sentience and the desire to alleviate suffering is the primary motivator for embracing veganism and a strict plant-based diet.

Also by Skye Michael Conroy

The Gentle Chef Cookbook - *Vegan Cuisine for the Ethical Gourmet*

The Non-Dairy Evolution Cookbook - *A Modernist Culinary Approach to Plant-Based Dairy-Free Foods*

Email: thegentlechef@gmail.com

Website: http://thegentlechef.com

Table of Contents

Gravies, Sauces and Glazes

Foreword

Many people who embrace a plant-based diet do so for ethical reasons and not because they dislike the flavor and texture of meat. But finding satisfying meat alternatives is not always easy for individuals who once enjoyed the flavors and textures associated with meat-based dishes, or for individuals who grew up with meat-based dishes as a traditional part of their family or ethnic heritage.

This cookbook focuses on approximating the appearance, flavors and textures of meat and meat products that many of us grew up with: foods that are familiar and represent tradition and foods that evoke a feeling of nostalgia.

My work may venture too closely into the realms of realism for some people's taste. I understand that. But people thrive on familiarity and if that familiarity can be satisfied, then there is a greater chance of success in maintaining a plant-based diet. Seitan (seasoned and cooked gluten) and other meat analogues are virtually unknown to most non-vegan Westerners, so name and appearance associations are very helpful in tempting people to try these new foods. I truly believe that most people are not looking for something entirely new; they're simply looking for the familiar done differently...and compassionately.

Personally, I have no desire to ever eat real meat again - because it was never about the meat itself; it was the various textures and flavors that I enjoyed. Meat analogues provide the satisfaction of eating something I can sink my teeth into; of hearty foods that fill me up and stick to my ribs, and foods that remind of holiday traditions, and cookouts and camping trips with friends and family in the summertime.

You won't find nutrition information included with the recipes because the cookbook wasn't written for individuals monitoring calorie and nutrient intake. However, the recipes were created using wholesome ingredients as much as possible and refined ingredients were included only when absolutely necessary to achieve proper textures.

Keep in mind too, that in order to win people over to plant-based cuisine, I'm aiming for the best flavors and textures and not always the healthiest options. I'm a chef and I love preparing rich, comforting and satisfying meals. However, I do enjoy the health benefits of a well-balanced plant-based diet, and I encourage breaking the reliance on commercially prepared and heavily processed foods as much as possible. Detailed instructions are included in the cookbook for preparing many of the components of my recipes with unprocessed, wholesome ingredients. My philosophy is: "everything in moderation". Even plant-based foods can be unhealthy and fattening if not consumed sensibly.

Regarding food allergies and sensitivities: I have none; and since this cookbook is based upon my personal experience with plant-based cuisine, I rely heavily on gluten and soy as the foundation for most of my recipes. A few of the recipes are gluten-free or soy-free by nature, but that was not the intent when creating them. If you have sensitivity to either gluten or soy, this cookbook isn't for you and I recommend doing some research for cookbooks and websites that specifically benefit individuals with food sensitivities.

My recipes are not the only way to produce these foods, nor are they necessarily the easiest or the best way. They're simply my way based upon what satisfies me. Creating superior quality meat analogues is a complex art and there is no doubt that I have many discoveries to make in the future. The recipes will continue to evolve as I continue to learn. I invite you to join me on my journey of discovery...

Introduction to Meat Analogues

Meat analogues, also called meatless meats and mock meats, are generally understood within the vegan context to mean 100% plant-based foods that mimic or approximate certain aesthetic qualities, such as texture, flavor and appearance, of specific types of meat. This differs from meat substitutes or meat alternatives. For example, a grilled piece of tofu can serve as a substitute or alternative to meat, but when it's used as ingredient and transformed in some way to replicate the texture of chicken, it becomes a meat analogue.

Many modern commercial meat analogues are made from textured wheat protein from gluten and isolated soy protein and these products closely approximate the texture of real meat. Plant proteins, in general, can be textured to mimic the properties of real meat (chicken, beef, pork or seafood) using different factory processes such as spinning, jet-cooking, steam treatment and extrusion cooking. Among these processes, extrusion has been the preferred technology.

Textured wheat protein is produced using twin-screw extrusion technology using a mix of wheat gluten and other processing additives to yield products that differ in size, shape and color. Other technologies include blasting soy and pea proteins through an alternating cascade of high heat and high pressure in a stainless steel machine in order to create a meat analogue which simulates the texture of chicken.

Yuba and textured vegetable/soy protein (TVP/TSP) are soy-based meat analogues. Yuba is made by layering the thin skin of protein which forms on top of boiled soy milk. Textured vegetable/soy protein, a by-product of soybean oil production, is a processed protein. The soy protein is extracted, extruded (a manufacturing process that causes a change in the structure of the soy protein) and then dried into various shapes and sizes. This results in a fibrous material that is similar in texture to meat when rehydrated.

However, for many people, including myself, commercial meat analogues are often not satisfying, whether due to inaccurate flavor, appearance and/or texture; the inclusion of too many refined and processed ingredients; or simply lack of availability. Commercially prepared meat analogues can be expensive too and are not an affordable means of maintaining a well-balanced and nutritious plant-based diet on a day-to-day basis.

This cookbook is an expansion of my early work with meat analogues in the Gentle Chef Cookbook. With these recipes we will explore new and different ways to approximate the texture, flavor and appearance of a wide variety of meats and meat-based products at home using wholesome plant-based ingredients and without the need for expensive factory equipment. There's also something inherently magical about preparing foods from scratch with your own two hands and knowing the quality of ingredients that goes into them.

Some home cooks may think that preparing meat analogues is too complex and may feel intimidated by the process, but this concern is unfounded as long as one can follow a recipe. While having some plant-based cooking experience is helpful, I've put a lot of forethought into writing the recipes in order for even the novice cook to achieve success.

If you are a former meat and seafood aficionado, please keep in mind that we can only approximate the aesthetic qualities of meat and seafood with plant-based ingredients and home kitchen equipment. If you curb your expectation of creating exact reproductions, then these recipes should sufficiently satisfy your desire for meat-like appearances, textures and flavors.

Seitan and Beyond

Seitan (pronounced "say-tan"), or wheat meat, is an amazingly versatile, protein-rich meat analogue made from wheat gluten. The word seitan is of Japanese origin and was coined in 1961 by George Ohsawa, a Japanese advocate of the macrobiotic diet. Gluten (from the Latin gluten, meaning "glue") is a protein complex that appears in foods processed from wheat and related species, including barley and rye. Wheat gluten is not a complete protein in itself (lysine is the missing amino acid) which means that additional ingredients must be added to complete its amino acid profile (tamari, nutritional yeast or bean flour, for example). Lysine can also easily be obtained by consuming other plant protein sources in the daily diet.

Unfortunately, some individuals cannot benefit from the nutrition and versatility of seitan due to gluten sensitivity or total intolerance (Celiac disease), and must obtain their protein from vegetables, legumes and gluten-free grain sources such as quinoa, amaranth or buckwheat (which is actually not a grain but a seed).

Vital wheat gluten (often labeled as "vital wheat gluten flour") is not the same as high gluten wheat flour. High gluten wheat flour is typically used in baking to give breads a chewy texture. It also contains a large proportion of starch, unlike isolated vital wheat gluten. Ironically, high gluten wheat flour is used in the traditional method of preparing seitan. In this rather labor-intensive method, the wheat dough is continually kneaded and rinsed in water to wash away the soluble starch, thus yielding a stringy mass of gluten.

Vital wheat gluten must be high-quality in order to develop the proper texture for meat analogues. Be sure the packaging is labeled at a minimum of 75% protein. Bargain and bulk gluten may be of lesser quality and/or it may contain a significant amount of starch. Vital wheat gluten can be found in health food stores, and many supermarkets now carry it as well. It can also be purchased through the internet. Bob's Red Mill™ produces high-quality vital wheat gluten and this is what I use for all of my meat analogues containing gluten.

While some of the meat analogues in this cookbook are entirely gluten-based, some are entirely tofu-based and some are made from textured vegetable/soy protein. Many others are prepared by combining gluten with tofu or textured vegetable/soy protein. While combining gluten and tofu together to create a meat analogue is not a new concept, the proportion of ingredients, seasonings and cooking methods are what make these meat analogues so unique.

Cooking methods vary depending upon the type of plant protein being used and the desired finished texture, flavor and appearance of the meat analogue. Each method was carefully determined to create the best texture, flavor and finished appearance.

Preparing meat analogues at home is an art and science unto itself, much like the art and science of baking. Whether the recipe calls for a teaspoon (tsp), a tablespoon (T) or a cup (and fractions thereof), always use level measurements.

Since volume measurements for dry ingredients can sometimes be unreliable, I have included metric weight measurements for primary recipe ingredients such as vital wheat gluten and tofu. Volume measurements for water used to prepare the meat analogues include both standard U.S. measurements and metric. And please, no "eye-balling" volume measurements - that may work for some cooking techniques but it doesn't work when preparing meat analogues.

The recipes provided in this cookbook were formulated to produce appetizing results, and have been tested many times in my own kitchen; therefore, experimenting with dry ingredient to liquid ingredient ratios is not recommended, as this can upset moisture balance and change textures significantly enough to negatively affect the finished product. While adjusting or substituting seasonings to suit your taste is to be expected, avoid substituting primary functional ingredients or adding large amounts of unspecified extra ingredients, as this can also upset moisture balance or change flavors and textures significantly enough to negatively affect results. In other words, be creative and have fun but don't make too many changes and then wonder why something didn't turn out properly.

Depending upon the desired texture of the finished product, kneading is utilized in varying degrees to develop the gluten and create meat-like textures. Gluten strands form as the glutenin and gliadin molecules cross-link to create a sub-microscopic network. Kneading promotes this formation.

Meat analogues combining gluten and tofu require vigorous kneading for several minutes in order to sufficiently develop the gluten strands in the dough. This development is essential for producing the best texture in the finished product. However, vigorous hand-kneading requires stamina and with this particular combination of proteins, it's actually not the most efficient method for accomplishing this task. For ease, expediency and efficiency, dough containing both gluten and tofu can be placed into a food processor fitted with a dough blade, or a stand mixer fitted with a paddle attachment, and then processed. Work smart and not hard and let these versatile kitchen appliances do the work for you.

Dough Blade for Food Processor

Stand Mixer with Paddle Attachment

Cooking Methods for Meat Analogues

Wheat gluten is not digestible in its raw state, therefore it must be cooked. For seitan, the traditional method is to simmer it in a seasoned broth. A very gentle simmer is essential when cooking seitan using this method alone. This means that the cooking pot needs to be monitored closely and the heat regulated to maintain the gentle simmer. Rapid simmering or boiling will produce a brainy, spongy texture and no amount of pan frying will save your finished product. Merely poaching in hot broth without simmering will produce a tough, rubbery texture, as not enough liquid will be absorbed.

Through a great deal of experimentation with cooking techniques using gluten, and blends of gluten and tofu, I discovered that better meat-like textures could be produced in some of the meat analogues by utilizing a combination cooking method that includes both baking and simmering. When using this combination method, prebaking sets the texture of the dough and simmering completes the cooking process. Prebaking also regulates the amount of liquid the dough will absorb, creating dense meaty textures while preventing spongy finished textures. While I still recommend a gentle (but active) simmer when using the combination cooking method, the temperature of the simmering broth is not as critical since prebaking has already set the texture of the dough. However, merely poaching in hot broth should be avoided, since not enough liquid will be absorbed to complete the cooking process.

Meat analogues containing gluten will expand up to twice their size through absorption of the broth during simmering, therefore, the broth should be generously seasoned to enhance the flavor of the finished product. If the broth has little flavor, it will "leach" the seasonings from the dough.

Fresh homemade broths are always best and are recommended since the complex flavor of the broth is infused into the meat analogue as it simmers. They are also more wholesome since they don't contain ingredients such as corn syrup solids, maltodextrin, or hydrolyzed corn or soy proteins, which are commonly found in commercial vegetarian broth cubes and bouillon paste. And nothing quite compares to the comforting aroma of a homemade broth filling the kitchen. The recipes for these broths can be found in their appropriate chapter for the specific meat analogue being prepared. They're not difficult to make but they do involve some chopping of vegetables and about an hour of cooking time. I realize that busy schedules and time constraints don't always allow the home cook to prepare every component of a recipe from scratch, so quick options are also provided for preparing the simmering broths.

An important point I'd like to mention is the quality of water used for preparing meat analogues and simmering broths, or in any recipe for that matter. Avoid unfiltered tap water if at all possible, since tap water is full of impurities. Faucet mounted filters (PUR™, for example) are a godsend for ensuring clean water. They're also economical and kinder to the environment than disposable plastic water containers.

Baking is used exclusively for some meat analogues and typically involves rolling or wrapping the dough in aluminum foil before placing in the oven. This not only creates and holds the shape but seals in moisture. It's very important that you use heavy-duty aluminum foil when baking (except for the individual hand-rolled sausages). Regular foil can easily rupture from expansion of the dough as it cooks (especially with gluten and tofu blends), and from steam pressure which builds up inside the foil. Always err on using too much foil rather than not enough and when in doubt, rewrap with an additional sheet of foil.

Please note that oven temperatures recommended in the recipes were determined using a conventional home oven (radiant heat). If you have a convection oven (fan-assisted), reduce the recommended temperature by 25°F or 10°C. All baking times should remain the same.

Steam cooking is used for the individual hand-rolled sausages and a few other meat and seafood analogues. You will need a large pot with a lid and a steamer insert for this method. The seasoned dough is either wrapped or rolled in aluminum foil before being steamed.

Heavy-duty aluminum foil is recommended for most steaming applications but pop-up aluminum foil is recommended for wrapping the sausages. Pop-up foil is commonly used in the restaurant industry for wrapping baked potatoes. It's very convenient because cutting foil to create wrappers is not required. While pop-up foil is not available in all supermarkets, it is commonly used in hair salons for hair coloring and can be found in beauty supply stores. It can also be purchased online. Pop-up foil is very thin and flimsy, so double wrapping the sausages is required so they do not burst open while steaming.

If you don't have pop-up foil, standard or heavy-duty aluminum foil can be used for the individual sausages; however, the foil will need to be cut with scissors to create the wrappers. Further information is provided in the introduction to the individual hand-rolled sausages.

Some individuals may express concern about their food coming into contact with aluminum foil. Theories abound that aluminum ingestion is linked to some degenerative diseases, such as Alzheimer's disease, but I've never come across scientific documented evidence that aluminum particles or ions actually transfer to the food from aluminum foil while cooking. However, if there is a concern or you have any doubt, there is a simple solution: cut a piece of parchment paper to line the foil before rolling or wrapping. This will keep the dough from coming into contact with the aluminum foil.

All meat analogues containing gluten, and combinations of gluten and soy, benefit from refrigeration after preparation and before finishing and serving. Chilling changes the structure of the cooked gluten in a beneficial way, which in turn enhances the texture of the meat analogue. So don't rush or omit this step. Meat analogues simply require a little pre-planning, so prepare them a minimum of 8 hours before you plan to finish and serve. Meat analogues and simmering broths should be cooled to near room temperature before refrigerating.

For meat analogues that have been simmered in broth, include about ¼ cup of the broth in the food storage container or bag before refrigerating as this will keep the product moist. Products containing gluten/soy blends can be refrigerated in this manner for up to 1 week, and up to 10 days for strictly gluten-based analogues.

All meat analogues containing gluten or a combination of soy and gluten can be frozen for up to 3 months and then thawed and reheated or finished at your convenience. Simmering broths can be frozen for up to 3 months. Simmered meat analogues should be frozen without the broth.

Most prepared meat analogues benefit from finishing in some manner before serving. This can include pan-searing, pan-glazing, sautéing, frying, broiling, pan-grilling, or outdoor grilling. For pan-searing, pan-glazing, sautéing and pan-grilling, use a non-stick skillet or grill pan, or a well-seasoned cast iron skillet, since meat analogues are notorious for sticking to stainless steel (even with cooking oil present).

For outdoor grilling, season the grill grating with cooking oil to discourage sticking. Brush meat analogues with cooking oil before placing under the broiler or on the grill. This applies even if the meat analogue was marinated or a sauce is being used. There is very little fat content in meat analogues, other than the trivial amount of oil that was added during preparation, and plant fat (oil) is what will keep the "meats" tender, juicy and flavorful.

Special Ingredients and Cooking Terms

Some ingredients and cooking terms in this cookbook may be very familiar while others may not be familiar at all. Before attempting the recipes, it's helpful to familiarize yourself with these terms and recipe ingredients and understand what they are and why they are being used. Some recipe ingredients can be prepared at home.

All-purpose flour simply refers to common white flour. All-purpose flour is made from a blend of high-gluten hard wheat and low-gluten soft wheat. It differs from whole wheat flour in that the bran and germ have been removed from the wheat kernel (berry) prior to grinding into flour. Unbleached all-purpose flour undergoes less processing than bleached all-purpose flour (which is usually bleached chemically) and is thus a better choice. Unbleached flour bleaches naturally as it ages.

Beet powder is used in a few meat analogues in this cookbook to provide the red color that would typically be produced by curing meats with nitrites and nitrates. *Betanin* is the pigment which imparts the intense reddish purple color. However, this pigment degrades completely when exposed to high cooking temperatures for extended periods (at least this has been my experience with preparing meat analogues); therefore, it is added to meat analogues after preparation is complete. It's not readily available in most markets but can be found in a few specialty food stores or purchased through the internet. Organic beet powder is also available commercially. Beet powder is notorious for forming hard "rocks" in its storage container and these rocks don't dissolve easily in water. So crush the "rocks" into powder before measuring and stirring into the water or brine. If you don't have beet powder in your pantry, the bright red liquid from fresh cooked or canned beets (not pickled) can be used, but you'll have to experiment with producing the correct color intensity.

Block tofu, extra-firm water-packed, is made from soymilk that has been coagulated and pressed into soft white blocks. It is of Chinese origin, and is also a part of East Asian and Southeast Asian cuisine such as Chinese, Japanese, Korean, Indonesian, Vietnamese, and others. Tofu is considered a staple in plant-based diets, because of its high protein content, low content of calories and fat, high calcium and iron content and the ability to substitute for meat and eggs in a variety of recipes.

Calcium sulfate (gypsum) is the traditional and most widely used coagulant to produce water-packed block tofu. The resulting tofu curd is tender yet firm in texture and the coagulant itself has no perceivable taste. Use of this coagulant also produces a tofu that is rich in calcium. The coagulant and soymilk are mixed together in large vats, allowed to curdle and the resulting curds are drained, pressed into blocks and then packaged.

Extra-firm water-packed block tofu is sold in plastic tub containers completely immersed in water to maintain its moisture content and it will always be found in the refrigerated section of the market. It ranges in density and texture from soft to extra-firm. For the purpose of meat analogue production in this cookbook, only extra-firm water-packed block tofu is used. Extra-firm silken tofu (which is usually sold in unrefrigerated aseptic cartons) has a delicate, custard-like texture and is only used in the seafood analogue recipes in this cookbook as a binder. It is essential to know the difference, as the type of tofu used will definitely affect the recipe results. See pg. 24 for details and instructions on preparing tofu for the recipes.

Before using extra-firm block tofu in the meat analogue recipes in this cookbook, it will need to be pressed to remove as much water as possible. This can be done using the standard method of pressing between absorbent lint-free towels, such as paper towels, or by pressing using a tofu press. The tofu press is a spring-loaded device which effectively presses water from a U.S. standard-size block of commercial water-packed tofu, with the added advantage of maintaining its block shape. The press creates a very dense and meaty texture and this works especially well when using the intact tofu itself as a meat alternative (in other words, without combining with gluten).

Browning liquid is used to create a rich brown color in soups, stews and gravies. In meat analogues, especially those approximating beef, it is used as a color enhancer to produce a more appetizing appearance. My own recipe for natural browning liquid made with organic sugar can be found on pg. 26. Commercial versions such as Gravy Master™ and Kitchen Bouquet™ can be found in most markets where jar gravy is located.

Cooking oil refers to vegetable/plant oils that can withstand high heat. The best oils for high temperature cooking are safflower, sunflower, canola, peanut, and soybean. Olive oil is excellent for medium heat sautéing.

Emulsion refers to a mixture of two or more liquids that are normally immiscible (non-mixable or un-blendable) and emulsifying or emulsification refers to the process in which two or more liquids which are normally immiscible are blended together to create an emulsion. During this process, larger fat globules are broken down into smaller, evenly distributed particles.

Garbanzo bean flour (also known as chickpea flour, besan flour, ceci flour or gram flour) is a gluten-free flour produced by grinding dried garbanzo beans. It is very affordable and can be found in most health food stores or natural markets. Bob's Red Mill™ produces high-quality garbanzo bean flour. Soy flour, fava bean flour or yellow pea flour can be substituted, if more convenient. Garbanzo bean flour can easily be prepared at home by grinding dry garbanzo beans in a high-powered blender and then sifting to remove any stray larger particles.

Glucomannan, also known as konjac root powder, is the special ingredient used in this cookbook to make Shirataki Scallops and Mock Lobster. Glucomannan is a pure soluble fiber derived from konjac root. It has no protein, no fat, no carbohydrates, and is gluten-free. As a food additive, it is used as an emulsifier and thickener. As a food ingredient, it is used commercially and at home for preparing Japanese shirataki noodles. Commercial shirataki noodles have a distinct "fishy" odor and those who have opened a package will be familiar with this odor. However, the aroma of freshly prepared konjac has a much milder seafood-like aroma. Glucomannan can sometimes be found in health food stores (where it is often sold as a diet aid) but can definitely be purchased through the internet (e.g., Amazon.com).

Jackfruit (*Artocarpus heterophyllus*), is a species of tree in the mulberry family. It is native to parts of South and Southeast Asia, and is believed to have originated in the southwestern rain forests of India. The jackfruit is the largest tree-borne fruit, reaching as much as 80 pounds.

Unripe or green jackfruit is useful in plant-based cooking as a meat alternative due to its stringy, meat-like texture. In this cookbook, it is used specifically as a substitute for shredded lump crabmeat and fish. It has a very faint fruity aroma and not much flavor of its own. The aroma is imperceptible in prepared dishes. Green jackfruit can be found in Indian and Asian markets or through the internet. Look for the label "Green Jackfruit" or "Young Green Jackfruit" and be sure that it's packed in water or brine, not syrup. You may notice cans of ripe jackfruit stocked nearby but don't be tempted to substitute as it is very sweet when ripe and packed in sugar syrup. Green jackfruit, unlike its ripe version, needs to be cooked before being consumed.

Liquid smoke is a water-based seasoning distilled from real wood smoke and is used in meat analogues to provide a "cold-smoked" flavor. Personally, I don't feel it quite captures the intensity of actual cold-smoking, so I tend to use it in generous amounts. Some people are sensitive to smoke flavors, or don't care for smoke flavors at all, so it can be reduced or replaced with equal amounts of water as desired, although this will significantly alter the intended flavor of the meat analogue or finished dish.

"Hickory" liquid smoke and "mesquite" liquid smoke are the most commonly available smoke flavors, but other wood flavors are available if you do a little searching. For most recipes, the "hickory" flavor is recommended and the "mesquite" flavor reserved for Southwestern/Tex-Mex and South American cuisine. Liquid smoke can found in most major grocery stores, usually alongside other condiments and marinades. It can also be purchased through the internet. If you enjoy true smoked foods, as I do, and you have a cold-smoker at home, the meat analogues can be briefly smoked to add that much desired smoke intensity.

Mild vegetable oil, as referenced in this cookbook, refers to any plant oil with a mild taste such as safflower, sunflower, grapeseed, canola or soybean oil. This should not be confused with commercial labeling, in which "vegetable oil" usually refers only to soybean oil. Olive oil, although refined and milder in flavor than virgin olive oil, is not as mild in flavor as these other oils. The best mild vegetable oils for high temperature cooking are safflower, sunflower, canola, peanut, and soy.

Mirin is an essential condiment used in Japanese cuisine and is an ingredient in a few of the sauces and marinades in this cookbook. It is a type of rice wine similar to sake, but with a lower alcohol content and higher sugar content.

Mise en place (pronounced *meez-ahn-plahs*) is an important culinary technique and one of the most often ignored. Mise en place is a French term (literally translated as "put in place") and refers to assembly and preparation of all ingredients and tools before cooking begins. This means that all ingredients should be cleaned, peeled, chopped or measured beforehand. Many people prepare and cook at the same time and this is a bad habit that often leads to mistakes and failures. Practice mise en place consistently and your cooking experience will be both a pleasure and success.

Miso paste is a seasoning which originated in Japan and is produced by the fermentation of soybeans (or chickpeas or barley) with salt and the fungus "kōjikin" (*aspergillis oryzae*). Miso adds umami (a Japanese word used to describe a pleasant savory flavor) to foods. Both mellow white miso paste and red miso paste (which has a stronger "bite") are used as a seasoning in many of the meat analogues in this cookbook.

Miso paste can be found in natural food markets and health food stores in the refrigerator section. It has a very long refrigerator shelf life, usually about 2 years. If you're new to miso, be aware that mellow white miso paste is actually beige or light brown in color and not actually white.

Non-stick cookware is mentioned frequently in this cookbook, so I felt it was worth mentioning here. I prefer and recommend the newer "Green" non-stick cookware over the older Teflon™ cookware. Green non-stick cookware uses ceramic-based nanotechnology to create a non-stick surface that is said to be resistant to flaking and more stable upon exposure to high heat than older non-stick technology such as Teflon™. Green cookware is safer too because it's made without perfluorooctanoic acid, known as PFOA, the potentially toxic chemical used in the manufacture of Teflon™ non-stick pans. Teflon™ appears to be inert and safe unless it's heated to high temperatures. Then it emits fumes toxic enough to poison pet birds (birds are more sensitive to these fumes than humans and other mammals). Teflon™ also flakes after continued heavy use, with the flakes often ending up in the food.

While stainless steel cookware is the safest and most durable for most cooking applications, meat analogues (due to the nature of the protein and their lack of fat) tend to stick while pan-searing or sautéing unless substantial amounts of oil are used. With "Green" non-stick cookware, a light misting of cooking oil is all that is required for pan-searing and sautéing. A well-seasoned cast iron skillet is the next best option for cooking foods with a tendency to stick if non-stick cookware is not being used.

Nutritional yeast flakes are used in this cookbook as a flavoring and coloring ingredient for preparing simmering broths, sauces, condiments and a few meat analogues. Nutritional yeast is a non-active form of yeast and a source of complete protein and vitamins, especially the B-complex vitamins. Some brands of nutritional yeast flakes are fortified with vitamin B12. The vitamin B12 is produced separately and then added to the yeast. It is naturally low in fat and sodium and is free of sugar and dairy. Nutritional yeast flakes can be found in most health and natural food stores or online through food retail websites such as Amazon.com. Bob's Red Mill™ produces superior quality, vitamin-fortified nutritional yeast flakes with a rich golden color. The conversion ratio for nutritional yeast flakes to powder is 2:1. In other words, if a recipe calls for 2 tablespoons nutritional yeast flakes, use 1 tablespoon nutritional yeast powder. Do not confuse nutritional yeast with brewer's yeast.

Olive oil is labeled by different names indicating the degree of processing the oil has undergone, as well as the quality of the oil itself. Extra-virgin olive oil is the highest grade available, followed by virgin olive oil. The word "virgin" indicates that the olives have been pressed to extract the oil; no heat or chemicals have been used during the extraction process, and the oil is pure and unrefined. Save the expensive extra-virgin and virgin oils for dressings and vinaigrettes, dipping crusty bread or drizzling over bruschetta, since they do not perform well in moderate to high heat applications such as sautéing and frying. The flavor of the virgin oils can also be too strong for many dishes. Pure olive oil, on the other hand, is more refined and filtered. It has a delicate, mild flavor that is suitable for most cooking applications and has a higher smoke point (410° F) than virgin or extra-virgin oils, which makes it ideal for sautéing over medium heat.

Store olive oil in its original container in a cool, dark place. If refrigerated, olive oil will return to its original liquid state when warmed to room temperature. Refrigeration does not harm most grades of olive oil, but it is not recommended. Pure olive oil should smell mild and have a delicate flavor; virgin olive oils should have a fresh, grassy aroma and flavor. If the oil smells acrid or tastes bitter, it has turned rancid and should be discarded.

Organic is a term used to describe agricultural farming practices as well as food production, although the "organic" standard is defined differently in different regions. In general, organic farming integrates biological and mechanical practices that encourages cycling of resources, promotes ecological balance, and conserves biodiversity in crop production. Synthetic pesticides and chemical fertilizers are generally not allowed, although non-synthetic and organically approved pesticides may be used under limited conditions.

In general, organic foods are not processed using irradiation, industrial solvents, or chemical food additives. Currently, the European Union, the United States, Canada, Japan and many other countries require producers to obtain special certification based on government-defined standards in order to market food as organic within their borders. If non-organic ingredients are present, at least a certain percentage of the food's total ingredients must be organic (95% in the United States, Canada, and Australia).

Organic sugar is made from organic sugar cane and should not be confused with refined white sugar. The juice is pressed from organic raw sugar cane, evaporated and then crushed into crystals. In adherence with strict Organic Standards, the fields are green cut and not burned or treated with herbicides or synthetic fertilizers. No chemicals or animal by-products are used to decolorize the sugar. This makes it very different from refined white sugar, which has typically been decolorized by filtering through animal bone char. Organic sugar is my sweetener of choice for cooking because of its availability, cost and neutral flavor. Organic powdered sugar can be made from organic sugar. Organic light and dark brown sugar can also be made from organic sugar, with the inclusion of organic blackstrap molasses. Recipes for both light and dark brown sugar can be found in this cookbook.

Parchment paper, also known as bakery release paper, is a cellulose-based paper that is used in baking as a disposable non-stick surface. In this cookbook, it is used as an alternate to a silicone baking mat for lining baking sheets and pans when baking meat analogues. It can also be used as an option for wrapping meat analogues prior to wrapping in aluminum foil when contact with aluminum foil is undesirable. To do so, wrap the meat analogue first with the paper and then follow the directions for wrapping with the foil prior to steaming or baking.

Porcini mushroom powder is used to add umami (a complex savory flavor) to beaf. It's also an instant way to add an incredible depth of earthy flavor to soups, stews, gravies and sauces. It can found in many specialty and gourmet food markets; through the internet; or it can easily be prepared by grinding dried porcini mushrooms in a dry blender, spice grinder or coffee grinder. If you absolutely cannot access porcini mushroom powder for the beaf recipes, substitute with an equal amount of garbanzo bean flour, although some of the umami flavor will be sacrificed. Please note that porcini mushroom powder has a very concentrated pungent aroma which may not be pleasing to some noses; however, only the umami flavor, and not the mushroom aroma, will be perceptible in the finished meat analogues.

Poultry seasoning is a blend of aromatic herbs and spices which is commonly used, as the name implies, for seasoning poultry. For our purpose it used as a flavoring ingredient in chikun and turky and their respective simmering broths. It can also be used to season stuffing or dressing, broths, soups, stews, gravies and sauces. Obviously, the term "poultry" is not used or acceptable in the ethical plant-based diet but the seasoning blend itself is traditional and available commercially under this name. It typically does not and should not contain any animal products. Poultry seasoning can easily be prepared at home using my own seasoning blend called "Aromatica" (pg. 34).

Raw apple cider vinegar is vinegar produced from organic and unpasteurized apple cider. The "mother" is made up of the yeasts and fermentation by-products that are produced when the cider ferments to vinegar. These by-products settle as sediment at the bottom of the bottle, therefore the bottle should be shaken before use. Most commercial companies pasteurize their vinegar and filter out this sediment. I prefer it in recipes because I feel it has a more complex flavor than filtered apple cider vinegar; however, if you don't have any in your pantry, the common and more economical filtered version can be substituted.

Rice flour is an inexpensive, gluten-free, starchy flour with a subtle flavor. It can be used as an alternative to all-purpose flour for preparing roux and for dredging purposes when frying.

Roux (pronounced "roo") is a primary thickening agent for soups, gravies, sauces and stews with origins dating back more than 300 years in French cuisine. A roux is made by cooking equal parts of all-purpose flour and plant fat (mild olive; non-dairy butter or margarine; or a mixture of the two) until the raw flour flavor is eliminated and the mixture has achieved the desired color. When a dark roux is desired, non-dairy butter or margarine is recommended since it browns better than oil when heated.

Precooking the flour allows the starch granules to swell and absorb moisture from added liquids without the flour clumping or forming lumps. A well-prepared roux promotes silky smoothness and a nutty flavor as it thickens hot liquids. When cooked to a golden or brown stage, a roux takes on a rich, toasted flavor and adds color to the dish (non-dairy butter or margarine is better for creating a dark roux).

A roux forms the foundation of soups, sauces, gravies and stews, whereas a slurry (a mixture of pure starch and water) can be added later if necessary for additional thickening (you wouldn't want to add an uncooked roux later because of the raw flour flavor).

A roux is also more stable in heated liquids than a slurry (it doesn't break down and lose its thickening power as quickly) because it contains more solids than pure starch. Appearance is a factor too, as a roux remains opaque in heated liquids, while a slurry produces a glossy appearance, which is undesirable in many dishes such as gravies and stews.

When preparing soups and stews, vegetables are often cooked in the hot oil before the flour is added, or more accurately sprinkled over the cooked vegetables. This is a French culinary technique called singer (pronounced sin-jay), which means to "lightly coat, dust or sprinkle with flour". After the flour is cooked with the oil and vegetables to remove the raw flour flavor, the liquids in the recipe are incorporated in increments while stirring to prevent clumping of the flour.

Shelf life refers to the length of time that a food may be stored without becoming unfit for consumption. However, shelf life alone is not an accurate indicator of how long a food can safely be stored. Many foods can remain fresh for several days past their recommended shelf life if stored and refrigerated properly. In contrast, if these foods have already been contaminated with harmful bacteria, the guideline becomes irrelevant. Shelf life also depends on the degradation mechanism of a specific food. Most foods can be influenced by several factors such as acid and salt content; exposure to light, heat and moisture; transmission of gases; and contamination by micro-organisms.

The general guideline for refrigerator shelf life of any prepared food that does not contain preservatives, heavy salt content or vinegar is 7 to 10 days.

A **silicone baking mat** is a non-stick, flexible baking sheet produced by several manufacturers (i.e., Silpat™ and Silchef™). It's made of silicone with a reinforced glass weave and is effective at temperatures ranging from -40°F to 480°F. It does not require greasing and provide even heat transfer. As such, it can be used as an alternate to parchment paper for lining the metal baking sheet when baking meat analogues. It can be found in gourmet shops, department store kitchenware sections or purchased online.

Silken tofu, extra-firm is a variety of tofu commonly used in plant-based cooking to produce sauces, thick creams and custard-like textures. It's also used in combination with other ingredients to replicate eggs in a variety of egg-free dishes. It has a smooth and very delicate texture compared to the firmer water-packed block tofu. In this cookbook, extra-firm silken tofu is used in a few of the seafood analogue recipes where it's blended with starch to act as a binder.

Magnesium chloride and calcium chloride are the coagulants (called nigari in Japan) used to make silken tofu. These coagulants are added to soymilk and the mixture is then sealed in 12.3 oz. aseptic cartons. In other words, the resulting bean curd is produced inside its own package, rather than being drained and pressed into blocks. Silken tofu packaged in this manner needs no refrigeration until the carton is opened. This gives it an extended shelf life, compared to fresh water-packed tofu sold in tub containers. However, silken tofu can now often be found in tub containers in the refrigerated section next to the water-packed block tofu. This can be somewhat confusing if you're new to tofu, so it's important to read labels and be aware of what you're purchasing.

Whenever my recipes call for extra-firm silken tofu, I'm referring specifically to the product packaged in 12.3 oz. aseptic cartons (such as Mori-Nu™). If you purchase extra-firm silken tofu in a refrigerated tub container, you will have to weigh the tofu before using in the recipe.

A **slurry** is a mixture of starch (usually cornstarch, unmodified potato starch or arrowroot) and cold water which is whisked together until smooth and then added to soups, sauces and gravies as a thickener. If a dry starch is added directly to a hot liquid, the starch granules cannot disperse easily and lumps will form. Once mixed with water, the slurry can be added directly to the hot liquid. The liquid must be brought up to a simmer each time to ensure the starch reaches its full thickening potential before more is added. Stir in a little at a time until you reach the desired consistency. A roux (see "Roux") is the primary base thickener for a soup, sauce or gravy, while a slurry can be added later if additional thickening in required.

A **stainless steel cooling rack** is a flat rack made from an open mesh network of closely arranged stainless steel wires set on short legs to raise it above surface level. While it's typically used for cooling baked goods, it is used in this cookbook for lining baking sheets prior to baking some of the meat analogues. The raised surface provides air circulation so the meat analogue doesn't excessively brown from contact with the hot baking surface and the rack is lined with parchment paper or a silicone baking mat to prevent sticking. It's important that the rack have thick, strong wires so it won't sag in the center.

Cooling racks can be round, square or rectangular and can range from small to large; however, for the purpose of this cookbook, the cooling rack should be rectangular and should fit inside a standard-size baking sheet.

T is the abbreviation for "tablespoon" and "tsp" is the abbreviation for "teaspoon".

Tamari, soy sauce or Bragg Liquid Aminos™ are liquid seasonings made from soybeans. Tamari and soy sauce can also include wheat. Reduced-sodium tamari and soy sauce is available for those wishing to lower their sodium intake. Although soy sauce (also known as *shoyu*) and tamari are both made from fermented soybeans, Japanese tamari has a smoother, more complex and well-balanced flavor compared to soy sauce (which is sharper due to the difference in raw materials and a stronger alcoholic fermentation).

Bragg Liquid Aminos™ are made from non-GMO soybeans and purified water. This product can be used as a replacement for tamari and soy sauce and contains 16 amino acids, including the nine essential amino acids. Bragg Liquid Aminos™ have not been fermented or heated and are alcohol and gluten-free. The packaging label states that the product has only a small amount of naturally occurring sodium, but I find it to be just as salty tasting as tamari and soy sauce, so use it in the same measurements as you would tamari or soy sauce.

Tempeh is a cultured food made by the controlled fermentation of cooked soybeans with the fungus *Rhizopus oligosporus* (aka tempeh "starter"). This fermentation binds the soybeans into a compact white cake. Tempeh is not related to TVP/TSP or tofu at all, other than the fact that all three are produced from soybeans. Tempeh has been a favorite food and staple source of protein in Indonesia for several hundred years. Although I don't use it much in my personal cooking, I've included it in this glossary because some may find it useful as a meat replacement, since it has a firm texture and a nutty mushroom flavor.

Typically, tempeh is sliced or cut into cubes and fried until the surface is crisp and golden brown. To mellow the flavor and make it better able to absorb marinades, cut the tempeh block in half and then simmer in water for about 10 minutes. Drain, blot dry and then slice or cube and place in the marinade. Chill for a minimum of one hour and even better overnight before frying.

It can also be crumbled or grated and used as a unique alternative to ground seitan and TVP/TSP in recipes such as Sloppy Joes, tacos, burritos or chili. Tempeh can also be used as an ingredient in soups, spreads, salads and sandwiches. Tempeh is now commonly available in many supermarkets, as well as in Asian markets and health food stores.

tsp is the abbreviation for "teaspoon" and "T" is the abbreviation for "tablespoon".

TVP (textured vegetable protein) and TSP (textured soy protein) are two terms, often interchangeably used, to describe a commercially produced soy-based meat analogue. This processed protein is actually a by-product of soybean oil production. The soy protein is extracted, extruded (a manufacturing process that causes a change in the structure of the soy protein) and then dried into various shapes and sizes. This results in a fibrous material that is similar in texture to meat when rehydrated. This process is done using factory equipment and is not something that can be produced in a home kitchen. TVP/TSP cooks quickly, contains no fat and has a protein content equal to that of meat. It is a very economical and versatile source of protein for the plant-based diet.

Many TVP/TSP producers use hexane (a chemical solvent) to separate soy fat from soy protein. Although the FDA claims that hexane is safe to use in the processing of soy proteins, there is very little available data on how much of the chemical residue remains after processing and what the possible long-term effects of consumption may be. It has been argued that TVP/TSP has been safely used in the food industry for decades, primarily as a meat extender in restaurants, prison kitchens and school cafeterias.

If you are concerned about the possibility of trace amounts of hexane in TVP/TSP and/or the use of genetically modified soybeans in its production, there is a solution to this concern: Organic TSP. Organic TSP is made from water-extracted, defatted soy flour (produced from organic, non-GMO soybeans) that is cooked, extruded and then dried. It contains no possible trace of hexane because hexane is not used in the extraction process. However, be aware that organic TSP may cost more. TVP can be found in natural food stores, some larger supermarket chains and online (e.g., Amazon.com). Organic TSP may be a bit more difficult to locate but can be found in some natural food stores or purchased online.

Unmodified potato starch is one of the less familiar starches used as a food thickener. It can be used in equal amounts as an alternate to cornstarch or arrowroot powder (personally, I prefer it over cornstarch or arrowroot). Do not confuse unmodified potato starch with potato flour, which is actually ground dehydrated potatoes and avoid modified potato starch (which has been physically, enzymatically, or chemically treated in such a manner that changes its properties). Bob's Red Mill™ produces high-quality and inexpensive unmodified potato starch.

Vital wheat gluten is the natural protein found in wheat. Vital wheat gluten is used in plant-based cooking to produce meat analogues. In baking, a small amount is often added to yeast bread recipes to improve the texture and elasticity of the dough.

In commercial vital wheat gluten production, a mixture of wheat flour and water is kneaded vigorously by machinery until the gluten forms into a mass. Approximately 65% of the water in the wet gluten is removed by means of a screw press; the remainder is sprayed through an atomizer nozzle into a drying chamber, where it remains at an elevated temperature a short time to evaporate the water without denaturing the gluten. The process yields a flour-like powder with a 7% moisture content, which is air cooled and transported to a receiving container. In the final step, the collected gluten is sifted and milled to produce a uniform product.

When preparing meat analogues, vital wheat gluten must be high-quality in order to develop the proper elasticity in the dough. Be sure it is labeled at a minimum of 75% protein. Bargain and bulk gluten is generally of lesser quality and may contain a significant amount of starch. Excess starch will yield a bread-like texture in the finished product.

Vital wheat gluten can be measured by volume, by scooping up the gluten with a measuring cup and leveling off the top with a table knife; or measured by weight (which is more accurate).

Wakame is a sea vegetable, or edible seaweed. It has a subtly sweet flavor and sturdy texture that holds up well in cooking and is my favored ingredient for creating a seafood flavor in seafood analogues.

Chef's tip: Store spices in a cool, dark place, not above your stove. Humidity, light and heat will cause herbs and spices to lose their flavor.

Preparing Tofu for the Recipes

Extra-firm water-packed tofu is used in many of the meat analogue recipes in this cookbook and can be found in the refrigerated section of the market. Do not confuse this with extra-firm silken tofu, such as Mori-Nu™; which is typically packaged in unrefrigerated aseptic cartons as it won't work for these applications (extra-firm silken tofu is however used in a few seafood analogue recipes).

Before using in the recipes, the extra-firm tofu will need to be pressed to remove as much water as possible. This is very important for success of the recipe. It may seem redundant to press the water from the tofu, only to add water back when preparing the dough. However, the reason for this is very simple: Water content in tofu varies from brand to brand and even from block to block. By removing the liquid from the tofu and then adding back a precise amount of water, the texture of the finished meat analogue remains consistent.

In the United States, extra-firm water-packed tofu is typically sold in standard blocks weighing about 14 ounces (397 grams) after draining the water in the carton but before pressing (packaging weight may differ in other countries). After thorough pressing, a standard block of tofu will generally yield about 10 to 12 ounces (280 to 340 grams).

Depending upon the recipe, pressed tofu will be used in one of three weight increments: 10 ounces/280 grams (about 1 block); 5 ounces/140 grams (about one-half block); or 2.5 ounces/70 grams (about one-quarter block). Minor weight variations slightly above these recommended amounts are acceptable and will not negatively affect the recipe results. Be sure to weigh the tofu after pressing. A precision digital ounce/gram scale is recommended for accuracy.

Pressing can be done ahead of time using a tofu press (allow about 12 hours of pressing time); or the tofu can be wrapped in several layers of paper towels or a lint-free kitchen towel and pressed on a flat surface using the palms of your hands assisted by your upper body weight. The advantage of using a tofu press first, is that it will remove a substantial amount water, which then saves on paper towel usage.

Even when using a tofu press, a small amount of water may still remain, so firmly blot the pressed tofu with towel(s) to ensure that any remaining water is removed. When pressed sufficiently, the tofu should feel barely damp and have a crumbly texture. Some stores now offer pre-pressed extra-firm block tofu. To reiterate, whether home-pressed or commercially pre-pressed, the tofu should feel barely damp and crumble easily.

If pressed ahead of time, keep the pressed tofu refrigerated in an airtight container for up to 3 days until ready to use.

Chef's tip: For expediency, use the tofu press for about an hour to remove the excess water and then finish pressing between a few layers of paper towels.

Recipe Essentials and Incidentals

Worcestershire Sauce

This is my signature plant-based version of the classic condiment. It's an essential ingredient for preparing beaf and beaf simmering broth and was placed into this chapter for that reason. Traditional commercial Worcestershire sauce contains anchovy paste and is not suitable for those adhering to a plant-based diet. There are a few brands of vegan Worcestershire Sauce on the market, and they are good, but they're not readily available to everyone. This recipe yields about 1 and ¼ cup. I use this condiment so frequently that I always double the recipe.

Ingredients

- 1 and ½ cup raw apple cider vinegar
- ½ cup dark balsamic vinegar
- ½ cup tamari, soy sauce or Bragg Liquid Aminos™
- 3 T dark brown sugar
- 1 medium onion, chopped
- 3 cloves garlic, crushed
- 1 piece ginger root (about 1 and ½ inch), peeled and sliced
- 1 tsp lemon zest, loosely packed
- 1 tsp orange zest, loosely packed
- 1 tsp liquid smoke
- 1 tsp whole cloves
- 1 tsp whole black peppercorns
- 1 tsp prepared Dijon mustard or ½ tsp whole mustard seeds
- 1 bay leaf

Preparation

Place all of the ingredients in a medium saucepan and bring to a boil over medium-high heat. Reduce the heat to a rapid simmer and cook until the sauce is reduced by half volume, about 30 to 40 minutes.

Let cool and then press and strain through a fine mesh sieve or a double layer of cheesecloth into a jar with a lid. Store the sauce in the refrigerator for up to 3 months.

———————————×( )×———————————

Browning Liquid

For purists like myself who prefer to make their own recipe components, I've developed what is to my knowledge the first and only browning liquid made with organic sugar. Browning liquid is useful for adding a rich brown color to meat analogues, sauces, gravies, soups and stews.

This browning liquid has no added caramel color, nor does it have the sweet undertaste of commercial browning liquids. As a general rule for soups, gravies and stews use 1 teaspoon per 4 cups of liquid. This recipe yields about ⅓ cup browning liquid. Gravy Master™ is a suitable commercial alternative to homemade browning liquid.

Warning: This recipe produces copious amounts of smoke. Do not attempt to prepare unless you have an overhead exhaust fan for your stove that vents outside!

Ingredients

- ¼ cup very hot water
- 2 T tamari, soy sauce or Bragg Liquid Aminos™
- 1 T dark balsamic vinegar
- ½ cup organic sugar

Preparation

In a small measuring cup, mix the very hot water, tamari and vinegar; set aside.

In a small saucepan, place the dry sugar over medium-low heat. The goal is to melt the dry sugar and bring it to a darkly caramelized stage (essentially burnt). Swirl or gently shake the saucepan back and forth occasionally as the sugar begins to melt but do not stir. Melting will take several minutes. Be sure to run an overhead stove exhaust fan as the sugar will produce smoke as it begins to burn.

As the sugar continues to melt and darken, it will begin to rise in the saucepan. At this point, begin stirring gently with a wire whisk. When the sugar reaches a very dark brown color, reduce the heat to low. Now, while whisking vigorously, add the broth mixture a little at a time to the melted sugar. The mixture will foam and sizzle, so don't be alarmed. Very hot steam will also be released, so try to keep your hands back as you stir with the whisk to avoid steam burns.

Continue to stir until the mixture is smooth and then remove the saucepan from the heat to cool. Once cooled, the browning liquid will have a syrupy consistency. The concentrated liquid will have a rather bitter, burnt flavor; however, when used in small amounts as recommended, it will add a beautiful brown color and enhance the flavor of your favorite recipes. Store the mixture in an airtight jar in your pantry; refrigeration is not necessary. Replace the mixture after 4 months.

Better Butter

Better Butter is a superior tasting, palm oil-free alternative to dairy butter and commercial dairy and non-dairy margarine. This recipe produces a buttery spread that looks like, tastes like and melts like dairy butter or margarine and can be used in any recipe, including baking, as you would dairy butter or margarine. Better Butter will brown and burn when exposed to high heat and therefore should not be used for high-heat sautéing; it works best with low to medium heat.

The best kitchen appliance for emulsifying the ingredients is an immersion blender. A food processor will also work. The ingredients can also be emulsified using a standard or high-speed blender; however, retrieving the thick spread from around the blades can be difficult. This recipe yields about 2 cups.

Ingredients

- 1 cup organic refined coconut oil (NOT virgin coconut oil)
- ⅓ cup mild vegetable oil
- ⅔ cup organic plain unsweetened soymilk or homemade almond milk
- 4 tsp/20 ml liquid soy lecithin or liquid sunflower lecithin*;
  or 24 grams soy or sunflower lecithin powder (about 2 T plus 2 tsp);
  or 24 grams soy or sunflower lecithin granules ground into a fine powder
- 1 tsp organic sugar
- ½ tsp lactic acid powder (or 1 tsp raw apple cider vinegar and 1 tsp fresh lemon juice)
- ¼ tsp to 1 tsp fine sea salt or kosher salt, according to taste
- 1 tsp nutritional yeast flakes
- ½ tsp guar gum, sodium alginate or xanthan gum

*Sunflower lecithin can be substituted for the soy lecithin for those who prefer a soy-free butter. However, sunflower lecithin lacks the rich golden hue of soy lecithin, so expect a color variation.

Soy lecithin powder, lactic acid powder, and guar gum, sodium alginate and xanthan gum are available from ModernistPantry.com

Preparation

You will need a 2-cup minimum food storage container with a lid to store the butter. If you prefer, the butter can be shaped in a flexible silicone form, or divided into several forms, and released after hardening.

Remove the lid from the coconut oil and place the jar or bottle into a microwave. Heat until melted (about 30 seconds to 1 minute depending upon the solidity of the coconut oil); avoid overheating the oil. Alternately, place the jar or bottle into a container filled with near boiling water and let stand until the oil melts.

Pour 1 cup of the coconut oil into a 2-cup measuring cup or other suitable container with a pouring "lip". Add ⅓ cup vegetable oil to the coconut oil and set aside.

Immersion Blender Method

Add the remaining ingredients to a 4-cup glass measuring cup or heavy glass/ceramic bowl. Insert the immersion blender and process the mixture for about 15 seconds. With the immersion blender running on high speed, begin slowly pouring the mixed oils into the blending cup or bowl. Move the blender up and down and side to side as you add the oils. Continue blending until the mixture is emulsified and thick. Transfer to a sealable container.

If soymilk was used as a base, cover the container and refrigerate until solid (if using one or several silicone molds, cover with plastic wrap). The butter can also be stored in the freezer for to 3 months. To release the butter from a form, simply wiggle the sides a bit to loosen and then press out onto a plate.

If almond milk was used as a base, cover and freeze until solid (if using one or several silicone molds, cover with plastic wrap). Once frozen, place the butter in the refrigerator until thawed before using; or it can be stored in the freezer for up to 3 months. To release the butter from a form, simply wiggle the sides a bit to loosen and then press out onto a plate.

Food Processor Method

Add the remaining ingredients to the processor and turn on the processor. Now begin to slowly pour the mixed oils into the mixture through the food chute. Continue to process until the mixture is emulsified and thick. Transfer to a sealable container.

If soymilk was used as a base, cover the container and refrigerate until solid (if using one or several silicone molds, cover with plastic wrap). The butter can also be stored in the freezer for to 3 months. To release the butter from a form, simply wiggle the sides a bit to loosen and then press out onto a plate.

If almond milk was used as a base, cover and freeze until solid (if using one or several silicone molds, cover with plastic wrap). Once frozen, place the butter in the refrigerator until thawed before using; or it can be stored in the freezer for up to 3 months. To release the butter from a form, simply wiggle the sides a bit to loosen and then press out onto a plate.

Seasoned Butter

Seasoned Butter is a blend of homemade Better Butter and specially selected herbs and spices. It's wonderful for sautéing and adding a flavorful crust to pan-seared meat analogues. It's also excellent for topping potatoes, corn on the cob, cooked grains and cooked vegetables.

Ingredients

- ½ cup Better Butter, softened to room temperature
- 1 T fresh lemon juice
- 1 tsp Worcestershire Sauce (pg. 25) or commercial vegan equivalent
- ½ tsp onion powder
- ½ tsp garlic powder
- ¼ tsp coarse ground black pepper
- ¼ tsp sweet paprika
- ¼ tsp fine sea salt or kosher salt
- 2 tsp minced fresh herbs of your choice (optional)

Preparation

Mash all ingredients together in a bowl. Refrigerate in a covered container until ready to use.

Black Garlic Truffle Butter

Black garlic is a slow-roasted and fermented form of garlic. It possesses a unique combination of molasses-like sweetness and tangy garlic undertones with a tender, creamy texture similar to soft dried fruit. Truffle oil has deep, earthy, mushroom undertones. This rich butter is superb for pan-browning beaf. It's also superb as a spread for crackers or toasted bread. Try topping with non-dairy parmesan for a uniquely different garlic bread; or drizzle the melted butter over freshly popped popcorn, sprinkle with sea salt and toss well. Black garlic and truffle oil can be found in gourmet and specialty food markets or purchased online.

Ingredients

- ½ cup non-dairy butter, softened to room temperature
- 1 head black garlic, peeled and mashed
- 1 tsp black or white truffle oil
- sea salt or kosher salt, to taste (optional)

Preparation

With a fork, mash the ingredients together in a small bowl. Cover and refrigerate until ready to use.

Honee Butter

Melted honee butter is superb for basting meat analogues when grilling to keep them moist and tender; or try brushing a little melted honee butter over fried chikun. Also serve on toast, warm rolls, scones, corn bread, waffles, pancakes, etc.

Ingredients

- ½ cup Better Butter, near room temp; works best when still slightly chilled
- 3 T organic raw agave syrup
- 1 T real maple syrup

Preparation

Whip the ingredients with an electric beater until fluffy. Transfer to a sealable container and chill to re-firm until ready to use.

Soy Cream

Soy cream works beautifully when preparing cooked sauces for meat analogues, as it will not cause delicate sauces to over-thicken. It has a silky smooth texture with no discernible grit and is very quick and easy to prepare. Soy cream has a refrigerator shelf life of up to 10 days. Cashew milk can be used as an alternate to soy cream for cooked sauces since it has natural thickening properties when heated.

Ingredients

- 1 and ½ cup organic plain unsweetened soymilk, room temperature
- ½ cup organic refined coconut oil (NOT virgin coconut oil)
- 1 tsp organic sugar or other natural sweetener (optional)
- ¼ tsp fine sea salt or kosher salt

Preparation

The soymilk must be at room temperature to emulsify properly with the coconut oil. If necessary, gently warm the milk in a saucepan over low heat or briefly in the microwave. If cold soymilk is used, the coconut oil will congeal when it comes into contact with the cold liquid and disrupt the emulsification process.

Remove the lid from the coconut oil and place the jar or bottle into a microwave. Heat until melted (about 30 seconds to 1 minute depending upon the solidity of the coconut oil); avoid overheating the oil. Alternately, place the jar or bottle into a container filled with near boiling water and let stand until the oil melts. Measure the coconut oil and set aside.

Pour the milk into a blender, put the cover in place but remove the center insert. Begin blending on low speed, gradually increasing to high speed (if the milk is splashing too much in the blender jar, reduce the speed slightly). Pour the coconut oil slowly into the milk through the opening in the blender jar's lid. Continue to process for 10 seconds after the oil has been incorporated to ensure homogenization.

Transfer the cream to a sealable container and refrigerate until well-chilled. The cream will thicken to the proper texture upon refrigeration. Shake well before using and consume within 10 days.

Cashew Milk

Cashew milk thickens naturally when heated and is included here because it works well as a dairy cream substitute and alternate to Soy Cream when preparing delicate cooked sauces for meat analogues (cashew cream is more concentrated and can quickly over thicken delicate cooked sauces; therefore, cashew cream works best in cold applications or in cooking applications where a significant amount of thickening is desirable). This recipe yields about 1 quart of cashew milk. Cashew milk has a refrigerator shelf life of up to 5 days.

Ingredients

- 1 cup (5 oz. by weight) whole raw cashews
- 3 and ½ cups water
- ¼ tsp fine sea salt or kosher salt

You will also need a blender and a nylon nut milk bag to strain the fine solids from the milk. A strainer lined with 4-layers of cheesecloth and a large spoon can be used in place of the nut milk bag.

Preparation

Rinse the cashews to remove any dust or debris, drain thoroughly and place them in a high-powered blender. Pre-soaking of the cashews is not required. Add the salt and process the contents on high speed for 2 full minutes.

The milk will now need to be strained to remove the solids. To do this, wash your hands thoroughly and then pour the milk into the nut milk bag over a large container.

While holding the top of the bag with one hand, gently knead the bag to help the milk pass through the ultra-fine mesh - but don't force the milk through.

Optionally, the milk can be poured (in increments) into a strainer lined with 4-layers of cheesecloth placed over a large container. Stir the milk gently with a spoon to help it pass through the layers of cheesecloth.

Cashews break down significantly when processed into milk, so there won't be much solid residue remaining in the nut milk bag or strainer (compared to soymilk or almond milk, which leaves a great deal of solid residue). Discard or compost the cashew solids.

For drinking purposes, sweeten the milk to taste if desired. Transfer to a sealable container and refrigerate. Shake well before using.

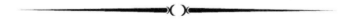

Quick Buttermilk

This quick and easy-to-make buttermilk has a tangy, refreshing flavor. Soymilk is essential for this formula since it thickens in the presence of lactic acid, which adds body to the buttermilk. It's excellent for breading and battering chikun for frying, or for any baking purpose. It's superb for salad dressings and dips too. This recipe yields 2 cups of buttermilk.

Ingredients

- 2 cups organic plain unsweetened soymilk
- 1 tsp lactic acid powder
  (available from ModernistPantry.com; sorry, no substitutes for lactic acid in this recipe)
- ¼ tsp fine sea salt or kosher salt

Preparation

Add the ingredients to a sealable container. Shake well and refrigerate until chilled before using. Quick buttermilk has a shelf life of up to 2 weeks.

Garbanzo Bean Flour

Garbanzo bean flour (also known as chickpea flour, besan flour, gram flour, chana flour or cici flour) is used a great deal in my recipes. However, if you have a difficult time finding it locally, a cost effective option is to grind your own. This can be done simply with a high-powered blender. Dry garbanzo beans are readily available in most supermarkets, usually in the aisle where dried beans and peas are found. If they're not there, check the aisle where Mexican and other ethnic foods are located. One pound of dried beans (about 2 cups) will yield one pound of ground flour. DO NOT use canned garbanzo beans!

Preparation

To grind your own flour, work in one cup batches. Add a cup of dried beans to a dry, high-powered blender, cover and process until finely powdered. Place a fine mesh sieve over a large bowl, add the flour and shake gently to sift the flour through the fine mesh. Discard any remaining particles in the sieve. Transfer the flour to a sealable container and repeat the process with the remaining dried beans.

Old-Fashioned Brown Sugar (Organic)

Homemade brown sugar is very easy to make. It has a warmer color and richer flavor compared to its commercially-processed counterpart.

Ingredients

- 1 cup organic cane sugar
- ¼ cup organic unsulfured molasses
  (for dark brown sugar)
  or 1 T organic unsulfured molasses
  (for light brown sugar)

Preparation

Place the organic sugar in a food processor with a standard chopping blade. Begin processing and drizzle the molasses into the food processor through the food chute. Continue processing until evenly combined. Store the brown sugar in an airtight container at room temperature.

Instant Chikun Bouillon Powder

This convenient instant powder can be used to prepare a comforting and savory chikun bouillon by the cup or the quart (bouillon is the French word for "broth"). Instant Chikun Bouillon Powder is also a convenient, nutritious and delicious alternative to chicken broth for vegan and vegetarian hospital patients restricted to a liquid diet.

Ingredients

- 1 cup nutritional yeast flakes
- 5 T fine sea salt or kosher salt
- ¼ cup onion powder
- 3 T organic sugar
- 1 T poultry seasoning
- 1 T garlic powder
- 1 T dried celery flakes
- 1 T dehydrated carrot flakes (optional)
- 2 tsp dried parsley flakes
- ½ tsp ground white pepper

Preparation

Process the ingredients in a dry blender until finely powdered; store in an airtight container for up to 6 months.

For a soothing mug of golden chikun broth, dissolve 1 level teaspoon bouillon powder, or more to taste, in 8 ounces of piping hot water. Stir well. A fine seasoning sediment will settle on the bottom of the mug, so stir occasionally while sipping or simply discard the sediment after consuming.

To prepare an instant chikun broth for soups and stews, use 1 level teaspoon of bouillon powder for each cup of simmering water, or more or less to taste. For chikun simmering broth, add 4 tablespoons (¼ cup) bouillon powder to 3 quarts (12 cups) simmering water. Add additional herbs and spices as desired to accommodate specific regional cuisines and season the prepared broth with salt to taste.

To clarify large quantities of broth, let the prepared broth cool to room temperature and pour into a sealable container, discarding any seasoning sediment that has settled on the bottom of the cooking pot. Refrigerate overnight, or for up to 10 days, which will allow any micro-fine seasoning sediment to further settle on the bottom of the container. Decant the clear portion of broth and use in recipes as needed.

Seasoning Blends

Aromatica

(aka Poultry Seasoning)

This highly aromatic blend of dried herbs and spices is my own homemade equivalent of commercial poultry seasoning. Use it for seasoning chikun and turky, stuffing, dressings, broths, soups, stews, gravies and sauces.

Ingredients

- 2 T dry rubbed sage
- 2 T dried thyme leaves
- 2 T dried marjoram leaves
- 2 T dried rosemary leaves or 1 tsp ground rosemary
- 1 tsp celery seed
- 1 tsp ground white pepper
- ¼ tsp ground nutmeg

Preparation

Process the dried herbs and spices in a spice grinder or dry blender until finely powdered; store in an airtight container for up to 6 months.

Garam Masala

(Indian Spice Blend)

Ingredients

- 2 T ground coriander
- 2 T ground turmeric
- 1 T ground cardamom (if you cannot find cardamom, substitute with ground ginger)
- 2 tsp ground cinnamon
- 2 tsp ground cloves
- 2 tsp ground nutmeg
- 1 tsp coarse ground black pepper

Preparation

Mix the spices together in a bowl. Store the mixture in an airtight container for up to 6 months.

Berber Spice Blend

This aromatic and peppery blend of traditional Berber spices is commonly used in Ethiopian cooking and is ideal for seasoning chikun prior to grilling.

Ingredients

- 3 T sweet paprika
- 1 T garlic powder
- 1 T ground ginger
- 1 T onion powder
- 1 T sea salt or kosher salt
- 1 and ½ tsp ground cayenne pepper
- 1 and ½ tsp ground cumin
- 1 and ½ tsp coarse ground black pepper
- 1 and ½ tsp ground fenugreek
- ¾ tsp ground cardamom
- ½ tsp ground cloves

Preparation

Mix the ingredients together and store in an airtight container for up to 6 months. For prepared chikun drumsticks or drummettes, rub the chikun with cooking oil and then generously rub with the mixture prior to grilling.

Montreal Seasoning

This flavorful blend is wonderful for seasoning beaf and portabella mushroom steaks before grilling. Try it for seasoning russet potato or sweet potato wedge fries too.

Ingredients

- ¼ cup coarse sea salt or kosher salt
- 2 T black peppercorns or mixed peppercorns
- 2 T dried minced or flaked onion
- 1 T dried rosemary leaves or ½ tsp ground rosemary
- 2 tsp garlic powder
- 2 tsp whole fennel seeds
- 2 tsp dried thyme leaves
- 1 tsp dried bell pepper powder
- 1 tsp smoked paprika
- ½ tsp ground dried orange peel

Preparation

Process all ingredients in a spice grinder or dry blender until finely ground; store in an airtight container for up to 6 months.

Jamaican Jerk Spice

Jerk is a style of cooking native to Jamaica in which chicken or pork is dry-rubbed or wet marinated with a very hot spice mixture called Jamaican jerk spice. For our purposes, it is used as a fiery seasoning for chikun and porq.

Ingredients

- 2 T onion powder
- 1 T dried thyme
- 1 T ground allspice
- 1 T sea salt or kosher salt
- 1 T organic sugar
- 2 tsp coarse ground black pepper
- 2 tsp cayenne pepper
- 2 tsp garlic powder
- ½ tsp grated nutmeg
- ½ tsp ground cinnamon

Preparation

Combine the ingredients in a bowl. Store the mixture in an airtight container for up to 6 months until ready to use.

For shredded Jamaican Jerk Chikun or Porq, rub the dough with 2 to 3 teaspoons of the mixture prior to baking.

For prepared chikun drumsticks or drummettes, rub the chikun with cooking oil and then generously rub with the mixture prior to grilling.

Cajun Dry Rub

Cajun dry rub is a spicy hot seasoning inspired by the cuisine of Louisiana. Use it as a spicy rub for chikun and porq.

Ingredients

- 3 T coarse sea salt or kosher salt
- 3 T sweet paprika
- 1 T onion powder
- 1 T garlic powder
- 1 T dried thyme leaves
- 1 T dried oregano leaves
- 2 tsp coarse ground black pepper
- 2 tsp cayenne pepper
- 1 bay leaf, crumbled

Preparation

Process the ingredients in a dry blender until the bay leaf is completely powdered. Store the mixture in an airtight container for up to 6 months until ready to use. For shredded Cajun Chikun or Porq, rub the dough with 2 to 3 teaspoons of the mixture prior to baking. For prepared chikun drumsticks, drummettes or porq chops, rub the meat with cooking oil and then generously rub with the mixture prior to grilling.

Basic Seitan

Traditional Seitan

Traditional seitan is particularly advantageous for those who don't have access to commercial vital wheat gluten. It is prepared by rinsing and kneading bread dough in water to remove the starch, leaving behind the protein portion of the wheat (gluten). As the starch is washed away, the gluten forms long, stringy strands. These protein strands create a meat-like texture in the finished seitan.

However, this method of preparation requires a substantial amount of wheat flour and is a bit time consuming and labor intensive. The seitan is also limited in applications, since you can't make specialty products such as sausages, roasts, meatballs, bacun, etc. Also, pre-seasoning the gluten doesn't work, since the seasoning is washed away during the rinsing process. Flavoring depends upon simmering the gluten dough in a heavily seasoned broth or marinating the simmered seitan before pan-frying or sautéing and serving.

White bread flour is recommended for preparing traditional seitan, since it is higher in gluten than standard all-purpose wheat flour and will yield more seitan. Don't bother using whole grain wheat flour since the bran will be washed away with the starch during the rinsing process (seitan is a protein food by nature and is not intended to be a source of fiber). Technique is crucial to success with the traditional preparation, so follow the directions carefully.

For optimum texture, traditional seitan requires refrigeration after simmering for a minimum of 8 hours before finishing and serving. This recipe yields about 1 lb.

Dough Ingredients

- 8 cups white wheat bread flour or all-purpose flour
- 3 and ¼ cups water

Simmering Broth

- 2 quarts (8 cups) seasoned vegetable broth

Preparation

Place the bread flour into a very large mixing bowl and create a "well" in the center. Begin slowly pouring the water into the well, a little at a time, while using a fork to incorporate the flour into the water. Now use your fingers to mix the dough until it comes together into a mass.

Begin kneading the dough in the bowl using the heel of your hand. If the dough feels too sticky, add a little more flour; if too dry, add a little more water. Keep kneading for a few minutes until the dough feels smooth and elastic.

Let the dough (and your arm) rest for 5 minutes and then knead again, about 50 strokes. Kneading is essential as it develops the gluten strands.

Form the dough into a ball. Place the bowl into the sink and fill with lukewarm water until the dough is submerged; let the dough rest in the water for 30 minutes.

During the last 10 minutes of soaking time, prepare the simmering broth in a large cooking pot, cover with a lid and place over high heat while you continue with the next step (if the broth comes to a full boil while rinsing the dough, simply reduce the heat until you are ready to add the gluten to the broth).

Begin kneading the dough in the bowl. Knead until the water is opaque and milky. Empty the bowl and refill with lukewarm water. Repeat kneading, emptying and refilling the bowl. The mass of dough will diminish in size as the starch is rinsed away. This process takes time, so be patient.

As the starch continues to be rinsed away, the mass of dough will feel like it's falling apart. This is normal and will change as the gluten strands develop.

After continued kneading and rinsing, the dough will develop long, stringy strands of gluten. This is exactly what you want. Keep kneading the strands until the water becomes a pale, translucent milky color - but not totally clear.

Here's where experience comes into play as you will need to make sure that enough starch is rinsed away, and at the same time you will want to retain enough starch so that the seitan is tender after simmering.

The dough should have a moderate degree of stretch before tearing but not fall apart in your hands. Smell the water; if it smells excessively starchy, rinse a bit more.

Drain the bowl and squeeze the ball of gluten firmly in your hands to remove excess water. Place the dough on a work surface, and with a sharp knife, slice the dough into cutlets or bite-sized nuggets. Gently lower the pieces of dough into the boiling broth. Immediately reduce the heat to a gentle, lazy simmer, and set a timer for 30 minutes.

Leave the cooking pot uncovered. The first ten minutes of simmering is the most crucial, as this is when the texture is set. Watch the pot and continue to adjust the heat by increments up or down as necessary to maintain a gentle simmer. If you catch the broth rapidly simmering, simply reduce the heat slightly. Turn the seitan pieces occasionally as they simmer.

When finished cooking remove the pot from the heat, cover and let the seitan cool in the broth. Transfer the seitan to a food storage bag or airtight container and refrigerate for a minimum of 8 hours, or for up to 10 days, before finishing. Chilling is very important in order to firm and enhance the texture. For extra flavor, store the seitan in a favorite marinade. Seitan can also be frozen for up to 3 months. Transfer the broth to a sealable container and refrigerate. During this time, any seasoning sediment will settle on the bottom of the container. Simply decant the clear portion for use in other recipes. The broth can be refrigerated for up to 10 days or frozen for future use at your convenience. Be sure to add back a little water as necessary before using, since the broth will have become concentrated from evaporation during simmering.

After simmering and chilling, seitan is completely cooked and edible but not very appetizing "as is". Therefore, the flavor and texture will benefit from pan-browning before serving. To do this, add a small amount of cooking oil to a non-stick skillet and place over medium heat. Sauté the seitan until the exterior is lightly crisp and golden brown. Serve with your favorite sauce or gravy if desired. For more flavor, seitan can be marinated, or tossed with an herb and spice blend before browning. Thin strips of seitan are well-suited for stir-frying and nuggets of seitan are well-suited for breading and quick deep-frying. Pan-browned seitan can also be diced, cubed or sliced into strips and added to soups and stews.

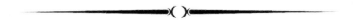

Quick Seitan

Quick seitan is a protein-rich and versatile meat-alternative that is quickly and easily prepared using concentrated vital wheat gluten, as opposed to the labor-intensive preparation of traditional seitan, which is made from rinsing the starch from bread flour. Quick seitan is cooked using the traditional simmer method and this is particularly advantageous during the hot summer months when using the oven is undesirable; however, it will not produce the remarkable meat-like textures that can be created from the beaf, chickun and porq recipes in this cookbook. For optimum results, classic seitan requires refrigeration after simmering for a minimum of 8 hours before finishing and serving. This recipe yields about 1 lb.

Dry Ingredients

- 1 cup (150 g) vital wheat gluten
- 2 T garbanzo bean flour or soy flour
- 1 T onion powder
- 1 and ½ tsp garlic powder
- ¼ tsp ground white pepper

Liquid Ingredients

- ⅔ cup (160 ml) water
- 2 T tamari, soy sauce or Bragg Liquid Aminos™
- 1 T mild vegetable oil

Simmering Broth

- 2 quarts (8 cups) seasoned vegetable broth

Preparation

Set the simmering broth over high heat in a large cooking pot while the dough is prepared.

Stir together the dry ingredients in a large mixing bowl. Mix the liquid ingredients in a separate bowl or measuring cup.

Pour the liquid mixture (not the simmering broth) into the dry ingredients in the mixing bowl and combine with a sturdy silicone spatula to form the dough and begin developing the gluten.

Transfer the dough to a work surface and knead just until it begins to feel slightly elastic. Avoid over-kneading or the finished seitan will be excessively chewy. With a sharp knife, cut the dough into 3 pieces. After simmering the pieces can be thinly sliced before finishing and using in recipes. For cutlets, cut the dough into 6 pieces and then stretch and flatten the pieces on your work surface. Alternately for nuggets, tear the dough into small chunks.

Once the simmering broth has come to a boil, gently lower the pieces of dough into the broth. Immediately reduce the heat to a gentle, lazy simmer, and set a timer for 40 minutes for larger pieces and 30 minutes for cutlets and nuggets. Leave the cooking pot uncovered.

The first ten minutes of simmering is the most crucial, as this is when the texture is set. Watch the pot and continue to adjust the heat by increments up or down as necessary to maintain a gentle simmer. If you catch the broth rapidly simmering, simply reduce the heat slightly. Turn occasionally once the seitan pieces float to the top of the pot.

When finished cooking, remove the pot from the heat, cover and let the seitan cool in the broth. Transfer the seitan to a food storage bag or airtight container and refrigerate for a minimum of 8 hours, or for up to 10 days, before finishing. The seitan will be soft at this stage. Chilling is very important as it will contract the gluten and thus firm and enhance the texture. Seitan can also be stored in the freezer for up to 3 months.

Transfer the broth to a sealable container and refrigerate. During this time, any seasoning sediment will settle on the bottom of the container. Simply decant the clear portion for use in other recipes. The broth can be refrigerated for up to 10 days or frozen for future use at your convenience. Be sure to add back a little water as necessary before using, since the broth will have become concentrated from evaporation during simmering.

Finishing Traditional Seitan

After simmering and chilling, seitan is completely cooked and edible but not very appetizing "as is". Therefore, the flavor and texture will benefit from pan-browning before serving. To do this, add a small amount of cooking oil to a non-stick skillet and place over medium heat. Sauté the seitan until the exterior is lightly crisp and golden brown. Serve with your favorite sauce or gravy if desired.

For more flavor, seitan can be marinated, or tossed with an herb and spice blend before browning. Thin strips of seitan are well-suited for stir-frying, and nuggets of seitan are well-suited for breading and quick deep-frying. Pan-browned seitan can also be diced, cubed or sliced into strips and added to soups and stews.

Chikun

Chikun is a versatile, plant-based meat created from a blend of wheat protein, soy protein from tofu and select seasonings (however, two recipes are offered that are entirely tofu-based). While combining gluten and tofu together to create a meat analogue is not a new concept, the proportion of ingredients, seasonings and cooking process is what makes these recipes so unique. The cooking process varies depending upon the type of chikun being prepared. Some recipes require baking only, while others require a combination of baking and simmering in a seasoned broth. Each method was carefully determined to create the best flavor and finished texture.

Chikun has an appetizing texture and "white meat" color, and virtually no wheat undertaste compared to traditional seitan. It's neutrally and lightly seasoned which allows for additional seasoning or marinating before grilling, sautéing, frying or stewing according to the specific cuisine being prepared.

A food processor with a dough blade or a stand mixer with a paddle attachment is recommended for kneading the dough in the recipes, which in turn will provide sufficient gluten development essential for proper texture. However, if you don't have this equipment, the dough can be hand-kneaded (be aware that lengthy and vigorous hand-kneading requires stamina and can cause fatigue in your hand and arm).

Be sure to begin the recipes a minimum of 8 hours before planning to serve (the day before being ideal). This will allow sufficient time for preparation and refrigeration before finishing. Refrigeration will firm and enhance the chikun texture, so this step should not be omitted or rushed. Chilling will also allow time for marinating if desired.

Please note that oven temperatures recommended in the recipes were determined using a conventional home oven (radiant heat). If you have a convection oven (fan-assisted), reduce the recommended temperature by 25°F or 10°C. All baking times should remain the same.

Chikun Simmering Broth

Chikun simmering broth is used for simmering chikun as directed in the recipes. It can also be used as a no-chicken base for preparing soups, stews, golden-colored sauces and gravies, or used in any recipe calling for chicken broth. Additional herbs or spices can be added to accommodate specific regional cuisines. This recipe yields about 3 quarts of prepared broth.

Ingredients

- 3 quarts (12 cups) water
- 3 large onions, peeled and chopped
- 3 ribs celery, chopped
- 1 large carrot, unpeeled and chopped
- 9 parsley stems
- 6 cloves garlic, crushed
- ¼ cup nutritional yeast flakes
- 4 tsp fine sea salt or kosher salt, or more to taste
- 1 T organic sugar
- 1 tsp whole black peppercorns
- 1 tsp dry rubbed sage
- 3 sprigs fresh thyme or ½ tsp dried thyme leaves
- 1 small sprig fresh rosemary

The sage, thyme and rosemary can be replaced with ¾ tsp poultry seasoning if desired.

Preparation

Combine all ingredients in a large cooking pot, cover and simmer for a minimum of 1 hour. Strain and discard the larger solids from the broth with a slotted spoon before simmering chikun. After simmering, let the broth cool and then strain into a sealable container to remove any remaining solids and refrigerate. During this time, any seasoning sediment will settle on the bottom of the container. The broth can be refrigerated for up to 1 week or frozen for future use at your convenience. To use, simply decant the clear portion and discard the fine sediment. Be sure to add back a little water as necessary before using, since the broth will have become concentrated from evaporation during simmering.

If using the broth immediately for other purposes, strain through a fine sieve into another cooking pot and discard the solids.

Quick Broth Options

Fresh homemade broth is always best and is recommended. However, for the sake of convenience and expediency, a quick chikun simmering broth can be made with Better Than Bouillon™ Vegetarian No Chicken Base (1 tsp for each cup water) or other commercial no-chicken broth cubes (½ cube for each cup water), or more or less to taste.

For a superb instant and homemade chikun broth, try my Instant Chikun Bouillon Powder (pg. 33) Add additional herbs and spices as desired to accommodate specific regional cuisines and season the prepared broth with salt to taste.

Chikun Cutlets, Tenders and Nuggets

For chikun cutlets, tenders, nuggets, the lightly seasoned dough is cut and shaped accordingly, prebaked to seal in the ingredients and set the texture, and then simmered in a seasoned broth to complete the cooking process before finishing and serving or using in recipes.

Dry Ingredients

- 1 cup (150 g) vital wheat gluten
- 2 tsp onion powder
- 1 tsp garlic powder

Simmering Broth

- 3 quarts (12 cups) chikun simmering broth (pg. 42) or similar

Blender Ingredients

- 5 oz (140 g) pressed extra-firm block tofu (see for instructions)
- ⅔ cup (160 ml) water
- 1 T mellow white miso paste
- 1 T mild vegetable oil
- ¾ tsp fine sea salt or kosher salt
- ¼ tsp poultry seasoning

Additional Items Needed

- baking sheet
- stainless steel cooling rack (not required but recommended)
- parchment paper or silicone baking mat

Preparation

Prepare the simmering broth and bring to a simmer in a large covered cooking pot. If preparing the broth from scratch, prepare and bring to a simmer 30 minutes before preparing and prebaking the dough. This will allow sufficient time to simmer the vegetables before adding the chikun.

Place a stainless steel cooling rack on a baking sheet and line the rack with parchment paper or a silicone baking mat. The cooling rack is not required, but it is recommended, as it will prevent excessive browning which would occur from direct contact with the hot baking sheet.

Preheat the oven to 350°F/180°C.

Combine the dry ingredients in a large mixing bowl. Crumble the pressed tofu into a blender and add the remaining blender ingredients. Process the contents until the tofu is completely liquefied and the mixture is smooth and creamy. This is essential! Stop the blender as necessary to scrape down the sides.

Scoop the tofu mixture into the dry ingredients (a small amount of the tofu mixture will remain in the blender; this is inconsequential). Combine with a sturdy silicone spatula until the tofu mixture is incorporated and a ball of dough begins to form. The mixture may seem a bit dry at first. Do not add more water; just keep mixing.

Place the dough into a food processor fitted with a dough blade and process for 1 full minute. Alternately, place the dough into a stand mixer fitted with a paddle and process on medium speed for 1 full minute.

If kneading by hand, knead the dough in the bowl vigorously for 3 full minutes. This is very important in order to develop the gluten. Test the dough by stretching it. If it tears easily, more kneading is required. The dough needs to exhibit a moderate degree of elasticity in order to produce the proper finished texture.

Cutlets: With a sharp knife, divide the dough into 6 pieces. Flatten the pieces with the palm of your hand. Stretch the dough against your work surface with your fingers and form into cutlet shapes. Flatten the cutlets again with the palm of your hand. If the dough is resistant to shaping, let it rest a few minutes to relax the gluten. Place the cutlets on the parchment paper or baking mat.

Tenders: Tenders are narrow strips of chikun. They're thicker than cutlets and longer than nuggets and are ideal for breading and frying. With a sharp knife, divide the dough into 6 pieces. Stretch a piece of dough until it begins to tear and then let it contract. Don't try to smooth the surface of the tender, as bumps and irregularities will yield a better finished texture and appearance. Place the tender on the parchment paper or baking mat and repeat with the other pieces.

Nuggets: Nuggets are one or two-bite pieces of chikun. Like tenders, they're also ideal for breading and frying. With a sharp knife, divide the dough into 12 pieces. Stretch a piece of dough as far as it can be stretched without tearing completely and then twist and wind it around your index finger, pinching the dough so it doesn't unwind (if the dough tears too easily, it needs additional kneading). Place the nugget on the parchment paper or baking mat and repeat with the other pieces. While this may seem like tedious work, the nuggets can be formed quickly once the technique is mastered.

Place the baking sheet on the middle rack of the oven. Bake uncovered for 20 minutes and then remove from the oven.

Bring the broth to a boil. If the broth was made from scratch, use a slotted spoon to remove and discard the larger solids. It's not necessary to strain the broth completely.

Please note that the surface of the chikun will darken slightly during prebaking, but the "white meat" appearance will return after simmering in the broth.

Lower the chikun pieces into the boiling broth and immediately reduce the heat to a gentle simmer. Leave the pot uncovered and set a timer for 20 minutes. Do not boil! Turn the pieces occasionally once they float to the top of the pot. After simmering, remove the cooking pot from the heat, cover and let the chikun cool in the broth for a few hours or until lukewarm.

Transfer the chikun to a food storage bag and add ¼ cup of broth, or a desired marinade. Handle the cutlets carefully as they can be fragile. Refrigerate for a minimum of 8 hours or for up to 1 week to firm and enhance the chikun texture before finishing and serving or using in recipes. Chilling is very important so do not omit this step. The cutlets, tenders and nuggets can be frozen without the broth for up to 3 months and then thawed and finished at your convenience.

Strain the cooled broth into a sealable container and refrigerate. During this time, any seasoning sediment will settle on the bottom of the container. The broth can be refrigerated for up to 1 week or frozen for future use at your convenience. Decant the clear portion for preparing gravies or sauces that can be served with the finished chikun; or use for other recipes as desired. Discard the sediment.

After chilling, the cutlets, tenders or nuggets are ready to be seasoned and finished as desired (if frying, lightly blot them with a paper towel to remove excess moisture before breading and placing in the hot oil).

For outdoor grilling, season the grill grating with cooking oil to discourage sticking. Brush the chikun with cooking oil before placing under the broiler or on the grill. This applies even if the chikun was marinated or a sauce is being used.

Chef's tip: If you find you need more oil in a skillet when sautéing, add it in a stream along the edges of the pan so that the oil is heated by the time it reaches the ingredient(s) being sautéed.

Chikun Piccata

"Piccata" refers to a method of preparing food in a piquant sauce. For this dish, tender chikun cutlets are lightly breaded, sautéed and served in a tangy sauce consisting of chikun broth, white wine, lemon juice, non-dairy butter, capers and parsley. Try serving it with your favorite pasta. Pressed tofu cutlets can stand in for the chikun if desired.

Ingredients

- 6 Chikun cutlets (pg. 43)
- coarse ground black pepper
- rice flour or all-purpose flour for dredging
- ¼ cup olive oil
- 1 shallot, finely chopped or ¼ cup finely chopped red onion
- 1 tsp rice flour or all-purpose flour
- ½ cup chikun simmering broth (pg. 42) or similar
- 6 T dry white wine (i.e., Chardonnay; Pinot Grigio; Sauvignon Blanc) or additional broth
- 2 T fresh lemon juice
- 2 T capers, drained
- 2 T non-dairy butter or margarine
- ¼ cup fresh chopped parsley
- optional garnish: caperberries
- optional garnish: fresh lemon slices

Preparation

Season the chikun with pepper. Dredge lightly in the flour, shaking off any excess.

In a large skillet, heat the olive oil over medium heat. When the oil is hot, add the cutlets and cook, turning every few minutes until the chikun is browned nicely. Remove the skillet from the heat and transfer the chikun to a plate and cover with foil to keep warm.

Return the skillet to the heat; add the shallots and garlic and sauté until the shallots are translucent. Sprinkle the flour over the shallots and garlic, stir to combine and cook for 1 minute. Incorporate the chikun broth in increments while stirring vigorously. Add the lemon juice, white wine and capers and bring the sauce to a boil. Whisk in the butter until melted and simmer for about 5 minutes or until the sauce thickens a bit. Stir in the chopped parsley.

Arrange the chikun on serving plates; pour the sauce over the chikun and garnish with optional caperberries and lemon slices. *Buon Appetito!*

Lemon Tarragon Marinade

A light and refreshing marinade for sautéing, broiling or grilling chikun cutlets.

Ingredients

- ¼ cup fresh squeezed lemon juice
- ¼ cup dry white wine (e.g., Chardonnay, Sauvignon Blanc)
- 2 T fresh tarragon, bruised and chopped
- 1 tsp fresh lemon zest
- 1 tsp sea salt or kosher salt
- ½ tsp coarse ground black pepper
- 2 T extra-virgin olive oil

Preparation

Combine all ingredients except for the olive oil in a bowl. Whisk in the olive oil until emulsified. Pour the marinade into a food storage bag and add the chikun, pressed tofu or tempeh. Press the air out of the bag, seal and refrigerate for a minimum of one hour, and even better overnight, before sautéing, broiling or grilling.

For outdoor grilling, season the grill grating with cooking oil to discourage sticking. Brush the chikun with cooking oil before placing under the broiler or on the grill. This applies even after the chikun has been marinated.

Chef's tip: When chopping herbs, sprinkle a little coarse salt onto the cutting surface; it will help keep the herbs from scattering about.

Murgh Makhani

(Butter Chikun)

Tender chikun is cooked in a deliciously rich and fragrant tomato cashew cream sauce. Murgh Makhani is traditionally served over basmati rice with a side of naan bread. This dish is an excellent introduction to Indian cuisine because the seasonings are not overwhelming to most uninitiated or timid palates.

Ingredients

- 1 recipe (about 16 oz) Chikun tenders or nuggets (pg. 43), torn into bite-size pieces
- ½ cup (2.5 oz by weight) whole raw cashews
- 2 tsp Garam Masala (pg. 34) or commercial equivalent
- 1 tsp ground cumin
- 1 tsp ground turmeric
- ½ tsp ground fenugreek
- ⅛ tsp cayenne pepper, or more to taste
- 1 and ½ cup chikun simmering broth (reserved from preparing the chikun)

- 1 T fresh lemon juice
- ¼ cup (4 T) olive oil
- 1 medium yellow onion, cut in half and thinly sliced
- 1 T fresh grated ginger root
- 3 cloves garlic, minced (1 T)
- 2 T non-dairy butter or margarine
- 1 can (15 oz) tomato sauce
- sea salt or kosher salt to taste

Preparation

Soak the cashews for a minimum of 8 hours in the refrigerator with just enough water to cover. To expedite softening, place the cashews in a bowl, cover with boiling water and let soak for about 30 minutes.

In a small bowl, combine the garam masala, cumin, turmeric, fenugreek and cayenne pepper; set aside.

Drain the cashews, discarding the soaking water and add to a blender. Add the broth and lemon juice and process for 2 full minutes; set aside.

Add 2 tablespoons olive oil to a large non-stick skillet and place over medium heat. Lightly brown the chikun in the oil. Remove and set aside.

In the same skillet over medium heat, add the remaining 2 tablespoons olive oil and the spices and stir until very fragrant. Add the onion and sauté until softened, about 5 minutes. Add the ginger and garlic and sauté an additional minute. Add the butter and stir until melted.

Add the tomato sauce and stir until combined. Add the chikun, bring the sauce to a simmer and then reduce the heat to just above low. Cover the skillet and cook for 20 minutes, stirring occasionally.

Tip: This is the ideal time to prepare the basmati rice separately. For extra flavor, cook the rice in some of the reserved simmering broth from preparing the chikun.

Now stir in the cashew cream mixture, bring to a simmer and cook, stirring frequently, for an additional 5 minutes or until the sauce is thickened. Season the dish with additional cayenne pepper and/or salt to taste, as desired. Serve over the basmati rice with a side of naan bread.

How to Grate Fresh Ginger

With a paring knife, slice away the tough skin. Place a box grater over a clean work surface and grate the ginger on the second to smallest holes on the grater. The fibrous material will remain on the outside of the grater; dispose of the fibrous material. The ginger pulp will either fall to the work surface or collect on the inside of the grater. Using your fingers, reach inside the grater and scrape out the pulp. Measure the amount needed and proceed with your recipe.

Triple-Dip Battered Chikun

This is my own batter recipe for creating an extra-crispy seasoned coating when frying chikun. Try using a 50/50 blend of all-purpose flour and rice flour for the dry mixture and batter for a superb texture.

Ingredients for the Dry Coating

- 1 and ½ cup all-purpose flour or rice flour (or ¾ cup each)
- 2 tsp onion powder
- 2 tsp garlic powder
- 2 tsp fine sea salt or kosher salt
- 2 tsp sweet paprika (or smoked paprika for a smoky flavor)
- 1 to 2 tsp coarse ground black pepper

Ingredients for the Batter

- 1 cup all-purpose flour or rice flour (or ½ cup each)
- 2 tsp baking powder (preferably aluminum-free)
- 1 tsp fine sea salt or kosher salt
- 1 and ½ cup non-dairy milk or non-dairy buttermilk
  (buttermilk recipes can be found in the Non-Dairy Evolution Cookbook)

Other ingredients

- high-temp cooking oil for frying

Preparation

Sift or whisk the dry ingredients together in a large bowl.

In a separate large bowl, whisk together the batter ingredients until smooth (small lumps are okay). The batter will thicken upon standing. A thick batter is ideal for this breading so do not dilute with additional milk.

Dredge the chikun in the dry mixture. Dip into the batter until coated evenly; shake off any excess. Dredge again into the dry mixture until coated evenly and set aside on a plate. Repeat with the remaining pieces of chikun.

Note: The batter is thick and messy, so you will need to frequently rinse or wipe your fingers while dipping, even when dipping the dry mixture with one hand and the batter with the other hand. Alternately, to avoid messy fingers, use a fork for dipping.

In a deep fryer, or deep skillet or wok, heat a sufficient amount of cooking oil to 350°F/180°C (test with an instant-read thermometer). Fry in the hot oil until golden brown, turning occasionally. Place on a plate lined with several layers of paper towels to drain. Serve hot or cold.

—✕( )✕—

Chikun Yakitori and Satay Marinade

A delicious grilling marinade for skewered chikun nuggets or tenders.

Ingredients

- 2 T reserved chikun simmering broth or water
- 2 T tamari, soy sauce or Bragg Liquid Aminos™
- 2 T rice vinegar
- 2 T mirin (Japanese sweet rice wine)
- 3 cloves garlic, minced (1 T)
- 2 tsp fresh grated ginger
- ½ tsp sesame oil
- ½ tsp sambal oelek or Sriracha™
- 2 T peanut oil or other cooking oil

Preparation

Combine all ingredients except for the vegetable oil in a bowl. Whisk in the vegetable oil until emulsified. The marinade can also be processed in a blender if preferred. Pour the marinade into a food storage bag and add the skewered chikun (exercise caution as the sharp points of the skewers can puncture the bag). Press the air out of the bag, seal and refrigerate for a minimum of one hour, and even better overnight, before pan-searing, broiling or grilling.

Any remaining marinade can also be used to create a dipping sauce. After marinating the chikun, drain the marinade into a small saucepan and bring to simmer. Reduce the heat to low to keep warm until ready to serve. Pour the dipping sauce into small bowls and garnish with chopped green onions or chopped cilantro.

Chikun Drumsticks and Drummettes

Drumsticks and Drummettes are prepared by wrapping lightly seasoned dough around wooden sticks and then prebaking until partially cooked. After prebaking, the drumsticks or drummettes are simmered in a seasoned broth to complete the cooking process before battering and frying or finishing on the grill. For the drumsticks, you will need 6 wooden craft sticks (the type used for ice cream treats). For the drummettes (mini-drumsticks), you will need 12 wooden hors d'oeuvre/party forks.

Dry Ingredients

- 1 cup (150 g) vital wheat gluten
- 2 tsp onion powder
- 1 tsp garlic powder

Blender Ingredients

- 5 oz (140 g) pressed extra-firm block tofu (see pg. 24 for instructions)
- ⅔ cup (160 ml) water
- 1 T mellow white miso paste
- 1 T mild vegetable oil
- ¾ tsp fine sea salt or kosher salt
- ¼ tsp poultry seasoning

Simmering Broth

- 3 quarts (12 cups) chikun simmering broth (pg. 42) or similar

Additional Items Needed

- baking sheet
- stainless steel cooling rack (not required but recommended)

Prepare the simmering broth and bring to a simmer in a large covered cooking pot. If preparing the broth from scratch, prepare and bring to a simmer 30 minutes before preparing and prebaking the dough. This will allow sufficient time to simmer the vegetables before adding the chikun.

Place a stainless steel cooling rack on a baking sheet. The cooling rack is not required, but it is recommended for propping up the drumsticks or drummettes, thus preventing flat spots from occurring from contact with the baking surface. It will also prevent excessive browning which would occur from direct contact with the hot baking sheet.

Preheat the oven to 350°F/180°C.

Combine the dry ingredients in a large mixing bowl. Crumble the pressed tofu into a blender and add the remaining blender ingredients. Process the contents until the tofu is completely liquefied and the mixture is smooth and creamy. This is essential! Stop the blender as necessary to scrape down the sides.

Scoop the tofu mixture into the dry ingredients (a small amount of the tofu mixture will remain in the blender; this is inconsequential) and combine with a sturdy silicone spatula until the tofu mixture is incorporated and a ball of dough begins to form. The mixture may seem a bit dry at first. Do not add more water; just keep mixing.

Place the dough into a food processor fitted with a dough blade and process for 1 full minute. Alternately, place the dough into a stand mixer fitted with a paddle and process on medium speed for 1 full minute.

If kneading by hand, knead the dough in the bowl vigorously for 3 full minutes. This is very important in order to develop the gluten. Test the dough by stretching it. If it tears easily, more kneading is required. The dough needs to exhibit a moderate degree of elasticity in order to produce the proper finished texture.

With a sharp knife, divide the dough into 6 pieces for drumsticks or 12 pieces for drummettes. Stretch a piece of dough as far as it can be stretched without tearing completely and then twist and wind it around a stick (if the dough tears too easily, it requires additional kneading). Be sure to leave about ½-inch of the stick free for grasping. Wind the dough narrow at the bottom and thicker towards the top to create a drumstick shape. Pinch the end of the dough so it doesn't unwind. Gently pinch the dough together with your fingers if necessary to hold the drumstick shape.

Insert the free end of the sticks into the slots in the rack, propping up the drumsticks/drummettes at a slight angle. Space them so they do not touch each other. Place the baking sheet on the middle rack of the oven. Bake uncovered 20 minutes for the drumsticks and 15 minutes for the drummettes and then remove from the oven.

Please note that the surface of the chikun will darken slightly during prebaking, but the "white meat" appearance will return after simmering in the broth.

Bring the broth to a boil. If the broth was made from scratch, use a slotted spoon to remove and discard the larger solids. It's not necessary to strain the broth completely.

Lower the pieces into the boiling broth and immediately reduce the heat to a gentle simmer. Leave the pot uncovered and set a timer for 20 minutes. Do not boil! Turn the pieces occasionally once they float to the top of the pot. After simmering, remove the cooking pot from the heat, cover and let the chikun cool in the broth for a few hours or until lukewarm.

Transfer the drumsticks or drummettes to a food storage bag and add ¼ cup of broth, or a desired marinade. Refrigerate for a minimum of 8 hours or for up to 1 week to firm and enhance the chikun texture before finishing and serving. Chilling is very important so do not omit this step. The drumsticks and drummettes can be frozen without the broth for up to 3 months and then thawed and finished at your convenience.

Strain the cooled broth into a sealable container and refrigerate. During this time, any seasoning sediment will settle on the bottom of the container. The broth can be refrigerated for up to 1 week or frozen for future use at your convenience. Decant the clear portion for preparing gravies or sauces that can be served with the finished chikun; or use for other recipes as desired. Discard the sediment.

After chilling, the drumsticks and drummettes are ready to be seasoned and finished as desired (if frying, lightly blot them with a paper towel to remove excess moisture before breading and placing in the hot oil).

For outdoor grilling, season the grill grating with cooking oil to discourage sticking. Brush the chikun with cooking oil before placing under the broiler or on the grill. This applies even if the chikun was marinated or a sauce is being used.

Ethiopian Chikun

Succulent chikun drumsticks are rubbed with a traditional blend of Berber spices, blackened in a hot skillet and served with wedges of fresh lemon.

Ingredients

- 1 recipe Chikun Drumsticks (pg. 50)
- cooking oil
  (peanut oil is ideal for this recipe)
- lemon wedges for serving

Berber Spice Blend

- 1 T sweet paprika
- 1 tsp garlic powder
- 1 tsp onion powder
- 1 tsp ground ginger
- 1 tsp sea salt or kosher salt
- ½ tsp ground cayenne pepper
- ½ tsp ground cumin
- ½ tsp coarse ground black pepper
- ½ tsp ground fenugreek
- ¼ tsp ground cardamom
- ⅛ tsp ground cloves

Preparation

Prepare the Chikun drumsticks according to the directions and chill them as directed after simmering.

Mix the spices together in a small bowl. In a large bowl, toss the spice mix with the drumsticks, coating them evenly. Add enough cooking oil to coat the bottom of a large non-stick skillet or wok and place over medium-high heat. When the oil is hot but not smoking, brown the drumsticks in the hot oil. Transfer to a serving platter and drizzle with a squeeze of fresh lemon juice. Serve with additional lemon wedges.

———————————————)( )(———————————————

Seasoned Breadcrumb Coating for Fried Chikun

This is my own seasoned breading recipe for creating a light and crispy coating when frying chikun.

Breading Ingredients

- 1 cup plain non-dairy milk
- ¾ cup rice flour or all-purpose flour
- 1 and ½ cup very fine plain dry breadcrumbs
- 2 tsp onion powder
- 1 and ½ tsp fine sea salt or kosher salt
- 1 tsp sweet paprika
- 1 tsp coarse ground black pepper
- 1 tsp garlic powder

Other Ingredients

- high-temp cooking oil for frying

Preparation

Whisk together the flour and milk in a bowl. Combine the remaining dry breading ingredients in a separate bowl. Dip the chikun in the batter, shake off the excess and then dredge in the breadcrumb mixture, coating evenly. Set aside on a plate to dry for about 10 minutes.

In a deep fryer, or deep skillet or wok, heat a sufficient amount of cooking oil to 350°F/180°C (test with an instant-read thermometer). Fry in the hot oil until golden brown, turning occasionally. Place on a plate lined with several layers of paper towels to drain. Serve hot or cold.

Chikun Satay

Chikun Satay is prepared by wrapping seasoned dough around bamboo skewers, prebaking the skewers until partially cooked and then simmering them in a seasoned broth to complete the cooking process. The skewers are then marinated or seasoned and finished on the grill. Satay is traditionally served with a dipping sauce, but this is optional. For the satay, you will need 8 six-inch long bamboo skewers.

Dry Ingredients

- 1 cup (150 g) vital wheat gluten
- 2 tsp onion powder
- 1 tsp garlic powder

Blender Ingredients

- 5 oz (140 g) pressed extra-firm block tofu (see pg. 24 for instructions)
- ⅔ cup (160 ml) water
- 1 T mellow white miso paste
- 1 T mild vegetable oil
- ¾ tsp fine sea salt or kosher salt
- ¼ tsp poultry seasoning

Simmering Broth

- 3 quarts (12 cups) chikun simmering broth (pg. 42) or similar

Additional Items Needed

- baking sheet
- stainless steel cooling rack (not required but recommended)
- parchment paper or silicone baking mat

Preparation

Prepare the simmering broth and bring to a simmer in a large covered cooking pot. If preparing the broth from scratch, prepare and bring to a simmer 30 minutes before preparing and prebaking the dough. This will allow sufficient time to simmer the vegetables before adding the chikun.

Place a stainless steel cooling rack on a baking sheet and line the rack with parchment paper or a silicone baking mat. The cooling rack is not required, but it is recommended, as it will prevent excessive browning which would occur from direct contact with the hot baking sheet.

Preheat the oven to 350°F/180°C.

Combine the dry ingredients in a large mixing bowl. Crumble the pressed tofu into a blender and add the remaining blender ingredients. Process the contents until the tofu is completely liquefied and the mixture is smooth and creamy. This is essential! Stop the blender as necessary to scrape down the sides.

Scoop the tofu mixture into the dry ingredients (a small amount of the tofu mixture will remain in the blender; this is inconsequential) and combine with a sturdy silicone spatula until the tofu mixture is incorporated and a ball of dough begins to form. The mixture may seem a bit dry at first. Do not add more water; just keep mixing.

Place the dough into a food processor fitted with a dough blade and process for 1 full minute. Alternately, place the dough into a stand mixer fitted with a paddle and process on medium speed for 1 full minute.

If kneading by hand, knead the dough in the bowl vigorously for 3 full minutes. This is very important in order to develop the gluten. Test the dough by stretching it. If it tears easily, more kneading is required. The dough needs to exhibit a moderate degree of elasticity in order to produce the proper finished texture.

With a sharp knife, divide the dough into 8 pieces. Stretch a piece of dough as far as it can be stretched without tearing completely and then twist and wind it around a bamboo stick (if the dough tears too easily, it needs additional kneading). Be sure to leave about ½-inch of the stick free on each end for grasping. Pinch the dough on each end so it doesn't unravel from the stick. Flatten the skewered dough with the palm of your hand and place the skewer on the parchment paper or baking mat. Repeat with the remaining pieces.

Place the baking sheet on the middle rack of the oven. Bake uncovered 20 minutes and then remove from the oven.

Bring the broth to a boil. If the broth was made from scratch, use a slotted spoon to remove and discard the larger solids. It's not necessary to strain the broth completely.

Lower the skewers into the boiling broth and immediately reduce the heat to a gentle simmer. Leave the pot uncovered and set a timer for 20 minutes. Do not boil! Turn the skewers occasionally once they float to the top of the pot. After simmering, remove the cooking pot from the heat, cover and let the skewers cool in the broth for a few hours or until lukewarm.

Transfer the skewers to a food storage bag and add ¼ cup of broth, or a desired marinade. Exercise caution so the sharp points of the skewers do not puncture the bag. Refrigerate for a minimum of 8 hours or for up to 1 week to firm and enhance the chikun texture before finishing and serving. Chilling is very important so do not omit this step. Satay can be frozen without the broth for up to 3 months and then thawed and finished at your convenience.

Strain the cooled broth into a sealable container and refrigerate. During this time, any seasoning sediment will settle on the bottom of the container. The broth can be refrigerated for up to 1 week or frozen for future use at your convenience. Decant the clear portion for preparing any sauces that can be served with the grilled satay; or use for other recipes as desired. Discard the sediment.

Finishing the Satay

After chilling, the skewers are ready to be grilled or broiled. For pan grilling, be sure to oil the pan to discourage sticking. Non-stick grill pans are recommended. For outdoor grilling, "season" the grill grating with cooking oil to discourage sticking. Brush the chikun with cooking oil before placing under the broiler or on the grill. This applies even if the chikun was marinated or a sauce is being used. Serve with additional sauce on the side for dipping.

Tandoori Chikun Marinade

Tandoori is a dish originating from the Indian subcontinent. The name comes from the type of cylindrical clay oven, a "tandoor", in which the dish is traditionally prepared. The marinade usually consists of yogurt and a blend of spices called tandoori masala. Grilling the chikun as opposed to roasting in the oven will keep it moist and tender.

Ingredients

- 1 cup Quick Greek-Style Yogurt (pg. 206) or commercial plain non-dairy yogurt
- 2 T peanut oil or other cooking oil
- juice of 1 large lemon (about 2 T)
- 3 cloves garlic, minced
- 1 tsp onion powder
- 1 tsp beet powder
- 1 tsp ground turmeric
- 1 tsp ground ginger
- 1 tsp ground coriander
- 1 tsp ground cumin
- 1 tsp smoked paprika
- ½ tsp fine sea salt or kosher salt
- ¼ tsp cayenne pepper

Preparation

Whisk together the ingredients in a bowl until thickened and add to a food storage bag with the chikun. Press to remove excess air from the bag and seal. Marinate the chikun for a minimum of several hours in the refrigerator, and even better overnight, before grilling.

Be sure to season the grill pan or outdoor grill grating with cooking oil before grilling to discourage sticking.

When outdoor grilling or oven broiling: Brush or mist the chikun with cooking oil, and then frequently with the marinade to keep it moist and tender. Garnish the grilled chikun with lemon wedges and sliced raw or lightly grilled onions.

Shredded Chikun

Shredded chikun is prepared from a blend of wheat protein from gluten, soy protein from tofu and select seasonings. It amazingly resembles baked and shredded chicken in flavor, aroma and texture and is ideal for use in recipes where a shredded texture is desired, such as chikun salad, hot or cold wraps or sandwiches, stir-fries, flash sautés, Mexican cuisine (tamales, enchiladas, taquitos, flautas and burritos). The chikun can also be torn into long "tenders" and battered and fried.

Shredded chikun can be added to soups and stews just before serving; however, for soups, stews, pot pies and saucy casseroles, Stewing Chikun (pg. 62) is a better option, since it retains a firmer texture when heated in sauces, gravies and broths.

Shredded chikun is minimally and neutrally seasoned which allows for additional seasoning when using in recipes; or try using a dry seasoning rub prior to wrapping and baking (such as a Jamaican Jerk dry rub). Several quick and easy seasoning and finishing suggestions follow the recipe.

A food processor with a dough blade or a stand mixer with a paddle attachment is highly recommended for kneading the sticky dough, which in turn will provide sufficient gluten development essential for this recipe. However, if you don't have this equipment, the dough can be hand-kneaded (be aware that lengthy and vigorous hand-kneading requires stamina and can cause fatigue in your hand and arm).

This recipe yields about 1 and ½ lb. or 24 oz.

Dry Ingredients

- 1 and ½ cup (225 g) vital wheat gluten
- 4 tsp onion powder
- 2 tsp garlic powder

Additional Item Needed

- 18-inch wide heavy-duty aluminum foil

Blender Ingredients

- 10 oz (280 g) pressed extra-firm block tofu (see pg. 24 for instructions)
- 1 and ¼ cup (300 ml) water
- 2 T mellow white miso paste
- 2 T mild vegetable oil
- 1 tsp fine sea salt or kosher salt
- ½ tsp poultry seasoning

Preparation

Warning! It is very important to use only heavy-duty aluminum foil for this recipe. Regular foil is not sturdy enough and can easily rupture from steam pressure which builds up inside the sealed package.

Preheat the oven to 350°F/180°C.

Combine the dry ingredients in a large mixing bowl.

Crumble the pressed tofu into a blender and add the remaining blender ingredients. Process the contents until the tofu is completely liquefied and the mixture is smooth and creamy. This is essential! Stop the blender as necessary to scrape down the sides.

Scoop the tofu mixture into the dry ingredients (a small amount of the tofu mixture will remain in the blender; this is inconsequential) and combine with a sturdy silicone spatula until the tofu mixture is incorporated and a sticky ball of dough begins to form. Let the dough rest about 5 minutes. This will give the gluten a chance to absorb the liquid and help reduce stickiness.

Place the dough into a food processor fitted with a dough blade and process for 2 full minutes. Alternately, place the dough into a stand mixer fitted with a paddle and process on medium speed for 2 full minutes.

If kneading by hand, knead the dough in the mixing bowl vigorously for a minimum of 5 full minutes. This is very important in order to develop the gluten. The dough will be sticky. Do not add additional gluten to the dough to reduce stickiness! Test the dough by stretching it. If it tears easily, more kneading is required. If it has a moderate degree of elasticity and fine web-like strands of gluten are visible when it begins to tear, it has been kneaded sufficiently.

Tear off a sheet of foil (about 18-inches) and place it on your work surface. Transfer the dough to the foil and shape into a compact slab. Shaping perfection is unnecessary. If you are using a dry rub seasoning, rub 2 to 3 teaspoons of the mixture over the dough. Fold the slab of dough in the foil (don't roll), creating a semi-flat package. Fold in the ends but leave a little room (about 1-inch on each side) to allow the dough to expand as it bakes. This is very important! Crimp the folded ends to seal the package.

Rewrap the package in a second sheet of foil and place the package directly on the middle rack of the oven. Bake for 2 hours.

Let the chikun cool in the foil to room temperature and then refrigerate for a minimum of 8 hours to firm and enhance its texture, or for up to 1 week, before pulling and using in recipes. You can also store the chikun in the freezer wrapped in the foil for up to 3 months.

Pulling the Chikun

Remove the foil and recycle. Using your hands, bend the roast in half to split it lengthwise; this will reveal the "grain". Tear the roast in half following where it has been split. Bend and tear those pieces in half lengthwise. Now, with your fingers, pull the chikun into long strings or shreds, following the grain as much as possible. Tear those pieces into smaller bite-size shreds, once again, following the grain as much as possible. Use in your favorite recipes as desired.

Note: The chikun will form its own "skin" as it bakes. If you don't care for the "skin", simply discard it when pulling the chikun. For battering and frying, simply pull the chikun into larger "tenders" rather than shredding into small pieces.

Troubleshooting

If the finished product is yielding a bread-like texture, check your gluten. A bread-like texture may indicate poor quality gluten that contains too much starch. The gluten must be guaranteed a minimum of 75% protein. Also be sure to process the tofu mixture until completely liquefied before adding to the dry ingredients.

A bread-like texture may also indicate that the dough was not kneaded sufficiently to develop the gluten strands. For this reason, a food processor with a dough blade or a stand mixer with a paddle attachment is recommended for sufficient gluten development.

Also check your oven temperature. If the oven is running too hot, it can overcook the chikun; and be sure to double-wrap the dough with the foil and seal securely to prevent moisture loss while baking. If you're using a fan-assisted convection oven, keep in mind that they can run about 25°f or 10°C hotter than a conventional radiant heat oven (unless they automatically adjust themselves), so manually adjust the temperature if necessary.

Tex-Mex Shredded Chikun

Preparation

Pull the prepared and chilled chikun into bite-size shreds.

Combine the chili powders and cumin in a small dish. Add the oil to a large non-stick skillet or wok and place over medium heat; sauté the onion until tender and translucent. Add the garlic and sauté 30 seconds.

Add the shredded chikun and sauté, tossing frequently, until lightly browned. Add the water, sprinkle in the seasonings and toss well to distribute.

Ingredients

- 12 oz Shredded Chikun (pg. 57)
- 2 tsp mild chili powder (such as ancho)
- 1 tsp ground cumin
- ¼ tsp chipotle chili powder, or more for extra heat
- 2 T cooking oil
- 1 medium onion, halved and thinly sliced
- 3 cloves garlic, minced (1 T)
- 2 T water
- sea salt or kosher salt, to taste

Continue to sauté until almost all the liquid has evaporated but the chikun is still moist; season with salt to taste. Use in your favorite Tex-Mex recipes as desired.

BBQ and Teriyaki Shredded Chikun

Ingredients

- 12 oz Shredded Chikun (pg. 57)
- 2 T cooking oil
- 1 medium onion, halved and thinly sliced
- 3 cloves garlic, minced (1 T)
- ½ cup BBQ sauce or teriyaki sauce, or more to taste

Preparation

Pull the prepared and chilled chikun into bite-size shreds.

Add the oil to a large non-stick skillet or wok and place over medium heat; sauté the onion until tender and translucent. Add the garlic and sauté 30 seconds.

Add the shredded chikun and sauté, tossing frequently, until lightly browned. Add the BBQ sauce or teriyaki sauce and toss well to distribute. Continue to cook until heated through.

Chef's tip: Never cook with fear; it can be tasted in the food. Relax, have fun, and remember that the more you cook, the better you will become.

Mediterranean Chikun

Tender shreds of chikun are sautéed in white wine, lemon juice and Mediterranean seasonings and then garnished with Kalamata olives and parsley for a light and refreshing flavor.

Ingredients

- 12 oz Shredded Chikun (pg. 57)
- 1 tsp dried basil leaves
- 1 tsp dried oregano leaves
- ½ tsp ground cumin
- ¼ tsp crushed red pepper
- 2 T dry white wine, such as Chardonnay or Sauvignon Blanc (if necessary, substitute with lemon juice)
- 1 T fresh lemon juice
- 1 medium onion, halved and thinly sliced
- 3 cloves garlic, minced (1 T)
- 2 T olive oil
- 2 T chopped parsley for garnish
- pitted Kalamata olives for garnish (optional)
- sea salt or kosher salt and coarse ground black pepper to taste

Preparation

Pull the prepared and chilled chikun into bite-size shreds.

Combine the basil, oregano, cumin and red pepper in a small dish; set aside. Combine the wine and lemon juice in separate small dish; set aside. Add the oil to a large non-stick skillet or wok and place over medium heat; sauté the onion until tender and translucent. Add the garlic and sauté 30 seconds.

Add the shredded chikun and sauté, tossing frequently, until lightly browned. Add the wine/lemon juice mixture and the seasonings and toss well to distribute. Continue to sauté until most of the liquid has evaporated but the chikun is still moist; season with salt and pepper to taste.

Serve on top of orzo, couscous or rice and garnish with the parsley and optional Kalamata olives. The seasoned chikun can also be served hot or cold in a flat-bread wrap or pita pocket with your favorite grilled or fresh vegetables and optional sauce (such as tahini or non-dairy Greek Tzatziki, pg. 207).

Chikun and Vegetable Stir-Fry

Ingredients

- 12 oz Shredded Chikun (pg. 57)
- 2 T tamari, soy sauce or Bragg Liquid Aminos™
- 1 T mirin (Japanese sweet rice wine)
- 2 T peanut oil (or other high-heat cooking oil)
- 2 tsp sesame oil
- 4 cups stir-fry vegetables of your choice, chopped, julienned or shredded (separate the cruciferous or crunchy vegetables from the tender, quick-cooking vegetables and place into separate bowls)
- 1 T fresh grated ginger
- 3 cloves garlic, minced (3 T) minced
- 1 to 2 T Sriracha™ or sambal oelek

Preparation

Pull the prepared and chilled chikun into bite-size shreds.

Combine the tamari and mirin in a small bowl; set aside. Combine the oils in a small dish; set aside.

Heat a wok until very hot. Swirl the oils around the sides of the wok. Add any cruciferous or crunchy vegetables and stir-fry until the colors are bright. Add the ginger and garlic and stir-fry for 30 seconds.

Add the shredded chikun and swirl the tamari/mirin mixture around the sides of the wok. Continue to stir-fry, tossing frequently, until the chikun has absorbed most of the liquid and the vegetables are tender crisp.

Add any quick-cooking vegetables (such as pea pods and bean sprouts) and toss for 30 seconds. Add the chili sauce and toss well just before removing from the heat. Serve immediately over jasmine rice, sticky rice or Asian noodles.

Stewing Chikun

Stewing chikun was specially formulated for high-moisture applications, such as soups, stews, pot pies, and saucy casseroles. This recipe yields about 1 lb. which should be ample for most stewing applications. For tender shredded chikun, which is better suited for cold dishes and reduced moisture applications, please see the recipe on pg 57.

Dry Ingredients

- 1 cup (150 g) vital wheat gluten
- 2 tsp onion powder
- 1 tsp garlic powder

Blender Ingredients

- 5 oz (140 g) pressed extra-firm block tofu (see pg. 24 for instructions)
- ¾ cup (180 ml) water
- 1 T mellow white miso paste
- 1 T mild vegetable oil
- ¾ tsp fine sea salt or kosher salt
- ¼ tsp poultry seasoning

Additional Item Needed

- 18-inch wide heavy duty aluminum foil

Preparation

Warning! It is very important to use only heavy-duty aluminum foil for this recipe. Regular foil is not sturdy enough and can easily rupture from steam pressure which builds up inside the sealed package.

Preheat the oven to 350°F/180°C.

Combine the dry ingredients in a large mixing bowl.

Crumble the pressed tofu into a blender and add the remaining blender ingredients. Process the contents until the tofu is completely liquefied and the mixture is smooth and creamy. This is essential! Stop the blender as necessary to scrape down the sides.

Scoop the tofu mixture into the dry ingredients (a small amount of the tofu mixture will remain in the blender; this is inconsequential) and stir with a sturdy silicone spatula until the tofu mixture is incorporated and a sticky ball of dough begins to form.

Place the dough into a food processor fitted with a dough blade and process for 2 full minutes. Alternately, place the dough into a stand mixer fitted with a paddle and process on medium speed for 2 full minutes.

If kneading by hand, knead the dough in the bowl vigorously for 5 full minutes. This is very important in order to develop the gluten. Test the dough by stretching it. If it tears easily, more kneading is required. The dough needs to exhibit a substantial degree of elasticity in order to produce the proper finished texture.

Tear off a sheet of foil (about 18-inches) and place it on your work surface. Transfer the dough to the foil and shape into a compact slab. Shaping perfection is unnecessary. If you are using a dry rub seasoning, rub about 2 teaspoons of the mixture over the dough. Fold the slab of dough in the foil (don't roll), creating a semi-flat package. Fold in the ends but leave a little room (about 1-inch on each side) to allow the dough to expand as it bakes. This is very important! Crimp the folded ends to seal the package.

Rewrap the package in a second sheet of foil and place the package directly on the middle rack of the oven. Bake for 1 hour and 30 minutes.

Let the chikun cool in the foil to room temperature and then refrigerate for a minimum of 8 hours to firm and enhance its texture, or for up to 1 week, before pulling and using in recipes. You can also store the chikun in the freezer wrapped in the foil for up to 3 months.

Preparing the Chikun for Stewing

Remove the foil and recycle. Using your hands, bend the roast in half to split it lengthwise; this will reveal the "grain". Tear the roast in half following where it has been split. Bend and tear those pieces in half lengthwise. Now, with your fingers, pull the chikun into long strips, following the grain as much as possible. Tear those pieces into smaller bite-size pieces. The pieces can also be cubed or diced. For pot pies and saucy casseroles, simply add to the recipe. For soups and stews, add the chikun the last 15 to 20 minutes of cooking time before serving. Alternately, the whole roast can be added to simmering liquids for 1 hour, and then transferred to a serving platter and shredded with a fork to serve.

Note: The chikun will form its own "skin" as it bakes. If you don't care for the "skin", simply discard it when preparing the chikun for stewing.

Thai Green Curry

Thai green curry paste is made from a blend of green chilies, Thai ginger (galangal), lemongrass and kaffir lime. This fragrant Thai curry with chikun is wonderful served with sticky rice. This is my own version of the traditional dish.

Ingredients

- 1 T cooking oil
- 1 medium onion, peeled and sliced
- 2 cans (13.5 oz each) organic unsweetened coconut milk
- 1 cup chikun simmering broth (pg. 42) or similar
- 3 T Thai green curry paste (e.g., Thai Kitchen™)
- 1 T coconut palm sugar or light brown sugar
- 1 medium zucchini, halved lengthwise and sliced
- ½ cup green peas, fresh or from frozen
- ¼ tsp crushed red pepper flakes, or more for additional heat
- 8 oz Stewing Chikun, torn into bite-size pieces or medium diced (pg. 62)
- juice of 1 large lime
- sea salt or kosher salt to taste
- ¼ cup chopped Thai basil or sweet basil, for garnish
- ¼ cup chopped cilantro, for garnish

Preparation

Add the oil to a cooking pot and place over medium-low heat. Sweat the onion (low sizzle; no browning) for about 10 minutes until tender.

Add the coconut milk, broth, curry paste, sugar, zucchini, peas and red pepper flakes. Bring to a gentle simmer, partially cover and cook for 15 minutes.

Add the chikun and lime juice. Return to a simmer and cook uncovered for 15 minutes. Season the curry with salt to taste. Ladle into bowls and garnish with the basil and cilantro. Serve plenty of sticky rice on the side to add to the curry while eating.

—◦( )◦—

Chef's tip: Taste, taste, taste! It seems like a rather obvious step when cooking but it's amazing how many cooks forget to taste every component of what they are cooking.

Succulent Roast Chikun

Succulent Roast Chikun is created from a special blend of wheat protein, soy protein from tofu and select seasonings. The roast is prebaked until partially cooked, which seals in the ingredients and sets the texture. The roast will also create its own "skin" while prebaking. The partially cooked roast is then simmered in a seasoned broth to complete the cooking process, infuse the roast with additional flavor and ensure that the roast remains moist and tender. This combination cooking method produces a tender, succulent, "white meat" roast with a delicate texture which cannot be achieved by baking or simmering alone. After simmering the roast, the ample amount of remaining seasoned broth can be used for sauces, gravies, soups and stews. The roast is finished by pan-glazing until golden brown before slicing and serving.

The roast requires refrigeration before pan-glazing and serving in order to enhance its texture, so prepare at least the night before (or up to 1 week ahead) and then pan-glaze and reheat when ready to serve. This recipe yields about 1.25 lbs.

Dry Ingredients

- 1 cup (150 g) vital wheat gluten
- 2 T all-purpose flour
- 2 tsp onion powder
- 1 tsp garlic powder

Blender Ingredients

- 5 oz (140 g) pressed extra-firm block tofu (see pg. 24 for instructions)
- ¾ cup (180 ml) water
- 1 T mellow white miso paste
- 1 T mild vegetable oil
- ¾ tsp fine sea salt or kosher salt
- ¼ tsp poultry seasoning

Simmering Broth

- 3 quarts (12 cups) chikun simmering broth (pg. 42) or similar

Pan-Glaze Ingredients

- 2 T non-dairy butter or margarine
- 1 T tamari, soy sauce or Bragg Liquid Aminos™
- 2 T dry white wine, lemon juice or reserved simmering broth
- 1 T minced herbs of your choice (optional)
- coarse ground black pepper or other dry spice seasonings of your choice, to taste

Additional Item Needed

- 18-inch wide heavy-duty aluminum foil

Preparation

Preheat the oven to 350°F/180°C.

Combine the dry ingredients in a large mixing bowl; set aside.

Crumble the pressed tofu into a blender and add the remaining blender ingredients. Process the contents until the tofu is completely liquefied and the mixture is smooth and creamy. This is essential! Stop the blender as necessary to scrape down the sides.

Scoop the tofu mixture into the dry ingredients (a small amount of the tofu mixture will remain in the blender; this is inconsequential) and combine with a sturdy silicone spatula until the tofu mixture is incorporated and a sticky ball of dough begins to form.

Place the dough into a food processor fitted with a dough blade and process for 1 full minute. Alternately, place the dough into a stand mixer fitted with a paddle and process on medium speed for 1 full minute.

If kneading by hand, knead the dough in the bowl vigorously for 3 full minutes. This is very important in order to develop the gluten. Test the dough by stretching it. If it tears easily, more kneading is required. The dough needs to exhibit a moderate degree of elasticity in order to produce the proper finished texture.

Tear off a sheet of foil (about 18-inches) and place it on your work surface. Place the dough onto the foil and shape it into a round ball. Now, lift the edge of the foil over the dough and begin rolling into a cylinder, pinching the ends closed simultaneously while rolling. The goal is to create a compact cylindrical package. Twist the ends tightly to seal, being careful not to tear the foil. Bend the twisted ends in half to lock them tight.

Tip: While the ends need to be twisted tightly to seal the package, avoid twisting inwards so far as to tightly compress the dough. The dough will expand significantly as it bakes. Leaving room on each end for expansion will relieve pressure on the foil and thus discourage rupturing.

Wrap with a second sheet of foil and twist the ends tightly to completely seal the package. If the foil tears at any point while twisting the ends, rewrap in a third sheet of foil.

Place the package directly on the middle rack of the oven and bake for 1 hour.

While the roast is prebaking, prepare the simmering broth. Add all of the broth ingredients to a large cooking pot and bring to a boil. Cover with a lid and reduce the heat to a gentle simmer. For quick broths, bring the water and bouillon paste, cubes or powder to a simmer in a large covered cooking pot after the roast has been removed from the oven.

Remove the roast from the oven and let cool for about 30 minutes. Unwrap the roast and with a fork, pierce the roast 4 times on the top and 4 times on the bottom.

If the broth was made from scratch, use a slotted spoon to remove and discard the larger solids. It's not necessary to strain the broth completely. Bring the broth to a boil and carefully lower the roast into the broth. Reduce the heat to a simmer and cook for 45 minutes. Turn the roast occasionally as it simmers. Monitor the pot frequently and adjust the heat as necessary to maintain the simmer. The broth should be gently bubbling. Do not boil, but do not let the roast merely poach in the hot broth either, as a gentle simmer is necessary to penetrate the roast and finish the cooking process.

Remove the pot from the heat, cover and let cool for a few hours or until lukewarm. Remove the roast, seal in a food storage bag with ¼ cup broth and refrigerate for up to 1 week. Chilling is very important so do not omit this step. To freeze the unfinished roast for future use, place it into a freezer bag without the broth and freeze for up to 3 months. If the roast was frozen, thaw for several days in the refrigerator before finishing.

Be sure to reserve the simmering broth for other recipes, such as soups or stews; or for gravies and sauces that can be served with the roast. Strain the cooled broth into a sealable container and refrigerate. During this time, any seasoning sediment will settle on the bottom of the container. Then decant the clear portion for use and discard the sediment. The broth can be refrigerated for up to 1 week or frozen for future use at your convenience.

Finishing the Roast

Bring the roast to room temperature for about 1 hour before finishing.

Preheat the oven to 350°F/180°C. Lightly blot the roast with a paper towel.

In a large, deep non-stick skillet or wok, melt the butter or margarine over medium heat. Add the roast and turn with 2 large spoons to coat the roast in the butter or margarine (wooden spoons are ideal, as they won't mar the surface of the roast). Continue to turn the roast occasionally until lightly browned. Add the tamari and continue to turn about 1 minute. Now add the wine, lemon juice or reserved broth, the optional herbs and a few pinches of black pepper (or a teaspoon of other dry spices as desired). Continue to pan-glaze until the liquid has evaporated and the roast achieves a beautiful golden brown color.

Transfer to a shallow baking dish, cover with foil and bake for 20 minutes to heat through.

Transfer the roast to a serving platter, slice and serve immediately. Store any leftover roast in a food storage bag or sealable container in the refrigerator. Consume within 1 week or freeze.

Tip: Thinly sliced cold leftover roast makes superb hot or cold sandwiches. For hot sandwiches, slice the cold roast and then wrap the slices securely in foil. Place the foil package in a hot oven or in a steamer until heated through. The slices can also be gently reheated in the microwave.

Chikun Roulades

Chikun roulades consist of thin cutlets of tender, moist chikun wrapped around a savory filling. The word roulade originates from the French word "rouler", meaning "to roll". For this application, the roulades are double wrapped in foil, steamed until cooked and then finished by pan-glazing in a skillet or by breading and frying in hot oil. Example recipes for filling and finishing the roulades are provided after the basic recipe and preparation instruction. This recipe yields 4 chikun roulades (4 servings).

Dry Ingredients for the Chikun

- 1 cup (150 g) vital wheat gluten
- 2 tsp onion powder
- 1 tsp garlic powder

Blender Ingredients for the Chikun

- 5 oz (140 g) pressed extra-firm block tofu (see pg. 24 for instructions)
- 1 cup (240 ml) water
- 1 T mellow white miso paste
- 1 T mild vegetable oil
- ¾ tsp fine sea salt or kosher salt
- ¼ tsp poultry seasoning

Filling Ingredients

The roulade filling can consist of any combination of most plant-based ingredients, as long as they are not too wet. For example:

- ❖ lightly steamed cruciferous and starchy vegetables
- ❖ lightly toasted and chopped nuts and seeds
- ❖ chopped fresh or dried herbs
- ❖ fresh or lightly toasted breadcrumbs
- ❖ diced dried fruits
- ❖ cooked grains
- ❖ thinly sliced meat analogues
- ❖ thinly sliced or shredded non-dairy cheese
- ❖ non-dairy butter mixed with herbs

Filling combinations are limited only by your imagination. Ingredients with high water content, such as onions, mushrooms, kale, mustard greens and spinach can certainly be used but should be sautéed first to evaporate the excess moisture. Squashes are not recommended because they will disintegrate into mush during the extended period of steaming. Each roulade can accommodate about ¼ cup of filling.

Additional Items Needed

- 8 foil wrappers (about 9"x10") cut from standard or heavy duty aluminum foil (do not use pop-up foil for this application; it's not sturdy enough)
- large cooking pot with a lid and a steamer insert

Preparation

Add enough water to the cooking pot to just reach the bottom of the steamer insert. Do not overfill or the foil packages will be sitting in water.

Set aside the filling(s) you will be using; lightly steam or sauté any ingredients that require preparation.

Combine the dry ingredients in a large mixing bowl. Crumble the pressed tofu into a blender and add the remaining blender ingredients. Process the contents until the tofu is completely liquefied and the mixture is smooth and creamy. This is essential! Stop the blender as necessary to scrape down the sides.

Scoop the tofu mixture into the dry ingredients (a small amount of the tofu mixture will remain in the blender; this is inconsequential) and combine with a sturdy silicone spatula until the tofu mixture is incorporated and a sticky dough begins to form. Let the dough rest about 5 minutes. This will give the gluten a chance to absorb the liquid and help reduce stickiness. The dough will be very soft.

Place the dough into a food processor fitted with a dough blade and process for 1 full minute. Alternately, place the dough into a stand mixer fitted with a paddle and process on medium speed for 1 full minute.

If kneading by hand, knead the dough in the mixing bowl vigorously for a minimum of 3 full minutes. This is very important in order to develop the gluten. Keep in mind that it will be soft and somewhat sticky due to its moisture content. Do not add additional gluten to the dough to reduce stickiness!

Divide the dough into 4 portions. Place a foil wrapper on your work surface. Place a portion of dough on the foil and press and stretch into a rectangular shape about ¼-inch thick. Spread ¼ cup filling (or layer thinly sliced ingredients) over the dough, avoiding the edges. When using herbed butter (such as for Chikun Kiev) place the solid, chilled lump of herbed butter near the edge where rolling will begin (rather than spreading it over the dough).

Pick up the end corners of the foil wrapper and use the foil to lift and fold the edge of the dough over to begin the roll. Fold in the sides of the dough and then complete rolling. The dough will be very soft, so this requires a bit of finesse and patience. When rolling herbed butter, fold the edge of the dough over the lump of butter to encase it completely, fold in the sides and then complete rolling. Pinch the seams of the roll thoroughly to prevent leaking of any melted cheese or butter in the filling while steaming (regardless of how well the dough is sealed, some melted butter will inevitably leak out).

Now, compress and shape the roll with your hands into a small, compact bundle, again making sure that any seams are pinched together. Roll the roulade inside the foil wrapper to create a cylinder and twist the ends tightly to seal the foil package. To ensure a complete seal, re-wrap each roulade with a second sheet of foil, again twisting the ends very tight. Repeat with the remaining pieces of dough and filling and set the foil packages aside.

Bring the water in the steamer to a rapid boil over high heat and add the foil packages. The water must be boiling to generate the proper amount of steam heat to cook the roulades thoroughly and evenly. Cover the pot and steam for 1 hour.

Check the pot at 20 minute intervals to monitor water loss (use an oven mitt to avoid steam burns) and add hot water to replace water lost to steam evaporation. Do not let the pot boil dry. If you're steaming in a smaller cooking pot with a shallow volume of water, it's not unusual to replace several cups of water during steaming. Replacing water should be unnecessary in larger steamers that hold a large volume of water.

When the roulades have finished steaming, remove the foil packages and let them cool to near room temperature. Refrigerate the roulades in their foil wrappers for a minimum of 8 hours, or up to 1 week, to firm and enhance the chikun texture before finishing.

Finishing the Roulades

Bring the foil wrapped roulades to room temperature for about 1 hour before finishing. This will help heat them through more efficiently (and subsequently help re-melt ingredients such as cheese and butter).

Finish the roulades by pan-glazing or breading and frying in hot oil. If necessary, the roulades can be placed in a microwave briefly to heat the center or placed in a shallow baking dish covered with foiled and warmed in a hot oven until heated through. Serve immediately.

Chef's tip: Read entire recipes from start to finish before proceeding. Take extra time before starting to assemble, measure and/or prepare ingredients. This is a French culinary term called "mise en place" which literally means to "put in place". The more organized you are before you begin, the better your results will be, and often with less stress.

Chikun Champignon

Tender chikun is wrapped around a filling of sautéed mushrooms, onions and melted white non-dairy cheese. The roulades are finished by pan-glazing in non-dairy butter and white wine until golden brown.

Filling Ingredients

- 2 T olive oil
- ¼ cup diced onion
- 6 oz fresh mushrooms of your choice, chopped
- ½ tsp dried thyme leaves
- sea salt or kosher salt and coarse ground black pepper
- ½ cup shredded non-dairy white cheese that melts
  (Suisse cheese from The Non-Dairy Evolution Cookbook is ideal for this recipe)

Pan-Glaze Ingredients

- 2 T non-dairy butter or margarine
- 2 T dry white wine or 1 T fresh lemon juice
- 1 tsp tamari, soy sauce or Bragg Liquid Aminos™
- coarse ground black pepper

Preparation

Combine the wine and tamari in a small dish; set aside.

Add the olive oil to a skillet and place over medium heat. Add the onions and mushrooms and season with the thyme and 2 pinches each of salt and pepper. Sauté the vegetables until golden brown; set aside to cool.

Prepare the chikun roulade dough according to the instructions on pg. 68. Divide the dough in the bowl into 4 portions.

Fill, wrap and steam the roulades according to the general instructions using 2 tablespoons of the sautéed vegetables and 2 tablespoons of the shredded cheese for each roulade.

When the roulades have finished steaming, remove the foil packages and let them cool to near room temperature. Refrigerate the roulades in their foil wrappers for a minimum of 8 hours, or up to 1 week, to firm and enhance the chikun texture before finishing.

Finishing the Roulades

Bring the foil wrapped roulades to room temperature for about 1 hour before finishing. This will help heat them through more efficiently (and subsequently help re-melt the cheese). Remove the foil and recycle.

Melt the butter in a non-stick skillet over medium heat and add the roulades. Sauté until golden, turning frequently; add the wine and tamari. Continue to sauté, turning frequently, until the roulades are nicely browned; season with pepper to taste. If necessary, the roulades can be placed in a microwave briefly to heat the center or placed in a shallow baking dish covered with foiled and warmed in a hot oven until heated through. Serve immediately.

Chikun Cordon Bleu

Tender chikun is wrapped around savory slices of vegan ham and melted non-dairy white cheese. After steaming the roulades are breaded and pan-fried until golden brown. Serve the roulades with Dijon mustard for an elegant and impressive dish.

Filling Ingredients

- 4 thin slices Country Garden Ham (pg. 122) or Deli-Style Garden Ham (pg. 125)
- 4 thin slices vegan white cheese that melts
  (Suisse cheese from The Non-Dairy Evolution Cookbook is ideal for this recipe)

Breading Ingredients

- ½ cup plain non-dairy milk
- 6 T rice flour or all-purpose flour
- 1 cup very fine plain dry breadcrumbs
- 1 tsp sweet paprika
- 1 tsp sea salt or kosher salt
- ½ tsp coarse ground black pepper
- cooking oil for frying

Preparation

Prepare the chikun roulade dough according to the instructions on pg. 68. Divide the dough in the bowl into 4 portions.

Fill, wrap and steam the roulades according to the general instructions using 1 slice of ham and 1 slice of cheese for each roulade.

When the roulades have finished steaming, remove the foil packages and let them cool to near room temperature. Refrigerate the roulades in their foil wrappers for a minimum of 8 hours, or up to 1 week, to firm and enhance the chikun texture before finishing.

Finishing the Roulades

Bring the foil wrapped roulades to room temperature for about 1 hour before finishing. This will help heat them through more efficiently (and subsequently help re-melt the cheese). Remove the foil and recycle.

Whisk together the flour and milk in a bowl. Combine the remaining dry breading ingredients in a separate bowl.

Dip each roulade in the batter and then roll the in the breadcrumb mixture, coating evenly. Set aside on a plate to dry for about 10 minutes.

In a large skillet or wok, add the cooking oil to ½-inch depth and place over medium heat-high heat. When the oil begins to shimmer, add the roulades and fry, turning occasionally, until golden brown. Transfer the roulades to a plate lined with paper towels to drain for 1 minute before serving. If necessary, the roulades can be placed in a microwave briefly to heat the center or placed in a shallow baking dish covered with foiled and warmed in a hot oven until heated through. Serve immediately.

Chikun Kiev

Tender chikun cutlets are wrapped around a mixture of garlic, herbs and non-dairy butter. After steaming, the roulades are then breaded and pan-fried until golden brown.

Filling Ingredients

- ½ cup non-dairy butter or margarine, softened
- 1 clove minced garlic
- 2 T fresh minced parsley or 2 tsp dried parsley
- 2 T fresh minced tarragon or 2 tsp dried tarragon
- ¼ tsp coarse ground black pepper
- pinch of sea salt or kosher salt

Breading Ingredients

- ½ cup plain non-dairy milk
- 6 T rice flour or all-purpose flour
- 1 cup very fine plain dry breadcrumbs
- 1 tsp sweet paprika
- 1 tsp sea salt or kosher salt
- ½ tsp coarse ground black pepper
- cooking oil for frying

Preparation

With a fork, mash together the butter or margarine, garlic, parsley, tarragon, black pepper and a pinch of salt in a bowl. Place the mixture back in the refrigerator to chill and firm before proceeding.

Prepare the chikun roulade dough according to the instructions on pg. 68. Divide the dough in the bowl into 4 portions.

Fill, wrap and steam the roulades according to the general instructions using ¼-portion of the chilled garlic herb butter for each roulade.

When the roulades have finished steaming, remove the foil packages and let them cool to near room temperature. Refrigerate the roulades in their foil wrappers for a minimum of 8 hours, or up to 1 week, to firm and enhance the chikun texture before finishing.

Finishing the Roulades

Bring the foil wrapped roulades to room temperature for about 1 hour before finishing. This will help heat them through more efficiently (and subsequently help re-melt the cheese). Remove the foil and recycle.

Whisk together the flour and milk in a bowl. Combine the remaining dry breading ingredients in a separate bowl.

Dip each roulade in the batter and then roll the in the breadcrumb mixture, coating evenly. Set aside on a plate to dry for about 10 minutes.

In a large skillet or wok, add the cooking oil to ½-inch depth and place over medium heat-high heat. When the oil begins to shimmer, add the roulades and fry, turning occasionally, until golden brown. Transfer the roulades to a plate lined with paper towels to drain for 1 minute before serving. If necessary, the roulades can be placed in a microwave briefly to heat the center or placed in a shallow baking dish covered with foiled and warmed in a hot oven until heated through. Serve immediately.

━━━━━━━━━━━━━━)( )(━━━━━━━━━━━━━

Soy Chikun Strips

Soy chikun strips are easy-to-make, gluten-free, and remarkably resemble grilled strips of seasoned chicken. The ingredients are simple: tofu and a seasoning marinade. The secret is in the preparation technique. A tofu press is recommended in order to compress the tofu properly and remove as much water as possible. However, the traditional plate and heavy weight method will work too, but the texture may not be as dense.

Each block of tofu will yield about 8 ounces of prepared chikun strips. Most households do not possess more than 1 tofu press, so if you wish to prepare additional chikun, press the first block and then store the block in the refrigerator in an airtight container while the additional block is pressed. For additional blocks, simple double or triple the water and seasonings in the recipe.

Ingredients

- 1 block (about 14 oz before pressing) extra-firm water-packed tofu (not silken tofu)
- ⅓ cup water
- 1 tsp nutritional yeast
- ½ tsp fine sea salt or kosher salt
- ½ tsp onion powder
- ¼ tsp poultry seasoning
- ¼ tsp garlic powder

Additional Items Needed

- baking sheet
- parchment paper or silicone baking mat

Preparation

Press the tofu until as much water has been removed as possible (keep stored in the refrigerator while pressing). A tofu press is ideal since this will compress the tofu while removing the water, thus creating a dense texture. This will take a minimum of 8 to 12 hours. Blot the tofu with a paper towel.

Preheat the oven to 350°F/180°C. Line a baking sheet with parchment paper or a silicone baking mat. Place the block(s) of tofu on the paper or mat and bake uncovered for 1 hour and 30 minutes. The tofu will develop a firm golden crust while baking. Let the block(s) cool completely after baking.

Trim the crust from the block(s) of baked tofu since the texture will be rather tough. Small amounts of crust may remain; that's okay. Slice the tofu into strips and then place into a food storage bag.

Now, in a small bowl, whisk together the remaining ingredients. The dry seasoning powders may take a moment to dissolve, so keep whisking until blended. Pour the seasoning marinade over the tofu in the bag. Press as much air out of the bag as possible; seal and refrigerate for several hours (overnight is best).

Other herbs and spices can be added to the marinade to impart specific ethnic food flavors:

For a Tex-Mex variation, prepare the marinade with the basic recipe and add 1 tsp mild chili powder, an additional ½ tsp onion powder, ½ tsp ground cumin, an additional ¼ tsp garlic powder and ¼ tsp chipotle chili powder.

For an Asian Stir Fry variation, marinate and sauté the chikun as directed and add a dash or two of tamari or soy sauce (or wheat-free tamari or Bragg Liquid Aminos™ for gluten-free). Toss with a tablespoon of chili garlic sauce just before removing from the skillet.

For a Mediterranean variation, prepare the marinade with the basic recipe but reduce the water to ¼ cup. Add 1 T lemon juice, 1 tsp dried basil, 1 tsp dried oregano, an additional ½ tsp onion powder and an additional ¼ tsp garlic powder. Finish with fresh ground black pepper.

The strips are now ready to be pan-grilled or sautéed. This step is necessary to prepare the chikun for serving or using in recipes. Lightly oil a non-stick skillet with cooking oil and place over medium heat. Add the chikun including any residual marinade. Sauté until the excess liquid has evaporated and the chikun is golden. Use a gentle touch while sautéing; the chikun is firm but can break apart if handled roughly. Use immediately in your favorite hot recipe or chill for use in cold recipes (wraps, salads, etc.) For soups and stews, the strips can be cubed or diced and added just before serving to avoid becoming too soft.

Store any leftovers in an airtight container in the refrigerator. Consume within 1 week or freeze up to 1 month.

Spicy Buffalo Soy Chikun Drummettes

If you've ever been "on the fence" about tofu because of its texture, these spicy, gluten-free nuggets may just change your mind. They're pre-baked to give them a dense, meaty and slightly chewy texture before breading and frying. I also experimented with a batter that seems to work rather well for getting the breading to actually adhere to the tofu. Serve them with vegan ranch or bleu cheese dressing. They're gluten-free too!

Ingredients for the Drummettes

- 1 block (about 14 oz before pressing) extra-firm water-packed tofu
- ¼ cup nutritional yeast flakes
- ¼ cup plain non-dairy milk
- 2 T No-Eggy Mayo (pg. 202) or commercial egg-free mayonnaise
- ¾ tsp sea salt or kosher salt
- ½ tsp poultry seasoning
- ¼ tsp coarse ground black pepper
- garbanzo bean flour, about 1 cup
- cooking oil for frying

Ingredients for the Sauce

- ¼ cup non-dairy butter or margarine
- ¼ cup red hot sauce (a thicker sauce, such as Sriracha™ works well)

Additional Items Needed

- baking sheet

75

- parchment paper or silicone baking mat

Preparation

Drain and slice the block of tofu lengthwise through the center to create 2 slabs. Lay each slab on its side and slice lengthwise down through the center to create 4 slabs total.

Thoroughly press the tofu until it is not releasing any more liquid. This is important: the drier the tofu, the better the texture of the finished dish (this can also be done with a tofu press using the whole intact block and then the block sliced after pressing).

Preheat the oven to 325°F/170°F.

Now cut each slab into 3 drummettes. Try slicing on a slight diagonal, turning the knife slightly to left on the first slice and then slightly to the right on the second slice so the drummettes are irregular rectangles, for a total of 12 drummettes. This will give them a more natural and less uniform appearance.

Line a baking sheet with parchment paper or a silicone baking mat and place the drummettes on the paper or mat in a single layer. Bake uncovered for 30 minutes, turning after 15 minutes. Remove to cool.

In a bowl, whisk together the nutritional yeast flakes, milk, mayo, salt and seasonings until smooth.

In a separate bowl, add the garbanzo bean flour.

Dip each drummette in the milk mixture and then dredge in the flour and set aside on a plate. Let the drummettes dry for about 10 minutes and then dredge them in the flour again. Replenish the flour as needed.

In a skillet or wok, heat about ½-inch of oil over medium-high heat until the oil begins to shimmer. Fry the drummettes in the hot oil for several minutes until golden brown. Remove to a plate lined with a paper towel to drain.

Meanwhile, melt the butter or margarine and whisk together with the hot sauce until smooth. Just before serving, drizzle the sauce over the drummettes in a bowl and turn the drummettes gently until they are thoroughly coated with the sauce. Transfer to a serving plate and serve immediately with the dipping dressing of your choice (e.g., vegan blue cheese or creamy ranch dressing).

Chef's tip: Is your oil is hot enough for frying? Stick the tip of a wooden skewer in the oil. If bubbles form around the wood, then you are good to go.

Beaf

"Beaf" is a hybrid word derived from the consonants of the word "beef" and the vowels of the word "wheat". It is a versatile, plant-based meat created from a blend of wheat protein (vital wheat gluten) and select seasonings. The cooking process varies depending upon the "cut" of beaf being prepared. Some recipes require baking only, while others require a combination of baking and simmering in a seasoned broth or brine. Each method was carefully determined to create the best flavor and finished texture.

Beaf is neutrally seasoned, which allows for additional seasoning or marinating before grilling, sautéing, frying, braising, or stewing according to the specific cuisine being prepared.

Be sure to begin the recipes a minimum of 8 hours before planning to serve (the day before being ideal). This will allow sufficient time for preparation and refrigeration before finishing. Refrigeration will firm and enhance the beaf texture, so this step should not be omitted or rushed. Chilling will also allow time for marinating if desired.

Please note that oven temperatures recommended in the recipes were determined using a conventional home oven (radiant heat). If you have a convection oven (fan-assisted), reduce the recommended temperature by 25°F or 10°C. All baking times should remain the same.

Beaf Simmering Broth

Beaf simmering broth is used for simmering beaf when directed in a recipe. It can also be used as a savory no-beef base for preparing brown sauces, gravies, 'jus', consommé, hearty soups and stews, or used in any recipe calling for seasoned beef broth. Additional herbs or spices can be added to accommodate specific regional cuisines. This recipe yields about 3 quarts of prepared broth.

Preparation

Combine all ingredients in a large cooking pot, cover and simmer for a minimum of 1 hour. Strain and discard the larger solids from the broth with a slotted spoon before simmering beaf.

After simmering, let the broth cool and then strain into a sealable container to remove any remaining solids and refrigerate. During this time, any seasoning sediment will settle on the bottom of the container.

The broth can be refrigerated for up to 1 week or frozen for future use at your convenience.

Ingredients

- 3 quarts water (12 cups)
- 3 large onions, peeled and quartered
- 3 ribs celery, chopped
- 1 large carrot, unpeeled and chopped
- 9 parsley stems
- 6 cloves garlic, crushed
- ½ cup tamari, soy sauce or Bragg Liquid Aminos™*
- 2 T nutritional yeast flakes
- 2 T dark brown sugar
- 1 T porcini mushroom powder (optional)
- 1 T Worcestershire Sauce (pg. 25) or commercial vegan equivalent
- 1 tsp fine sea salt or kosher salt, or more to taste
- 1 tsp whole black peppercorns

To use, simply decant the clear portion and discard the fine sediment. Be sure to add back a little water as necessary before using, since the broth will have become concentrated from evaporation during simmering.

If using the broth immediately for other purposes, strain through a fine sieve into another cooking pot and discard the solids.

For Beaf Consommé: Clarify the broth as described above. Create a slurry by dissolving 1 tablespoon of unmodified potato starch, cornstarch or arrowroot powder in 1 tablespoon of water. Bring the broth to a simmer in a large saucepan and whisk in the slurry. The slurry will add body and gloss. Serve piping hot.

Quick Broth Options

Fresh homemade broth is always best and is recommended. However, for the sake of convenience and expediency, a quick beaf simmering broth can be made with any commercially prepared low-sodium vegetable stock or broth, plus 2 tsp tamari, soy sauce or Bragg Liquid Aminos™ for each cup, or more or less to taste. Add additional herbs and spices as desired to accommodate specific regional cuisines and season the prepared broth with salt to taste.

A quick broth can also be made with Better Than Bouillon™ Vegetarian No Beef Base (1 tsp for each cup water), or more or less to taste. For some reason, this product has become increasingly more difficult to find (more reason to make your own broth from scratch). However, it can be purchased directly from the manufacturer, BetterThanBouillon.com, if you cannot locate it anywhere else.

Tournedos of Beaf

Tournedos (pronounced "toor-ni-dohz") are thick, tender medallions of beaf (an option for creating thin steak cutlets is included in the recipe). For this application, the seasoned beaf dough is cut into filets and prebaked to set their texture. The partially cooked medallions are simmered in a hearty broth to complete the cooking process and then chilled to firm and enhance their texture before finishing.

The medallions are finished by pan-glazing in a skillet to seal in juices and create a flavorful brown crust. If desired they can be served 'au jus', with a sauce of your choice, or simply smothered in sautéed mushrooms and onions. Tournedos of beaf are ideal for preparing Steak Diane, Steak Medici and Steak au Poivre (see the following recipes), or for any recipe requiring tender steak. Alternately, the medallions can be marinated, brushed with cooking oil to keep them moist and finished on the grill.

The medallions require chilling for a minimum of 8 hours after simmering to firm and enhance their texture before finishing, so plan accordingly. This recipe yields 4 meaty medallions.

Dry Ingredients

- 1 and ½ cup (225 g) vital wheat gluten
- 2 T porcini mushroom powder
- 4 tsp onion powder
- 2 tsp garlic powder
- ½ tsp ground white pepper

Liquid Ingredients

- 1 cup (240 ml) water
- 3 T tamari, soy sauce or Bragg Liquid Aminos™
- 2 T mild vegetable oil
- 2 tsp Worcestershire Sauce (pg. 25) or commercial vegan equivalent
- 1 tsp Browning Liquid (pg. 26) or commercial equivalent

Simmering Broth

- 3 quarts (12 cups) beaf simmering broth (pg. 78)

Pan-Glaze Ingredients for Finishing

- 2 T non-dairy butter or margarine
- 2 T dry red wine or reserved simmering broth
- 2 tsp Worcestershire Sauce (pg. 25) or commercial vegan equivalent
- a few pinches coarse ground black pepper
- ground spices and/or fresh or dried herbs of your choice (optional)

Additional Items Needed

- baking sheet
- stainless steel cooling rack (not required but recommended)
- parchment paper or silicone baking mat

Preparation

Prepare the simmering broth and bring to a simmer in a large covered cooking pot. If preparing the broth from scratch, prepare and bring to a simmer 30 minutes before preparing and prebaking the dough. This will allow sufficient time to simmer the ingredients before adding the beaf.

Place a stainless steel cooling rack on a baking sheet and line the rack with parchment paper or a silicone baking mat. The cooling rack is not required, but it is recommended, as it will prevent excessive browning which would occur from direct contact with the hot baking sheet. Preheat the oven to 350°F/180°C.

Combine the dry ingredients in a large mixing bowl. Stir together the liquid ingredients in a separate bowl or measuring cup.

Pour the liquid mixture (not the simmering broth) into the dry ingredients and combine thoroughly with a sturdy silicone spatula to form the dough and begin developing the gluten.

Transfer the dough to a work surface and knead vigorously until very elastic. Pick up the dough and stretch it into a long strand until it begins to tear. Place it on your work surface and then loosely roll it up into a lumpy mass. Knead a few strokes. Repeat the stretching, rolling and kneading technique until the dough is separating into stringy strands when stretched, finishing by loosely rolling it into a lumpy mass on your work surface. The goal of this technique is to isolate the strands of gluten, which in turn will create the proper beaf texture in the finished product.

Now, stretch and shape the lumpy mass of dough into a rough log shape, about 8-inches long. Don't try to smooth the surface, as bumps and irregularities will yield a better finished texture and appearance. With a sharp knife, cut the log into 4 pieces. Place the pieces with the cut side up/down on the parchment paper or baking mat and compress them with the palm of your hand to about 1 inch thick.

Place the baking sheet on the middle rack of the oven. Bake uncovered for 30 minutes and then remove from the oven. The medallions will form a dry crust while baking. This is normal and will disappear when the medallions are simmered.

Optionally, for thin steak cutlets, divide the dough into 8 pieces. Press and stretch each piece against your work surface and shape into a thin cutlet. If the dough is resistant to shaping, let the dough relax a few minutes and then press, stretch and shape again. Place the cutlets on the parchment paper or baking mat and prebake for 25 minutes. Simmer for 20 minutes and continue to follow the directions for chilling to firm and enhance the beaf texture before finishing. Steak cutlets are ideal for pan-grilling or breading and frying. Steak cutlets can also be sliced into strips, which make them ideal for fajitas and stir-fries.

Bring the broth to a boil. If the broth was made from scratch, use a slotted spoon to remove and discard the larger solids. It's not necessary to strain the broth completely.

Lower the prebaked medallions into the boiling broth and immediately reduce the heat to a gentle simmer. Leave the pot uncovered and set a timer for 30 minutes. Monitor the pot frequently to make sure the broth is maintained at a simmer. Do not boil the medallions but don't let them merely poach in hot broth either. Turn the medallions occasionally once they float to the top of the pot to ensure even cooking. After simmering, remove the cooking pot from the heat, cover and let the medallions cool in the broth for a few hours or until lukewarm.

Transfer the medallions to a food storage bag and add ¼ cup of broth, or a desired marinade. Refrigerate for a minimum of 8 hours, or for up to 1 week, to firm and enhance the beaf texture before finishing.

Chilling is very important so do not omit this step. The medallions can be frozen without the broth for up to 3 months and then thawed and finished at your convenience.

Strain the cooled broth into a sealable container and refrigerate. During this time, any seasoning sediment will settle on the bottom of the container. The broth can be refrigerated for up to 1 week or frozen for future use at your convenience. Decant the clear portion for preparing gravies or sauces that can be served with the finished beef; or use for other recipes as desired. Discard the sediment.

Finishing the Medallions

Combine the wine or reserved broth with the Worcestershire in a small dish. Stir in any desired optional seasonings.

In a large non-stick skillet, melt the butter or margarine over medium heat. Pan-sear the medallions, turning frequently until lightly browned on all sides.

Add the wine/broth mixture. Continue to pan-sear the medallions in the mixture, turning frequently until most of the liquid has evaporated and the medallions are nicely browned; season with black pepper to taste. Arrange the medallions on individual serving plates and serve immediately.

Alternately, the medallions can be broiled; or they can be finished in a non-stick grill pan or on an outdoor grill. Brush or spray the grill pan or grill grating with cooking oil to discourage sticking. Brush the medallions with cooking oil before broiling or grilling, even when a marinade or sauce is being used. There is little fat content in meat analogues, other than the trivial amount of oil that was added during preparation, and plant fat (oil) is what will keep the beef tender, juicy and flavorful when grilling.

Steak Diane

Steak Diane consists of tender tournedos of beaf flambéed and served with a rich mushroom, shallot and cognac cream sauce; serves 4.

Ingredients

- 4 Tournedos of Beaf (pg. 79)
- 2 T olive oil, or more as needed
- 2 T non-dairy butter or margarine
- 1 small shallot, finely chopped
- 1 cup sliced crimini or white mushrooms
- 2 cloves garlic, minced
- 1 T Worcestershire Sauce (pg. 25) or commercial vegan equivalent
- 1 T Dijon mustard
- ⅓ cup brandy or cognac
- 1 cup Soy Cream (pg. 30) or plain unsweetened cashew milk
- ¼ cup chopped parsley

Preparation

Prepare the Tournedos of Beaf according to the recipe. Chill them as directed but omit the finishing instructions.

Season the medallions on both sides with coarse black pepper. In a large non-stick skillet, add the olive oil and place over medium heat. Pan-sear the medallions until lightly browned. Transfer the medallions back to the plate and cover to keep warm until the sauce is prepared. Do not wipe or clean the skillet.

If the skillet is dry, add a tablespoon of olive oil. Add the shallots and sauté over medium heat until softened. Add the mushrooms and a pinch of salt. Sauté until the mushrooms have released their moisture and are beginning to lightly brown. Add the garlic and sauté an additional minute. Add the butter or margarine and stir until melted. Stir in the Worcestershire sauce and mustard and heat for about 30 seconds.

Remove the skillet momentarily from the heat and add the cognac or brandy. Place the skillet back over the heat and carefully ignite the alcohol with a long match or long-stemmed butane lighter. Shake the skillet gently until the flames die.

WARNING! Exercise caution when igniting the alcohol as it will produce a rather dramatic flame. Hold the skillet away from your body and away from anything flammable such as kitchen curtains, etc.

Stir in the cream and allow the sauce to slightly thicken before reducing the heat to medium-low.

Introduce the medallions back to the skillet with 2 tablespoons of parsley and cook briefly until heated through, about 1 minute.

Arrange the medallions on individual serving plates. Spoon the sauce over the medallions and sprinkle with the remaining parsley.

Steak Medici

Steak Medici consists of tender tournedos of beaf pan-seared until nicely browned and served with sautéed mushrooms in a port wine glaze; serves 4.

Ingredients

- 4 Tournedos of Beaf (pg. 79)
- 2 T olive oil, or more as needed
- 2 T non-dairy butter or margarine
- 1 cup sliced crimini or white mushrooms
- ½ cup port wine
- ¼ cup chopped parsley

Preparation

Prepare the Tournedos of Beaf according to the recipe. Chill them as directed but omit the finishing instructions.

In a large non-stick skillet, add the olive oil and place over medium heat. Pan-sear the medallions until lightly browned. Transfer the medallions back to the plate and cover to keep warm until the sauce is prepared. Do not wipe or clean the skillet.

If the skillet is dry, add a tablespoon of olive oil. Add the mushrooms and a pinch of salt. Sauté until the mushrooms have released their moisture and are beginning to lightly brown. Add the butter or margarine and stir until melted.

Introduce the medallions back to the skillet. Add the port wine and 2 tablespoons of parsley and cook briefly until heated through, about 1 minute.

Arrange the medallions on individual serving plates. Spoon the mushrooms and sauce around the medallions and garnish with the remaining parsley.

Chef's tip: For a spicy balsamic steak marinade and glaze, combine ½ cup apple juice or cider, 2 tablespoons dark balsamic vinegar, 2 tablespoons tamari, soy sauce or Bragg Liquid Aminos™, 2 tablespoons organic raw agave syrup and ½ tsp crushed red pepper flakes. Marinate the steaks for several hours or overnight. Add 2 tablespoons of the marinade while pan-browning the steaks to create a spicy and sweet caramelized glaze.

Steak au Poivre

Tender tournedos of beaf are encrusted with cracked black pepper, pan-seared until nicely browned and topped with a cognac cream sauce flavored with mustard and thyme; serves 4.

Preparation

Prepare the Tournedos of Beaf according to the recipe. Chill them as directed but omit the original finishing instructions.

In a small bowl, whisk together the cream, broth, mustard and thyme. Set aside.

Scatter a generous amount (about 1 tablespoon) of cracked black pepper on a plate and press the medallions into the pepper. Use more pepper as needed.

In a large non-stick skillet, add the olive oil and place over medium heat.

Ingredients

- 4 Tournedos of Beaf (pg. 79)
- 2 T olive oil, or more as needed
- 2 T non-dairy butter or margarine
- cracked black pepper, as needed
- 1 small shallot, finely chopped
- ⅓ cup reserved simmering broth (from preparing the tournedos)
- 2 tsp Dijon mustard
- ½ tsp dried thyme leaves
- ⅓ cup cognac or brandy
- ⅔ cup Soy Cream (pg. 30) or plain unsweetened cashew milk

Pan-sear the medallions until lightly browned. Transfer the medallions back to the plate and cover to keep warm until the sauce is prepared. Do not wipe or clean the skillet.

If the skillet is dry, add a tablespoon of olive oil. Add the shallots and sauté until translucent. Add the butter or margarine and stir until melted.

Remove the skillet momentarily from the heat and add ⅓ cup cognac or brandy. Place the skillet back over the heat and carefully ignite the alcohol with a long match or long-stemmed butane lighter. Shake the skillet gently until the flames die.

WARNING! Exercise caution when igniting the alcohol as it will produce a rather dramatic flame. Hold the skillet away from your body and away from anything flammable such as kitchen curtains, etc.

Stir in the broth and cream mixture. Continue to cook until the sauce has slightly thickened. Remove the skillet from the heat.

Arrange the medallions on individual serving plates. Pour the sauce over the medallions and serve immediately.

Steak Bites

To create steak bites, the seasoned dough is cut into small nuggets. The nuggets are prebaked to set their texture and then simmered in a hearty broth to complete the cooking process before finishing. Steak bites can be finished by pan-glazing in a skillet or they can be threaded onto long skewers to create brochettes/shish kebab for the grill.

Please note: Steak bites require chilling for a minimum of 8 hours after simmering to firm and enhance their texture before finishing, so plan accordingly.

Dry Ingredients

- 1 and ½ cup (225 g) vital wheat gluten
- 2 T porcini mushroom powder
- 4 tsp onion powder
- 2 tsp garlic powder
- ½ tsp ground white pepper

Simmering Broth

- 3 quarts (12 cups) beaf simmering broth (pg. 78)

Additional Items Needed

- baking sheet
- stainless steel cooling rack (not required but recommended)
- parchment paper or silicone baking mat

Optional Pan-Glaze Ingredients for Finishing

- 2 T non-dairy butter or margarine
- 2 T dry red wine or reserved simmering broth
- 2 tsp Worcestershire Sauce (pg. 25) or commercial vegan equivalent
- a few pinches coarse ground black pepper
- ground spices and/or fresh or dried herbs of your choice (optional)

Liquid Ingredients

- 1 cup (240 ml) water
- 3 T tamari, soy sauce or Bragg Liquid Aminos™
- 2 T mild vegetable oil
- 2 tsp Worcestershire Sauce (pg. 25) or commercial vegan equivalent
- 1 tsp Browning Liquid (pg. 26) or commercial equivalent

Preparation

Prepare the simmering broth and bring to a simmer in a large covered cooking pot. If preparing the broth from scratch, prepare and bring to a simmer 30 minutes before preparing and prebaking the dough. This will allow sufficient time to simmer the ingredients before adding the beaf.

Place a stainless steel cooling rack on a baking sheet and line the rack with parchment paper or a silicone baking mat. The cooling rack is not required, but it is recommended, as it will prevent excessive browning which would occur from direct contact with the hot baking sheet. Preheat the oven to 350°F/180°C.

Combine the dry ingredients in a large mixing bowl. Stir together the liquid ingredients in a separate bowl or measuring cup.

Pour the liquid mixture (not the simmering broth) into the dry ingredients and combine thoroughly with a sturdy silicone spatula to form the dough and begin developing the gluten.

Transfer the dough to a work surface and knead vigorously until very elastic. Pick up the dough and stretch it into a long strand until it begins to tear. Place it on your work surface and then loosely roll it up into a lumpy mass. Knead a few strokes. Repeat the stretching, rolling and kneading technique until the dough is separating into stringy strands when stretched, finishing by loosely rolling it into a lumpy mass on your work surface. The goal of this technique is to isolate the strands of gluten, which in turn will create the proper beaf texture in the finished product.

Now, with a sharp knife, cut the dough into 1-inch chunks and place them on the parchment paper or baking mat. Place the baking sheet on the middle rack of the oven. Bake uncovered for 25 minutes and then remove from the oven. The steak bites will form a dry crust while baking. This is normal and will disappear when the steak bites are simmered.

Bring the broth to a boil. If the broth was made from scratch, use a slotted spoon to remove and discard the larger solids. It's not necessary to strain the broth completely.

Lower the prebaked steak bites into the boiling broth and immediately reduce the heat to a gentle simmer. Leave the pot uncovered and set a timer for 20 minutes. Monitor the pot frequently to make sure the broth is maintained at a simmer. Do not boil the steak bites but don't let them merely poach in hot broth either. Move the steak bites occasionally in the broth once they float to the top of the pot. After simmering, remove the cooking pot from the heat, cover and let the steak bites cool in the broth for a few hours or until lukewarm.

Transfer the steak bites to a food storage bag and add ¼ cup broth, or a desired marinade. Refrigerate for a minimum of 8 hours, or for up to 1 week, to firm and enhance the beaf texture before finishing. Chilling is very important so do not omit this step. The steak bites can be frozen without the broth for up to 3 months and then thawed and finished at your convenience.

Strain the cooled broth into a sealable container and refrigerate. During this time, any seasoning sediment will settle on the bottom of the container. The broth can be refrigerated for up to 1 week or frozen for future use at your convenience. Decant the clear portion for preparing gravies or sauces that can be served with the finished steak bites; or use for other recipes as desired. Discard the sediment.

Finishing the Steak Bites

Combine the wine or reserved broth with the Worcestershire in a small dish. Stir in any desired optional seasonings. In a large non-stick skillet or well-seasoned cast iron skillet, melt the butter or margarine over medium heat. Sauté the steak bites, moving them frequently until lightly browned on all sides. Add the wine/broth mixture. Continue to sauté the steak bites in the mixture, turning frequently until most of the liquid has evaporated and the steak bites are nicely glazed; season with black pepper to taste. Arrange the steak bites on a serving platter, insert toothpicks and serve immediately.

To skewer and grill the steak bites, refer to the technique for Beaf en Brochette, Shish Kebab and Satay on the following page.

Please note: While the steak bites can certainly be used in soups and stews, they must be prebaked, simmered, chilled, and then browned in a skillet before re-adding to simmering liquids. Do not simply add the prebaked steak bites to soups and stews; the finished texture will not be correct. For this reason, consider Stewing Beaf as an option.

Beaf en Brochette, Shish Kebab and Satay

"En brochette" is the French term and "shish kebab or shish kabob" is the Middle Eastern term for skewered and grilled chunks of meat with or without vegetables. "Satay" is the Indonesian term for seasoned, skewered and grilled meat, typically served with a dipping sauce. Steak bites have a high moisture content and tender texture which makes them ideal for skewering and grilling.

Preparation

Prepare the steak bites according to the recipe on pg. 85. Marinate if desired and chill them as directed. For mini appetizer skewers, use 6-inch bamboo skewers and you may want to cut or tear the steak bites into smaller pieces before skewering. When using bamboo skewers, soak them in water for several hours before skewering and grilling to prevent the wood from burning.

For beaf en brochette and shish kebab, skewer the steak bites with any vegetables of your choice, such as thickly sliced zucchini, eggplant, cherry tomatoes, mushrooms and chunks of onion and bell pepper (pineapple is ideal for skewering and grilling too). Satay is not typically skewered with vegetables. Season or brush the skewers with a favorite grilling sauce.

Brush or spray a non-stick grill pan or outdoor grill grating with cooking oil before grilling to keep the beaf and vegetables from sticking. Brush the beaf with cooking oil before broiling or outdoor grilling, and then generously and frequently with the marinade or sauce of your choice while broiling or grilling to keep the beaf moist and tender.

Beaf Satay Marinade

Preparation

Combine all ingredients except for the olive oil in a bowl. Whisk in the olive oil until emulsified. The marinade can also be processed in a blender if preferred. Pour the marinade into a food storage bag and add the beaf. Press the air out of the bag, seal and refrigerate for a minimum of one hour, and even better overnight, before pan-searing, broiling or grilling.

Any remaining marinade can also be used to create a dipping sauce. After marinating the beaf, drain the marinade into a small saucepan and bring to simmer.

Ingredients

- 2 T reserved beaf simmering broth, or water
- 2 T tamari, soy sauce or Bragg Liquid Aminos™
- ¼ cup fresh lime juice
- 1 T dark brown sugar
- 3 cloves garlic, minced (1 T)
- 2 tsp fresh grated ginger
- ½ tsp sesame oil
- ½ tsp sambal oelek or Sriracha™
- 2 T extra-virgin olive oil

Reduce the heat to low to keep warm until ready to serve. Pour the dipping sauce into small bowls and garnish with chopped green onions or chopped cilantro.

Chef's note: Sambal oelek is a hot red chile sauce and a staple in Malaysian and Thai cooking.

Beaf Short-Ribz

Beaf short ribz are prepared by stretching and wrapping seasoned dough around short, split stalks of fresh sugarcane. The ribz are prebaked until partially cooked and then simmered in a seasoned broth to complete the cooking process. The ribz are finished on the grill and basted with a grilling sauce of your choice. This recipe yields 12 short ribz.

Please note: Short ribz require chilling for a minimum of 8 hours after simmering to firm and enhance their texture before grilling, so plan accordingly.

Dry Ingredients

- 1 and ½ cup (225 g) vital wheat gluten
- 2 T porcini mushroom powder
- 4 tsp onion powder
- 2 tsp garlic powder
- ½ tsp ground white pepper

Liquid Ingredients

- 1 cup (240 ml) water
- 3 T tamari, soy sauce or Bragg Liquid Aminos™
- 2 T mild vegetable oil
- 2 tsp Worcestershire Sauce (pg. 25) or commercial vegan equivalent
- 1 tsp Browning Liquid (pg. 26) or commercial equivalent

Simmering Broth

- 3 quarts (12 cups) beaf simmering broth (pg. 78)

Additional Items Needed

- two 12-inch pieces of raw sugarcane
- baking sheet
- stainless steel cooling rack (not required but recommended)
- parchment paper or silicone baking mat

Preparation

Lightly peel the cane with a vegetable peeler to expose the pulp. With a sharp cleaver, carefully make 2 crosswise cuts to create three 4-inch segments from each piece of cane. Carefully split the segments lengthwise through the center to create a total of 12 pieces. These pieces will be used as the 'bones" for the short-ribz.

Prepare the simmering broth and bring to a simmer in a large covered cooking pot. If preparing the broth from scratch, prepare and bring to a simmer 30 minutes before preparing and prebaking the dough. This will allow sufficient time to simmer the ingredients before adding the ribz.

Place a stainless steel cooling rack on a baking sheet and line the rack with parchment paper or a silicone baking mat. The cooling rack is not required, but it is recommended, as it will prevent excessive browning which would occur from direct contact with the hot baking sheet. Preheat the oven to 350°F/180°C.

Combine the dry ingredients in a large mixing bowl. Stir together the liquid ingredients in a separate bowl or measuring cup.

Pour the liquid mixture (not the simmering broth) into the dry ingredients and combine thoroughly with a sturdy silicone spatula to form the dough and begin developing the gluten.

Transfer the dough to a work surface and knead vigorously until very elastic. Test the dough by stretching. If it tears easily, knead a little longer and test again. The dough should be able to stretch considerably without tearing.

With a sharp knife, cut the dough into 12 roughly equal pieces. Stretch a piece of dough as far as it can be stretched without tearing completely and then wrap and press it around a sugarcane "bone". Be sure to leave about ½-inch of the cane free on each end for grasping. Pinch the dough together on each end so it doesn't unravel and place it on the parchment paper or baking mat. Repeat with the remaining pieces.

Place the baking sheet on the middle rack of the oven. Bake uncovered for 20 minutes and then remove from the oven. The ribz will form a dry crust while baking; this is normal and will disappear when the ribz are simmered.

Bring the broth to a boil. If the broth was made from scratch, use a slotted spoon to remove and discard the larger solids. It's not necessary to strain the broth completely.

Lower the short-ribz into the boiling broth and immediately reduce the heat to a gentle simmer. Leave the pot uncovered and set a timer for 20 minutes. Monitor the pot frequently to make sure the broth is maintained at a simmer. Do not boil the ribz but don't let them merely poach in hot broth either. Move the ribz occasionally in the broth once they float to the top of the pot. After simmering, remove the cooking pot from the heat, cover and let the ribz cool in the broth for a few hours or until lukewarm.

Transfer the ribz to a food storage bag and add ¼ cup of broth, or a desired marinade. Refrigerate for a minimum of 8 hours, or for up to 1 week, to firm and enhance the beaf texture before finishing. Chilling is very important so do not omit this step. The ribz can be frozen without the broth for up to 3 months and then thawed and finished at your convenience.

Strain the cooled broth into a sealable container and refrigerate. During this time, any seasoning sediment will settle on the bottom of the container. The broth can be refrigerated for up to 1 week or frozen for future use at your convenience. Decant the clear portion to use for other recipes as desired. Discard the sediment.

Finishing the Short-Ribz

Brush or spray a non-stick grill pan or outdoor grill grating with cooking oil before grilling to discourage the ribz from sticking. Brush the ribz with cooking oil before broiling or outdoor grilling and then generously and frequently with the sauce of your choice while broiling or grilling to keep the beaf moist and tender.

Prime Cut Roast Beaf

Succulent and tender prime cut roast beaf slices are delicious served 'au jus' or with your favorite gravy or sauce. Leftovers are superb for hot or cold deli-style sandwiches too. This recipe yields about 1 and ½ lb. Please note: Prime cut roast beaf requires chilling for a minimum of 8 hours after simmering to firm and enhance its texture before pan-glazing, so plan accordingly.

Dry Ingredients

- 1 and ½ cup (225 g) vital wheat gluten
- 2 T porcini mushroom powder
- 4 tsp onion powder
- 2 tsp garlic powder
- ½ tsp ground white pepper

Liquid Ingredients

- 1 cup (240 ml) water
- 3 T tamari, soy sauce or Bragg Liquid Aminos™
- 2 T mild vegetable oil
- 2 tsp Worcestershire Sauce (pg. 25) or commercial vegan equivalent
- 1 tsp Browning Liquid (pg. 26) or commercial equivalent

Pan-Glaze Ingredients

- 2 T non-dairy butter or margarine
- 2 T dry red wine or dry sherry (optional)
- 2 tsp Worcestershire Sauce (pg. 25) or commercial vegan equivalent
- a few pinches coarse ground black pepper
- optional: ground spices and/or fresh or dried herbs of your choice

Preparation

Prepare the simmering broth and bring to a simmer in a large covered cooking pot.

If preparing the broth from scratch, prepare and bring to a simmer 30 minutes before preparing and prebaking the dough. This will allow sufficient time to simmer the ingredients before adding the beaf.

Preheat the oven to 350°F/180°C.

Simmering Broth

- 3 quarts (12 cups) beaf simmering broth (pg. 78)

Additional Items Needed

- baking sheet
- stainless steel cooling rack (not required but recommended)
- parchment paper or silicone baking mat

Place a stainless steel cooling rack on a baking sheet and line the rack with parchment paper or a silicone baking mat. The cooling rack is not required, but it is recommended, as it will prevent excessive browning which would occur from direct contact with the hot baking sheet.

Combine the dry ingredients in a large mixing bowl. Stir together the liquid ingredients in a separate bowl or measuring cup.

Pour the liquid mixture (not the simmering broth) into the dry ingredients and combine thoroughly with a sturdy silicone spatula to form the dough and begin developing the gluten.

Transfer the dough to a work surface and knead vigorously until very elastic. Test the dough by stretching. If it tears easily, knead a little longer and test again. The dough should be able to stretch considerably without tearing.

Now, form the dough into a thick, compact slab. Don't worry about smoothing the surface too much, as some bumps and irregularities will yield a more natural finished appearance. Transfer the dough to the parchment paper or baking mat.

Place the baking sheet on the middle rack of the oven. Bake uncovered for 45 minutes and then remove from the oven. The roast will form a dry crust while baking. This is normal and will disappear when the roast is simmered.

Bring the broth to a boil. If the broth was made from scratch, use a spider or slotted spoon to remove and discard the larger solids. It's not necessary to strain the broth completely.

Lower the roast into the boiling broth and immediately reduce the heat to a gentle simmer. Leave the pot uncovered and set a timer for 45 minutes. Monitor the pot frequently to make sure the broth is maintained at a simmer. Do not boil the roast but don't let it merely poach in hot broth either. Turn the roast occasionally in the broth as it simmers to ensure even cooking. After simmering, remove the cooking pot from the heat, cover and let the roast cool in the broth for a few hours or until lukewarm.

Transfer the roast to a food storage bag and add ¼ cup of broth, or a desired marinade. Refrigerate for a minimum of 8 hours, or for up to 1 week, to firm and enhance the beaf texture before finishing. Chilling is very important so do not omit this step. The roast can be frozen without the broth for up to 3 months and then thawed and finished at your convenience.

Strain the cooled broth into a sealable container and refrigerate. During this time, any seasoning sediment will settle on the bottom of the container. The broth can be refrigerated for up to 1 week or frozen for future use at your convenience. Decant the clear portion for preparing 'au jus', gravy or sauce that can be served with the sliced roast; or use for other recipes as desired. Discard the sediment.

Finishing the Roast

Bring the roast to room temperature for about 1 hour before finishing.

Combine the wine or broth and tamari in a small dish; set aside. In a large, deep non-stick skillet, melt the butter or margarine over medium heat. Add the roast and turn it to coat with the butter or margarine. Lightly brown the roast, turning frequently. Add the liquid seasonings. The mixture will sizzle and begin to caramelize, turning the roast a beautiful deep brown color. Add the pepper and optional spices and herbs and continue to turn in the mixture to form a crust. Transfer to a serving platter and slice.

Note: If pan-glazing has not sufficiently reheated the roast, place it in a shallow baking dish, cover securely with foil and reheat in a 350°F/180°C oven for 15 to 20 minutes. The roast can also be briefly heated in the microwave before slicing and serving.

Quick Pan Gravy for Roast Beef

To make a quick pan gravy for sliced roast beef, add 4 tablespoons non-dairy butter or margarine to the same non-stick skillet used for pan-glazing the roast and heat on a medium setting until the butter or margarine melts.

Sprinkle in ¼ cup all-purpose flour or rice flour and stir to form a thick, smooth paste (roux). Cook the roux until it emits a nutty aroma, about 1 to 2 minutes.

Incorporate 2 cups of reserved beef simmering broth in small increments, whisking vigorously until smooth after each addition of broth. Continue to whisk, loosening any caramelized bits of glaze stuck to the skillet as you stir. To enrich the brown color, add ½ teaspoon to 1 teaspoon Browning Liquid (pg. 26) or a commercial equivalent. Increase the heat to medium-high and stir frequently until the mixture is bubbling and begins to thicken; season with salt and pepper to taste. Reduce the heat to low to keep warm until ready to serve, stirring occasionally.

Yam Neua

(Spicy Thai Beef Salad)

Assorted greens, bean sprouts, cucumber, scallions, red onion, cilantro and mint are topped with freshly grilled beaf seitan and then dressed with a spicy, peppery tamari lime dressing.

Ingredients

- ⅓ cup fresh lime juice (about 3 limes)
- 3 T tamari, soy sauce or Bragg Liquid Aminos™
- 1 T seeded and finely minced fresh Thai, serrano or jalapeno chili
- 1 T organic sugar
- 1 T finely chopped fresh mint
- assorted spring greens (about 5 cups)
- 2 scallions, chopped
- ½ red onion, thinly sliced
- 1 large cucumber, peeled, halved lengthwise, seeded and cut into ¼-inch slices
- 1 handful bean sprouts
- ¼ cup chopped fresh cilantro
- 2 T olive oil
- 10 oz Prime Cut Roast Beef (pg. 90), thinly sliced
- coarse ground black pepper, to taste
- ¼ cup unsalted peanuts, coarse chopped

Preparation

To make the dressing, whisk together the lime juice, tamari, chili and sugar in a small bowl until the sugar is dissolved. Stir in the mint and set aside.

Toss together the greens, scallions, red onion, cucumber, bean sprouts and cilantro in a large bowl; set aside.

Heat the oil in a large skillet over medium-high heat until hot but not smoking. Briefly pan-sear the beaf until lightly browned. Season the beaf with a dash of tamari and black pepper while pan-searing. Remove from the heat and let cool for 5 minutes.

Add the sliced beaf to the salad. Drizzle with the dressing, and toss. Sprinkle with the peanuts and serve.

Sauerbraten

In German "sauerbraten" means "sour roast". Actually, the roast and gravy boast a wonderful combination of sweet and sour flavors. Serve with German red cabbage, potatoes of your choice or Spätzle or Knöpfle. Wunderbar! Be sure to prepare the roast the day before planning to serve to allow a minimum of 8 hours for marinating.

Preparation

The day before planning to serve, prepare the Prime Cut Roast Beaf according to the directions on pg. 90. Let the roast cool in the broth until lukewarm and then transfer to a food storage bag. Add ¼ cup simmering broth and ¼ cup red wine vinegar or raw apple cider vinegar, seal and refrigerate for a minimum of 8 hours. Strain the remaining simmering broth into a sealable container and refrigerate. Discard the solids. A portion of the broth will be used for preparing the Sauerbraten gravy.

When ready to proceed, bring the roast to room temperature for about 1 hour. Spray a large non-stick skillet with cooking oil and place over medium heat. Drain the broth and vinegar marinade from the bag and reserve for the gravy. Brown the roast on both sides in the hot skillet. Transfer to a heat proof plate or shallow baking dish and cover with foil. Place in a low oven (about 250°F/120°C) to keep warm while the gravy is prepared.

Gravy Ingredients

- ¼ cup non-dairy butter or margarine
- ¼ cup all-purpose flour or rice flour
- 4 cups reserved simmering broth from preparing the roast, diluted as needed with water
- broth/vinegar marinade reserved after marinating the roast
- 1 large onion, peeled and chopped
- 1 large carrot, unpeeled and chopped
- 2 T dark brown sugar

- 1 bay leaf
- 12 juniper berries (optional)
- 1 tsp Dijon mustard
- 1 tsp ground ginger
- ½ tsp ground cloves
- ½ tsp ground black pepper
- ¼ cup seedless raisins
- sea salt or kosher salt, to taste
- chopped parsley for garnish (optional)

Gravy Preparation

Add ¼ cup butter or margarine to a large cooking pot and melt over medium heat. Sprinkle in the flour and stir to create a thick paste (roux). Cook until the roux emits a nutty aroma, about 1 to 2 minutes.

Incorporate the reserved broth in small increments while whisking vigorously until smooth after each addition of broth. Add the reserved broth and vinegar marinade and all remaining ingredients except the parsley garnish. Bring the mixture to a boil, stirring frequently. Reduce the heat to a simmer and cook partially covered for 45 minutes. Taste the gravy and season with salt if needed.

Remove the roast from the oven and thinly slice. Transfer the slices to a serving platter.

Strain the gravy through a sieve and discard the solids. Generously ladle the gravy over the sliced sauerbraten and garnish with the optional chopped parsley. Place additional gravy into a boat to serve on the side. Serve immediately. Leftovers can be refrigerated for up to 1 week or frozen for up to 3 months.

Chinese Pepper Beaf

Tender beaf, green bell peppers, onions and sliced garlic are stir-fried and tossed in a savory tamari-based sauce.

Preparation

Stir together the water, tamari and sugar in a bowl or measuring cup and set aside.

Add 1 tablespoon of cooking oil to a non-stick wok or deep skillet and place over medium heat. Brown the sliced beaf. Remove to a plate and set aside.

Add the remaining tablespoon of cooking oil to the wok or skillet and sauté the onions and peppers until the onions are golden, about 5 minutes. Add the garlic, ginger and red pepper flakes and sauté an additional minute.

Stir in the tamari mixture, bring to a simmer and cover the wok or skillet (an exact fitting lid is unimportant, just as long as it can hold in the steam). Simmer for 5 minutes.

While the vegetables are simmering, create a slurry by mixing the starch with a little water in a small dish until dissolved.

Ingredients

- ¾ cup water
- ¼ cup tamari, soy sauce or Bragg Liquid Aminos™
- 2 tsp dark brown sugar
- 2 T cooking oil
- 12 oz Prime Cut Roast Beaf (pg. 90), thinly sliced and cut into bite-size pieces
- 2 green bell peppers; stems, core, seeds and membrane removed and cut into bite-size pieces
- 1 large white or yellow onion, peeled and cut into bite-size pieces
- 3 cloves garlic, thinly sliced
- 2 tsp fresh grated ginger
- ½ tsp red pepper flakes, or more to taste
- 1 T unmodified potato starch, cornstarch or arrowroot powder

Stir the slurry into the wok contents and cook until the mixture begins to thicken. Add the beaf slices back to the wok and toss gently to combine and heat through. Serve hot over steamed rice.

Stewing Beaf

Stewing Beaf, as the name implies, is ideal for pot roast, stews, soups and pot pies or any recipe that involves simmering in hot liquids. It was formulated differently from the other beaf recipes in order to produce a shreddable texture when simmered that is remarkably similar to beef that has been slow-simmered for hours. Stewing beaf is neutrally seasoned which allows it to absorb additional herb and spice flavors from simmering liquids. This recipe yields about 1lb., after simmering, which should be ample for most recipes.

Please note: Stewing beaf requires chilling for a minimum of 8 hours after baking to firm and enhance its texture before stewing, so plan accordingly.

Dry Ingredients

- 1 cup (150 g) vital wheat gluten
- 1 T porcini mushroom powder
- 2 tsp onion powder
- 1 tsp garlic powder
- ¼ tsp ground white pepper

Blender Ingredients

- 2.5 oz (70 g) pressed extra-firm block tofu (see pg. 24 for instructions)
- ⅔ cup (160 ml) water
- 2 T mellow white miso paste
- 1 T mild vegetable oil
- 2 tsp Worcestershire Sauce (pg. 25) or commercial vegan equivalent
- 1 and ½ tsp Browning Liquid (pg. 26) or commercial equivalent
- ½ tsp fine sea salt or kosher salt

Additional Item Needed

- 18-inch-wide heavy-duty aluminum foil

Preparation

Warning! It is very important to use only heavy-duty aluminum foil for this recipe. Regular foil is not sturdy enough and can easily rupture from steam pressure which builds up inside the sealed package.

Preheat the oven to 350°F/180°C.

Combine the dry ingredients in a large mixing bowl.

Crumble the pressed tofu into a blender and add the remaining blender ingredients. Process the contents until the tofu is completely liquefied and the mixture is smooth and creamy. This is essential! Stop the blender as necessary to scrape down the sides.

Scoop the tofu mixture into the dry ingredients (a small amount of the tofu mixture will remain in the blender; this is inconsequential) and stir with a sturdy silicone spatula until the tofu mixture is incorporated and a sticky ball of dough begins to form.

Place the dough into a food processor fitted with a dough blade and process for 2 full minutes. Alternately, place the dough into a stand mixer fitted with a paddle and process on medium speed for 2 full minutes.

If kneading by hand, knead the dough in the bowl vigorously for 5 full minutes. This is very important in order to develop the gluten. Test the dough by stretching it. If it tears easily, more kneading is required. The dough needs to exhibit a substantial degree of elasticity in order to produce the proper finished texture.

Tear off a sheet of foil (about 18-inches) and place it on your work surface. Transfer the dough to the foil and shape into a compact slab. Shaping perfection is unnecessary. If you are using a dry rub seasoning, rub about 2 teaspoons of the mixture over the dough. Fold the slab of dough in the foil (don't roll), creating a semi-flat package. Fold in the ends but leave a little room (about 1-inch on each side) to allow the dough to expand as it bakes. This is very important! Crimp the folded ends to seal the package.

Rewrap the package in a second sheet of foil and place the package directly on the middle rack of the oven. Bake for 1 hour and 30 minutes and then remove from the oven to cool completely.

Refrigerate the foil package for a minimum of 8 hours, or for up to 1 week, to firm and enhance the beaf texture before stewing. Chilling is very important so do not omit this step. You can also store the beaf in the freezer wrapped in the foil for up to 3 months.

Preparing the Beaf for Stewing

Remove the foil and recycle. The exterior of the beaf will be hard and shriveled; this is normal and will resolve once the beaf is stewed. Using your hands, bend the roast in half to split it lengthwise; this will reveal the "grain". Tear the roast in half following where it has been split. Bend and tear those pieces in half lengthwise. Now, with your fingers, pull the beaf into long strips, following the grain as much as possible. Tear those pieces into smaller bite-size pieces. The pieces can also be cubed or diced. For pot pies and saucy casseroles, mix the diced beaf with the other ingredients before baking. For soups and stews, add the beaf the last 20 minutes of cooking time before serving.

For pot roasts or slow cooker recipes, leave the entire piece of beaf intact. After simmering, transfer to a serving platter and shred with a fork into chunks.

Classic Pot Roast

Preparation

Prepare the Stewing Beaf according to the recipe and then chill for 8 hours in the foil package. Prepare and strain the broth; this can be done in advance or just prior to making the pot roast.

Add the oil to a large cooking pot and place over medium heat. Add the flour and stir to create a paste (roux). Cook about 2 minutes until the flour emits a nutty aroma. Incorporate the broth in small increments while vigorously whisking the mixture.

Add the entire intact piece of stewing beaf and the remaining ingredients. Bring to a brief boil, partially cover the pot and reduce the heat to just above low. Let the beaf and vegetables cook until very tender, about 1 hour and 15 minutes; season with salt and additional black pepper to taste.

Transfer the beaf to a serving platter and tear into chunks using the tines of a fork. Using a slotted spoon, remove the vegetables and place around the beaf. Remove the rosemary and thyme stems. Ladle some of the gravy over the beaf and vegetables. Garnish with chopped parsley.

Ingredients

- 1 recipe Stewing Beaf, intact (pg. 95)
- 2 T olive oil
- 2 T all-purpose flour or rice flour
- 4 cups beaf simmering broth (pg. 78) or similar
- ¼ cup dry red wine, such as Cabernet Sauvignon or Merlot (optional)
- ¼ tsp coarse ground black pepper, or more to taste
- 3 sprigs fresh thyme or ½ tsp dried thyme leaves
- 2 sprigs fresh rosemary
- 2 large onions, peeled and cut into large chunks
- 4 large carrots, peeled and cut into large chunks
- 2 russet potatoes, peeled and cut into large chunks
- 3 cloves garlic, chopped
- sea salt or kosher salt to taste
- chopped parsley for garnish (optional)

Serve with prepared horseradish if desired. Leftover beaf and gravy is superb for open-faced pot roast sandwiches.

Shredded Beaf

Shredded beaf amazingly resembles slow-cooked shredded beef in flavor and texture and is ideal for any plant-based recipe where a shredded beaf texture is desired such as hot wraps or sandwiches, stir-fries, flash sautés and Mexican cuisine (tamales, enchiladas, taquitos, flautas and burritos).

Ingredients

- 1 recipe Stewing Beaf (pg. 95)
- 2 T cooking oil
- 1 medium onion, halved and thinly sliced
- 3 cloves garlic, minced, or more as desired
- ¼ cup water (except when using a sauce)
- optional fresh or dry herbs and spices as desired

Preparation

Prepare and then chill the Stewing Beaf according to the directions.

Remove the foil and recycle. Using your hands, bend the roast in half to split it lengthwise; this will reveal the "grain". Tear the roast in half following where it has been split. Bend and tear those pieces in half lengthwise. Now, with your fingers, pull the beaf into long strings or shreds, following the grain as much as possible. Tear those pieces into smaller bite-size shreds.

Add the oil to a large non-stick skillet or wok and place over medium heat; sauté the onion until tender and translucent. Add the garlic and sauté 30 seconds.

Add the shredded beaf and sauté, tossing frequently, until lightly browned. Add the water (omit when using a sauce), sprinkle in any optional seasonings and toss well to distribute. Continue to sauté until almost all the liquid has evaporated but the beaf is still moist; season with salt and pepper to taste. Use in your favorite recipes as desired. When using a sauce, simply toss with the pan-browned beaf and cook until heated through.

Chef's tip: Season your foods from start to finish while cooking. Seasoning in stages brings the most out of the ingredients and produces a better finished flavor.

Corned Beaf Brisket

Corned beaf is delicious anytime of the year but is especially appropriate for celebrating St. Patrick's Day or the Spring Equinox. This recipe requires time for marinating and chilling the brisket, so begin preparation a day ahead or at least early in the day before planning to serve. The corned beaf is prepared as a larger cut, and yields about 2 lbs., which allows it to be served as an entrée with ample leftover for sandwiches.

Aromatic Brine Ingredients

- 12 cups (3 quarts) water
- 2 T fine sea salt or kosher salt
- 2 T organic sugar
- aromatic spice blend:

  - 1 tsp whole cloves
  - 1 tsp whole allspice berries
  - 1 tsp whole juniper berries, lightly crushed
  - 2 bay leaves
  - 1 tsp whole black peppercorns
  - 1 tsp whole coriander seeds
  - 1 tsp caraway seeds
  - 1-inch piece ginger root, sliced
  - ½ stick whole cinnamon
  - ¼ tsp yellow mustard seeds

  or

  2 Tbsp commercial pickling spice blend plus 1 tsp caraway seeds

Dry Ingredients

- 2 cups (300 g) vital wheat gluten
- 2 T garbanzo bean flour
- 2 T onion powder
- 1 T garlic powder
- ¼ tsp ground white pepper

Coloring Brine Ingredients

- 2 cups (480 ml) cooled aromatic brine
- 1 T beet powder

Liquid Ingredients

- 1 and ¾ cup (420 ml) water
- 2 T tamari, soy sauce or Bragg Liquid Aminos™
- 2 T mild vegetable oil
- 1 tsp fine sea salt or kosher salt

Additional Items Needed

- 18-inch wide heavy-duty aluminum foil

Preparation

Warning! It is very important to use only heavy-duty aluminum foil for this recipe. Regular foil is not sturdy enough and can easily rupture from steam pressure which builds up inside the sealed package.

Prepare the aromatic brine by combining the brine ingredients in a large cooking pot. Cover, bring to a boil and then reduce heat to a gentle simmer for 20 minutes. Remove from the heat to cool.

While the brine is cooling, which requires a few hours, prepare and bake the brisket. Preheat the oven to 350°F/180°C.

Combine the dry ingredients in a large mixing bowl. Combine the liquid ingredients in a separate bowl or measuring cup and stir until the salt dissolves.

Pour the liquid mixture (not the aromatic brine or coloring brine) into the dry ingredients and combine thoroughly to develop the gluten. Knead the dough in the bowl until it feels elastic, about 1 minute.

Tear off a large sheet of foil (about 24-inches) and place it on your work surface. Place the dough onto the foil and flatten it into a slab about 1-inch thick.

Flat wrap the dough in the foil (don't roll), folding over several times to create a flattened package. Fold in the ends and crimp to seal the foil. Place the package on a second sheet of foil and rewrap in a similar fashion. Place the package directly on the middle rack of the oven and bake for 2 hours. Remove the package from the oven and let cool until it can be handled comfortably.

While the package is cooling, prepare the coloring brine mixture. Strain the aromatic brine to remove the spice solids and discard the solids. Combine 2 cups of the cooled aromatic brine with the beet powder and stir until completely dissolved (beet powder has a tendency to clump and form hard "rocks", so crush with the back of a spoon before mixing with the brine). Be sure to reserve the remaining uncolored brine for reheating the brisket later; do not discard!

Unwrap and transfer the brisket to a cutting board. With a sharp knife, trim away the thin layer of dry crust from the ends of the brisket and discard. Slice the brisket in half and trim away the thin layer of crust from the broad sides of the brisket and discard. Slice the brisket as thinly as possible and transfer the slices to a food storage bag.

Pour the coloring brine mixture into the food storage bag. Seal and turn the bag repeatedly to coat the slices with the mixture. Refrigerate for a minimum of 8 hours, or overnight, to allow sufficient marinating and staining with color. The brisket can also be stored in the coloring brine for up to 1 week before reheating and serving.

Finishing and Serving

To heat and serve the brisket, bring the reserved aromatic brine to a simmer in a cooking pot and then remove from the heat. Drain and discard the coloring brine mixture from the bag and transfer the slices to the hot brine. Cover and let stand for 10 minutes (as well as reheating, this will also help remove any excess color). Remove the slices with a spider or slotted spoon and transfer to a serving platter. Discard the brine. Serve warm with grainy mustard, prepared horseradish or Creamy Horseradish Sauce (pg. 195).

Note: If you wish to cook cabbage in the aromatic brine, cook and remove it before adding the color-infused brisket; otherwise the cabbage will be stained by the beet color.

Leftover corned beef can be reheated by wrapping securely in foil and placing in a 350°F/180°C oven, or a steamer, for 15 to 20 minutes. The slices can also be gently reheated in a lightly oiled skillet over medium-low heat. Leftovers should be consumed within 1 week or frozen for up to 3 months.

Deli-Style Pastrami

My signature meatless pastrami captures all the taste, texture and appearance of real pastrami without the animal cruelty or grisly fat. It has a smoky flavor and is generously seasoned with black pepper and other select spices. This recipe yields about 1 lb.

Dry Ingredients

- 1 cup (150 g) vital wheat gluten
- 1 T garbanzo bean flour
- 1 T onion powder
- 2 tsp garlic powder
- 1 tsp ground coriander
- ½ tsp smoked paprika
- ½ tsp dry ground mustard
- ¼ tsp ground allspice
- ¼ tsp ground cloves

Liquid Ingredients

- ¾ cup plus 2 T (210 ml) water
- 2 T tamari, soy sauce
  or Bragg Liquid Aminos™
- 1 T liquid smoke
- 1 T olive oil
- 1 tsp Worcestershire Sauce (pg. 25)
  or commercial vegan equivalent

Coloring Brine Ingredients

- 2 cups water
- 1 T dark brown sugar
- 1 T liquid smoke
- 1 tsp fine sea salt or kosher salt
- 2 tsp beet powder

Additional Seasoning Ingredient

- 1 and ½ tsp coarse ground black pepper

Additional Item Needed

18-inch wide heavy-duty aluminum foil

Preparation

Preheat the oven to 350°F/180°C.

Sift together the dry ingredients in a large mixing bowl. Combine the liquid ingredients in a separate bowl or measuring cup.

Pour the liquid mixture (not the coloring brine) into the dry ingredients and combine thoroughly to develop the gluten. Knead the dough in the bowl until it feels elastic, about 1 minute.

Tear off a sheet of foil (about 18-inches) and place it on your work surface. Place the dough onto the foil and flatten it into a slab about 1-inch thick. Sprinkle the surface of the dough with ¾ teaspoon black pepper. Flip the slab over and repeat with the remaining pepper.

Flat wrap the dough in the foil (don't roll), folding over several times to create a flattened package. Fold in the ends and crimp to seal the foil. Place the package on a second sheet of foil and rewrap in a similar fashion.

Place the package directly on the middle rack of the oven and bake for 1 hour and 30 minutes. Remove the package from the oven and let it cool to room temperature. Refrigerate for a minimum of 8 hours before proceeding. Chilling will not only firm and enhance the texture but make thin slicing easier.

Remove the foil and slice the pastrami as thin as possible, by hand or using an electric slicer. Transfer the slices to a food storage bag.

Stir together the coloring brine ingredients in a measuring cup or bowl and stir until the sugar, salt and beet powder dissolves (beet powder has a tendency to clump and form hard "rocks", so crush with the back of a spoon before mixing with the brine). Pour the coloring brine into the food storage bag. Seal and turn the bag repeatedly to coat the slices with the mixture. Refrigerate for a minimum of 30 minutes, to allow sufficient marinating and staining with color. The pastrami slices can be stored in the refrigerator for up to 1 week before reheating and serving.

Finishing and Serving

Drain and discard the coloring brine and gently pat the slices with paper towels to remove excess liquid. Lightly coat a non-stick skillet with cooking oil and place over medium-low heat. Gently toss the slices in the skillet until heated through. Leftovers should be consumed within 1 week or frozen for up to 3 months.

Lightly-Seasoned Beaf Crumbles

Lightly-seasoned beaf crumbles are an excellent gluten-based meat alternative for any recipe calling for cooked and crumbled ground beef, such as pasta with "meat" sauce, chili, casseroles, Mexican cuisine, etc.

For this application, the seasoned dough is wrapped in foil and steamed until almost completely cooked. The beaf is ground in a food processor, chilled to firm and enhance the texture and then lightly browned in a skillet to complete the cooking process (beaf crumbles are not intended to be used for preparing burgers, meatballs, meatloaf, etc.) Additional seasonings can be added as desired while browning the crumbles in the skillet.

This recipe yields about ¾ lb. of lightly-seasoned cooked beaf crumbles (which is roughly equivalent to 1lb. of lean ground beef after cooking).

Dry Ingredients

- 1 cup (150 g) vital wheat gluten
- 2 tsp onion powder
- 1 tsp garlic powder
- ¼ tsp ground white pepper

Finishing Ingredients

- 2 T olive oil
- 1 medium onion, finely diced
- 3 cloves garlic, minced
- sea salt or kosher salt and coarse ground black pepper, to taste
- optional fresh or dry herbs and spices as desired

Liquid Ingredients

- ⅔ cup (160 ml) water
- 2 T tamari, soy sauce or Bragg Liquid Aminos™
- 1 T mild vegetable oil
- 1 tsp Worcestershire Sauce (pg. 25) or commercial vegan equivalent
- 1 tsp Browning Liquid (pg. 26) or commercial equivalent

Additional Item Needed

- 18-inch wide heavy-duty aluminum foil

Preparation

For steaming, you will need a large cooking pot with a lid and a steamer insert. Add enough water to the pot to just reach the bottom of the steamer insert. Do not overfill or the foil package will be sitting in water.

Combine the dry ingredients in a large mixing bowl. Combine the liquid ingredients in a separate bowl or measuring cup. Pour the liquid mixture into the dry ingredients and combine thoroughly with a silicone spatula to form the dough and begin developing the gluten. Knead the dough in the bowl until elastic, about 1 minute.

Shape the dough into a compact flattened slab and wrap securely in heavy-duty aluminum foil. Be sure the package is tightly sealed. Steam the package over high heat for 45 minutes. Remove to cool for 30 minutes or until the package can be handled comfortably. Please note that the beaf will be fully cooked around the exterior but slightly undercooked in the center. This is normal. Cut the beaf into chunks and grind in a food processor with a standard chopping blade to the desired texture. Place in a food storage bag and refrigerate until thoroughly chilled. Chilling is necessary to firm and enhance the beaf texture.

Finishing the Beaf Crumbles

Add the oil to a skillet and place over medium heat; sauté the onion until tender, about 5 minutes. Add the minced garlic and any optional herbs and spices of your choosing and sauté an additional minute.

Add the ground beef, mix well and cook, stirring frequently until the crumbles are lightly browned. Season the crumbles with salt and pepper to taste. Use in your favorite recipe as desired.

Lightly-Seasoned Textured Soy Crumbles

Lightly-seasoned textured soy crumbles are an excellent soy-based meat alternative for any recipe calling for cooked and crumbled ground beef, such as pasta with "meat" sauce, chili, casseroles, Mexican cuisine, etc. Additional seasonings can be added as desired while cooking the crumbles in the skillet.

This recipe yields about 3 cups. Since TVP/TSP has a short shelf life once reconstituted, refrigerate any unused portion and consume within 3 days.

Seasoning Mixture Ingredients

- 1 and ⅓ cup water
- 2 T tamari, soy sauce or Bragg Liquid Aminos™
- 1 T Worcestershire Sauce (pg. 25) or commercial vegan equivalent
- 1 tsp onion powder
- 1 tsp Browning Liquid (pg. 26) or commercial equivalent
- optional fresh or dried herbs and spices as desired

Basic Sauté Ingredients

- 2 T olive oil
- 1 medium onion, finely diced
- 3 cloves garlic, minced
- 1 cup dry TVP/TSP granules (textured vegetable/soy protein)
- sea salt or kosher salt
- coarse ground black pepper, to taste

Preparation

In a bowl, whisk together the seasoning mixture ingredients; set aside.

Add the oil to a skillet and place over medium heat. Sauté the onion until tender, about 5 minutes. Add the minced garlic and sauté an additional minute.

Add the seasoning mixture to the skillet. Stir thoroughly to combine and bring the mixture to a boil.

Add the dry TVP/TSP granules and mix well. Reduce the heat to low and cover the skillet for 10 minutes.

Remove the cover and continue to cook over low heat, stirring frequently until the excess moisture begins to evaporate and the texture becomes firm (avoid cooking away all the moisture). Season the crumbles with salt and pepper to taste. Use in your favorite recipe as desired.

Porq

Porq is a versatile, plant-based meat. Some variations are created from a blend of vital wheat gluten, soy protein from tofu and select seasonings while others are created solely from vital wheat gluten and select seasonings. The cooking process varies depending upon the type of porq being prepared. Some recipes require baking only, while others require a combination of baking and simmering in a seasoned broth. Each method was carefully determined to create the best flavor and finished texture.

A food processor with a dough blade or a stand mixer with a paddle attachment is recommended for kneading the dough in the Pulled Porq recipe. This will provide sufficient gluten development essential for proper texture. However, if you don't have this equipment, the dough can be hand-kneaded (be aware that lengthy and vigorous hand-kneading requires stamina and can cause fatigue in your hand and arm).

Be sure to begin the recipes a minimum of 8 hours before planning to serve (the day before being ideal). This will allow sufficient time for preparation and refrigeration before finishing. Refrigeration will firm and enhance the porq texture, so this step should not be omitted or rushed. Chilling will also allow time for marinating porq chops and cutlets if desired.

Please note that oven temperatures recommended in the recipes were determined using a conventional home oven (radiant heat). If you have a convection oven (fan-assisted), reduce the recommended temperature by 25°F or 10°C. All baking times should remain the same.

Porq Simmering Broth

Porq simmering broth is used for simmering porq when directed in a recipe. It can also be used as an all-purpose vegetable broth base for preparing sauces, gravies, soups and stews, or used in any recipe calling for seasoned vegetable broth. Additional herbs or spices can be added to accommodate specific regional cuisines. This recipe yields about 3 quarts of prepared broth.

Ingredients

- 3 quarts (12 cups) water
- ¼ cup tamari, soy sauce or Bragg Liquid Aminos™
- 3 large onions, peeled and quartered
- 3 ribs celery, chopped
- 2 large carrots, unpeeled and chopped
- 9 parsley stems
- 6 cloves garlic, crushed
- 2 T nutritional yeast
- 2 tsp fine sea salt or kosher salt, or more to taste
- 1 tsp whole black peppercorns
- 1 bay leaf
- 3 sprigs fresh thyme or ½ tsp dried thyme

Preparation

Combine all ingredients in a large cooking pot, cover and simmer for a minimum of 1 hour. Strain and discard the larger solids from the broth with a slotted spoon before simmering porq. After simmering, let the broth cool and then strain into a sealable container to remove any remaining solids and refrigerate. During this time, any seasoning sediment will settle on the bottom of the container. The broth can be refrigerated for up to 1 week or frozen for future use at your convenience. To use, simply decant the clear portion and discard the fine sediment. Be sure to add back a little water as necessary before using, since the broth will have become concentrated from evaporation during simmering.

If using the broth immediately for other purposes, strain through a fine sieve into another cooking pot and discard the solids.

Variation

For a richer, deeper vegetable flavor, toss the chopped onion, celery, carrot and garlic with 1 tablespoon olive oil on a baking sheet and roast in a 400°F/200°C oven for 45 minutes, or until caramelized around the edges. Add to the cooking pot with the remaining ingredients and continue to follow the recipe as directed.

Quick Broth Options

Fresh homemade broth is always best and is recommended. However, for the sake of convenience and expediency, a quick porq simmering broth can be made with Better Than Bouillon™ Organic Vegetable Base (1 tsp for each cup water) or other commercial vegetable broth cubes (½ cube for each cup water) - or more or less to taste. Pre-prepared commercial vegetable broths are also available in aseptic cartons from most markets. Add additional herbs and spices as desired to accommodate specific regional cuisines and season the prepared broth with salt to taste.

Chops and Cutlets

Chops and cutlets are prepared from a blend of wheat protein, soy protein from tofu and select seasonings. For this application, the seasoned dough is shaped into 6 thick chops or 6 cutlets, prebaked to set the texture and then gently simmered in a seasoned broth. For optimum texture, the chops or cutlets require refrigeration for a minimum of 8 hours before finishing and serving, so plan accordingly.

Prepared chops and cutlets can be lightly dusted in seasoned flour and browned in a skillet with a small amount of cooking oil. They can also be marinated and then pan-seared in an oiled skillet or grill pan; or they can be breaded and fried.

Dry Ingredients

- 1 and ½ cup (225 g) vital wheat gluten
- 2 T onion powder
- 1 T garlic powder
- ½ tsp ground white pepper

Blender Ingredients

- 5 oz (140 g) pressed extra-firm block tofu (see pg. 24 for instructions)
- ¾ cup (180 ml) water
- 2 T tamari, soy sauce or Bragg Liquid Aminos™
- 2 T mellow white miso paste
- 2 T cooking oil

Simmering Broth

- 3 quarts (12 cups) porq simmering broth (pg. 106) or any seasoned vegetable broth

Preparation

Prepare the simmering broth and bring to a simmer in a large covered cooking pot. If preparing the broth from scratch, prepare and bring to a simmer 30 minutes before preparing and prebaking the dough. This will allow sufficient time to simmer the ingredients before adding the chops/cutlets.

Place a stainless steel cooling rack on a baking sheet and line the rack with parchment paper or a silicone baking mat. The cooling rack is not required, but it is recommended, as it will prevent excessive browning which would occur from direct contact with the hot baking sheet.

Preheat the oven to 350°F/180°C. Combine the dry ingredients in a large mixing bowl.

Crumble the pressed tofu into a blender and add the remaining blender ingredients. Process the contents until the tofu is completely liquefied and the mixture is smooth and creamy. This is essential! Stop the blender as necessary to scrape down the sides.

Scoop the tofu mixture into the dry ingredients (a small amount of the tofu mixture will remain in the blender; this is inconsequential) and combine with a sturdy silicone spatula until the tofu mixture is incorporated and a stiff dough begins to form. The mixture may seem a bit dry at first; just keep mixing.

Transfer the dough to a clean work surface (do not flour the work surface) and knead vigorously until it is springy and elastic, about 2 minutes.

Stretch the dough until it begins to tear and then roll it up into a mass. If it tears too easily, knead an additional minute or until it can be stretched a bit before tearing. Shape the mass into a compact log shape.

To create chops, slice the dough with a sharp knife into 6 roughly equal-sized pieces. Flatten each piece with the heel of your hand to ½-inch thick. Try not to taper the edges when pressing (chops should have a sharper blocked edge as opposed to cutlets which have a tapered edge). Use your fingers to create the characteristic "chop" shape (chops are wide at the top and narrow towards the bottom with a gentle "C" shaped curve on one side). If the dough is resistant to shaping, let it rest for a minute or two to relax the gluten.

To create cutlets, slice the dough with a sharp knife into 6 roughly equal-sized pieces. Press and stretch the dough against your work surface into flat cutlets. If the dough is resistant to shaping, let it rest for a minute or two to relax the gluten.

Place the chops/cutlets on the parchment paper or baking mat. Bake uncovered on the middle rack of the oven for 30 minutes and then remove from the oven.

Bring the broth to a boil. If the broth was made from scratch, use a slotted spoon to remove and discard the larger solids. It's not necessary to strain the broth completely.

Lower the chops/cutlets into the boiling broth and immediately reduce the heat to a gentle simmer. Leave the pot uncovered and set a timer for 20 minutes. Monitor the pot frequently to make sure the broth is maintained at a simmer. Do not boil. Turn the chops/cutlets occasionally once they float to the top of the pot. After simmering, remove the cooking pot from the heat, cover and let the chops/cutlets cool in the broth for a few hours or until lukewarm.

Transfer the chops/cutlets to a food storage bag and add ¼ cup of broth, or a desired marinade. Refrigerate for a minimum of 8 hours, or for up to 1 week, to firm and enhance the porq texture before finishing and serving. Chilling is very important so do not omit this step.

Strain the cooled broth into a sealable container and refrigerate. During this time, any seasoning sediment will settle on the bottom of the container. The broth can be refrigerated for up to 1 week or frozen for future use at your convenience. Decant the clear portion for preparing gravies or sauces that can be served with the finished chops/cutlets; or use for other recipes as desired. Discard the sediment.

Finishing the Chops/Cutlets

Once chilled, the chops/cutlets are ready to be seasoned as desired and pan-glazed in a non-stick skillet, grill pan or well-seasoned cast iron skillet; or they can be dredged in seasoned flour or breading and fried until golden brown. Blot the chops/cutlets with toweling to remove excess moisture before breading and frying. Chops can be basted and broiled or grilled outdoors. Be sure to brush or spray the grill pan or grill grating with cooking oil before grilling to discourage the chops from sticking. Brushing the chops with cooking oil before grilling will help keep them moist and tender even when a sauce or glaze is being used.

Tamari Citrus Glazed Chops

Ingredients

- 6 Porq Chops (see preceding recipe)
- ¼ cup tamari, soy sauce or Bragg Liquid Aminos™
- ¼ cup fresh lime juice
- 2 T organic sugar
- 1 T olive oil
- 1 T rice vinegar or raw apple cider vinegar
- 2 tsp fresh grated ginger
- 1 tsp Sriracha or other hot red pepper sauce
- 4 cups chopped mixed spring greens for plating
- ¼ cup chopped cilantro, for garnish

Preparation

Prepare the chops as directed. After cooling for 2 hours in the simmering broth, blot the chops lightly with toweling to remove excess moisture. Transfer them to a food storage bag and add the marinade. Seal and chill for a minimum of 8 hours.

When ready to prepare the dish, remove the chops from the marinade and set aside on a plate. Pour the remaining marinade into a small saucepan and bring to s simmer over medium heat. Remove from the heat and set aside.

Mist a non-stick skillet with cooking oil spray and place over medium heat. When the skillet is hot, pan sear the chops until golden brown on both sides. While the chops are browning, line serving plates with the greens. Top the greens with the chops and drizzle with the warmed marinade. Garnish with the chopped cilantro and serve.

Tonkatsu

Tonkatsu, which originated in Japan in the 19th century, consists of crispy panko-breaded and fried Porq cutlets served with a tangy, savory and sweet Katsu sauce.

Tonkatsu Ingredients

- 6 Porq cutlets (pg. 107)
- 1 cup plain non-dairy milk
- ¾ cup rice flour or all-purpose flour
- 1 tsp sea salt or kosher salt
- ½ tsp onion powder
- ¼ tsp garlic powder
- ¼ tsp ground white pepper
- 1 cup fine panko bread crumbs, or more as needed (fine crumbs adhere better to the cutlets; crush in a food processor if necessary)
- cooking oil for frying

Katsu Sauce Ingredients

- ½ cup tomato ketchup
- ½ cup water
- ¼ cup dark brown sugar
- 3 T tamari, soy sauce or Bragg Liquid Aminos™
- 1 T Worcestershire Sauce (pg. 25) or commercial vegan equivalent
- ½ tsp hot red pepper sauce
- ¼ tsp garlic powder
- 1 tsp unmodified potato starch, cornstarch or arrowroot powder mixed with 2 tsp water in small dish to create a slurry

Sauce Preparation

Whisk together all of the sauce ingredients except for the starch slurry in a small saucepan and bring to a simmer over medium heat. Whisk in the starch slurry and stir until thickened. Reduce the heat to low to keep warm until ready to serve. Stir occasionally. The sauce can also be used at room temperature.

Tonkatsu Preparation

In a bowl, whisk together the milk, flour, starch, yeast, salt, onion and garlic powder and white pepper until smooth.

Place the finely crushed panko crumbs into a separate bowl.

Dip the cutlets first in the batter, shake off any excess and then dredge them in the panko crumbs, making sure they are evenly coated. Set them aside on plate to dry while the oil is heated.

Add ½-inch of oil to a skillet or wok and place over medium-high heat. Test the temperature of the oil by dropping in a few panko crumbs. If the crumbs brown quickly, the oil is sufficiently hot.

Gently place the cutlets into the hot oil and fry until golden brown on each side. Transfer the cutlets to a plate lined with paper towels to blot any excess oil.

Garnish serving plates with the Katsu sauce. When the cutlets are cool enough to handle, slice them and place the slices onto the serving plate. Serve immediately with additional Katsu sauce on the side.

Pulled Porq

Pulled Porq is prepared from a blend of wheat protein from gluten, soy protein from tofu and select seasonings. It amazingly resembles pulled pork in flavor and texture and is ideal for any plant-based recipe where a shredded texture is desired, such as Mexican cuisine (carnitas, tamales, burritos, etc.), Cuban and Polynesian pulled porq and BBQ or teriyaki pulled porq sandwiches.

Pulled Porq is neutrally seasoned which allows for additional seasoning when using in recipes; or try using a dry seasoning rub prior to baking (such as a Cajun dry rub). Several quick and easy seasoning and finishing suggestions are offered after the recipe.

A food processor with a dough blade or a stand mixer with a paddle attachment is highly recommended for kneading the sticky dough, which in turn will provide sufficient gluten development essential for this recipe. However, if you don't have this equipment, the dough can be hand-kneaded (be aware that lengthy and vigorous hand-kneading requires stamina and can cause fatigue in your hand and arm).

This recipe yields about 1 and ½ lb. or 24 oz.

Dry Ingredients

- 1 and ½ cup (225 g) vital wheat gluten
- 2 T onion powder
- 1 T garlic powder
- ½ tsp ground white pepper

Blender Ingredients

- 10 oz (280 g) pressed extra-firm block tofu (see pg. 24 for instructions)
- 1 cup (240 ml) water
- 2 T mellow white miso paste
- 2 T tamari, soy sauce or Bragg Liquid Aminos™
- 2 T mild vegetable oil
- 1 tsp liquid smoke
- ½ tsp Browning Liquid (pg. 26) or commercial equivalent

Additional Item Needed

- 18-inch wide heavy-duty aluminum foil

Preparation

Warning! It is very important to use only heavy-duty aluminum foil for this recipe. Regular foil is not sturdy enough and can easily rupture from steam pressure which builds up inside the sealed package.

Preheat the oven to 350°F/180°C. Combine the dry ingredients in a large mixing bowl.

Crumble the pressed tofu into a blender and add the remaining blender ingredients. Process the contents until the tofu is completely liquefied and the mixture is smooth and creamy. This is essential! Stop the blender as necessary to scrape down the sides.

Scoop the tofu mixture into the dry ingredients (a small amount of the tofu mixture will remain in the blender; this is inconsequential) and stir with a sturdy silicone spatula until the tofu mixture is incorporated and a sticky ball of dough begins to form. Let the dough rest about 5 minutes. This will give the gluten a chance to absorb the liquid and help reduce stickiness.

Place the dough into a food processor fitted with a dough blade and process for 2 full minutes. Alternately, place the dough into a stand mixer fitted with a paddle and process on medium speed for 2 full minutes.

If kneading by hand, knead the dough in the mixing bowl vigorously for a minimum of 5 full minutes. This is very important in order to develop the gluten. The dough will be sticky. Do not add additional gluten to the dough to reduce stickiness! Test the dough by stretching it. If it tears easily, more kneading is required. If it exhibits a moderate degree of elasticity and fine web-like strands of gluten are visible when it begins to tear, it has been kneaded sufficiently.

Tear off a sheet of foil (about 18-inches) and place it on your work surface. Transfer the dough to the foil and shape into a compact slab. Shaping perfection is unnecessary. If you are using a dry rub seasoning, rub 2 to 3 teaspoons of the mixture over the dough. Fold the slab of dough in the foil (don't roll), creating a semi-flat package. Fold in the ends but leave a little room (about 1-inch on each side) to allow the dough to expand as it bakes. This is very important! Crimp the folded ends to seal the package.

Rewrap the package in a second sheet of foil and place the package directly on the middle rack of the oven. Bake for 2 hours.

Let the porq cool in the foil to room temperature and then refrigerate for a minimum of 8 hours to firm and enhance its texture, or for up to 1 week before shredding and using in recipes. You can also store the porq in the freezer wrapped in the foil for up to 3 months.

Pulling the Porq

Remove the foil and recycle. Using your hands, bend the roast in half to split it lengthwise; this will reveal the "grain". Tear the roast in half following where it has been split. Bend and tear those pieces in half lengthwise. Now, with your fingers, pull the porq into long strings or shreds, following the grain as much as possible. Tear those pieces into smaller bite-size shreds. Use in your favorite recipes as desired.

Troubleshooting

If the finished product is yielding a bread-like texture, check your gluten. A bread-like texture may indicate poor quality gluten that contains too much starch. The gluten must be guaranteed a minimum of 75% protein. Also be sure to process the tofu mixture until completely liquefied before adding to the dry ingredients.

A bread-like texture may also indicate that the dough was not kneaded sufficiently to develop the gluten strands. For this reason, a food processor with a dough blade or a stand mixer with a paddle attachment is recommended for sufficient gluten development.

Also check your oven temperature. If the oven is running too hot, it can overcook the porq; and be sure to double-wrap the dough with the foil and seal securely to prevent moisture loss while baking. If you're using a fan-assisted convection oven, keep in mind that they can run about 25°f or 10°C hotter than a conventional radiant heat oven (unless they automatically adjust themselves), so manually adjust the temperature if necessary.

BBQ and Teriyaki Pulled Porq

Ingredients

- 12 oz Pulled Porq (pg. 111)
- 2 T cooking oil
- 1 medium onion, halved and thinly sliced
- 3 cloves garlic, minced (1 T)
- ½ cup BBQ sauce or teriyaki sauce, or more to taste

Preparation

Pull the prepared and chilled porq into bite-size shreds.

Add the oil to a large non-stick skillet or wok and place over medium heat; sauté the onion until tender and translucent. Add the garlic and sauté 30 seconds.

Add the pulled porq and sauté, tossing frequently, until lightly browned. Add the BBQ sauce or teriyaki sauce and toss well to distribute. Continue to cook until heated through.

Cuban-Style Pulled Porq

Tender shreds of porq are sautéed in fresh citrus juices with onions and an abundance of garlic for this popular and favorite Cuban-style dish. Serve with rice and beans and soft flour tortillas.

Preparation

Pull the prepared and chilled porq into bite-size shreds.

Combine the citrus juices in a small bowl; set aside.

Add the oil to a large non-stick skillet or wok and place over medium heat; sauté the onion until tender and translucent. Add the garlic, oregano, orange zest and lime zest and sauté 30 seconds.

Add the pulled porq and sauté, tossing frequently, until lightly browned. Drizzle in the citrus juices and toss well to distribute. Continue to sauté until almost all the liquid has evaporated but the porq is still moist; season with salt and pepper to taste.

Transfer to a serving platter. Garnish with lime wedges.

Ingredients

- 24 oz Pulled Porq (pg. 111)
- ¼ cup fresh orange juice
- 2 T fresh lime juice
- 2 T cooking oil
- 1 large onion, halved and thinly sliced
- 9 cloves garlic, minced (3 T)
- ½ tsp fresh orange zest
- ½ tsp fresh lime zest
- 1 T fresh minced oregano
  or 1 tsp dried oregano
- sea salt or kosher salt and
  coarse ground black pepper to taste

Carnitas

(Mexican Pulled Porq)

Tender shreds of porq are sautéed with onions, green chile pepper, garlic, lime juice and south of the border seasonings for this classic Mexican dish.

Ingredients

- 24 oz Pulled Porq (pg. 111)
- 1 tsp ground cumin
- 1 tsp ground coriander
- 1 tsp dried oregano
- 1 tsp dried marjoram
- ¼ cup fresh lime juice
- 2 T cooking oil
- 1 large onion, halved and thinly sliced
- 1 large jalapeno or serrano pepper, seeded and minced
- 6 cloves garlic, minced (2 T)
- sea salt or kosher salt and coarse ground black pepper to taste

Preparation

Pull the prepared and chilled porq into bite-size shreds. Combine the cumin, oregano and marjoram in a small dish; set aside.

Add the oil to a large non-stick skillet or wok and place over medium heat; sauté the onion and chile pepper until tender. Add the garlic and sauté 30 seconds.

Add the pulled porq and sauté, tossing frequently, until lightly browned. Add the lime juice and seasonings and toss well to distribute. Continue to sauté until almost all the liquid has evaporated but the porq is still moist; season with salt and pepper to taste. Garnish with plenty of chopped cilantro and serve with warm tortillas and guacamole.

Polynesian Pulled Porq

Tender shreds of smoky and salty porq are sautéed with onion, garlic and ginger for this Polynesian island-style favorite.

Preparation

Pull the chilled porq into bite-size shreds. Combine the liquid smoke, water and salt in a small dish and stir until the salt dissolves; set aside.

Add the oil to a large non-stick skillet or wok and place over medium heat; sauté the onion until tender and translucent. Add the garlic and ginger and sauté 30 seconds.

Add the pulled porq and sauté, tossing frequently, until lightly browned. Add the smoke mixture and toss well to distribute.

Ingredients

- 24 oz Pulled Porq (pg. 111)
- 2 T liquid hickory smoke
- 2 T water
- 1 tsp Hawaiian red alae salt (or coarse sea salt or kosher salt), or more to taste
- 2 T cooking oil
- 1 large sweet yellow or Maui onion, halved and very thinly sliced
- 6 cloves garlic, minced (2 T)
- 2 tsp minced fresh ginger

Continue to sauté until almost all the liquid has evaporated but the porq is still moist; season with additional salt to taste (Polynesian porq should be a bit salty). Serve over sticky rice with your favorite island-style side dishes.

Chili Verde

Tender white beans and shreds of porq are simmered in a zesty tomatillo and green chile pepper-based sauce, garnished with chopped cilantro, non-dairy sour cream and shredded cheese and then served with warm flour tortillas.

Ingredients

- 12 oz Pulled Porq (pg. 111)
- 1 can (28 oz) tomatillos, drained
- 1 cup vegetable broth
- 2 T olive oil
- 1 large onion, diced
- 2 large jalapeno or serrano peppers, seeded, membrane removed and finely diced
- 5 cloves garlic, minced
- 2 cans (4 oz each) diced mild green chilies
- 1 can (15 oz) white beans, such as cannellini, navy or great northern
- 1 tsp dried oregano
- ½ tsp ground cumin
- ½ tsp ground coriander
- ½ tsp coarse ground black pepper
- sea salt or kosher salt to taste
- chopped cilantro, for garnish

Preparation

Pull the chilled porq into bite-size shreds.

Drain the canned tomatillos and place in a blender with the broth; pulse the blender a few times to chop the tomatillos while retaining some texture. Pour the mixture into a large cooking pot and place over low heat.

Add the olive oil to a skillet and place over medium heat. Add the onions and fresh chile peppers and sauté until the onions are translucent. Add the garlic and continue to sauté until the onions are just beginning to lightly brown. Transfer to the saucepan.

Add the diced mild chilies, white beans, oregano, cumin, coriander and black pepper to the cooking pot. Bring the mixture to a simmer and reduce the heat to medium-low. Partially cover and cook for 30 minutes, stirring occasionally.

Stir the pulled porq into the cooking pot and simmer for 5 minutes; season with salt to taste. Ladle the chili into individual serving bowls and top with the cilantro, shredded cheese and sour cream as desired. Serve with warm tortillas.

Country-Style Ribz and Rack Ribz

Country-Style Ribz ("boneless") and Rack Ribz ("bone-in") are particularly well-suited for outdoor grilling or anytime when using a grill pan or broiler. While the Rack Ribz require a little more work, they're fun to make and barbecued ribz are always better when you have something to grasp onto while eating. This is my new and original recipe for ribz that are chewy on the outside and moist and tender on the inside with a wonderful "pull-apart" texture. The secret to the texture is the tofu and shredded onion. This recipe yields 4 servings.

Dry Ingredients

- 1 cup (150 g) vital wheat gluten
- 2 tsp onion powder
- 1 and ½ tsp garlic powder
- ¼ tsp ground white pepper

Blender Ingredients

- 2.5 oz (70 g) pressed extra-firm block tofu (see pg. 24 for instructions)
- ½ cup (120 ml) water
- 1 T tamari, soy sauce or Bragg Liquid Aminos™
- 1 T mellow white miso paste
- 1 T mild vegetable oil
- ¼ tsp Browning Liquid (pg. 26) or commercial equivalent

Wet Ingredients

- ¼ cup fresh shredded onion (about 1 medium onion; see the recipe for instructions)

Additional Items Needed for Country-Style Ribz

- 8-inch square baking pan lined with parchment paper or aluminum foil
- grilling sauce or glaze of your choice

Additional Items Needed for Rack Ribz

- 12 wooden craft sticks (ice cream sticks)
- 18-inch wide heavy-duty aluminum foil
- grilling sauce or glaze of your choice

Dough Preparation

Preheat the oven to 350°F/180°C.

Combine the dry ingredients in a large mixing bowl; set aside.

Shred the onion on the largest holes of a box grater. The shredded onion will be very wet. Shred enough of the onion to pack ¼ cup. Set aside.

Crumble the pressed tofu into a blender and add the remaining blender ingredients. Process the contents until the tofu is completely liquefied and the mixture is smooth and creamy. This is essential! Stop the blender as necessary to scrape down the sides. Stir the shredded onion into the blender contents (do not process once the onion has been added).

Scoop the tofu mixture into the dry ingredients (a small amount of the tofu mixture will remain in the blender; this is inconsequential) and combine with a sturdy silicone spatula until the tofu mixture is incorporated and the dough begins to form. Knead the dough in the bowl until it begins to exhibit some elasticity, about 1 minute.

For Country-Style Ribz ("Boneless")

Pick up the dough, stretch it (like stretching pizza dough) and place it into the baking pan. Press, stretch and flatten the dough with your fingers to completely fill the bottom of the pan.

Cover the pan with a large sheet of foil and press the foil into the pan covering the surface of the dough. Seal the foil around the edges of the pan. The foil needs to be in contact with the surface of the dough to seal in moisture.

Note: If you wish to prevent the foil from coming into contact with ribz, cover with a sheet of parchment paper cut to fit inside the pan, and then cover with the foil as described.

Place the pan on the middle rack of the oven and bake for 45 minutes.

Remove the pan from the oven to cool with the foil in place. Refrigerate the pan for a minimum of 8 hours to firm and enhance the texture of the ribz.

To finish the ribz, skip the next section and then follow the instructions for finishing.

For Rack Ribz ("Bone-In")

With a knife, cut the dough into 4 roughly even pieces. Cut each quarter into 3 roughly even pieces for a total of 12 pieces.

Tear off a large sheet of foil (about 24-inches) and place it horizontally on your work surface.

Pick up a piece of dough, roll it between the palms of your hands to create a short "rope" and then gently stretch it as far as you can. If it tears too easily, knead the dough with your fingers until it can be stretched. Wrap the dough around the stick, leaving ½-inch of the stick free for grasping. Pinch both ends to prevent the dough from unwinding. If the dough tears while wrapping, simply press the dough together at the breaking point and continue. Perfection is not required. Place the individual "rib" onto the foil.

Repeat with another piece of dough and wooden stick and place the rib next to the first rib. Repeat with the remaining dough, lining up the ribz so they are touching each other. This may seem time consuming but it's not, once you've mastered the technique.

With the palms of your hands, firmly flatten the ribz and at the same time, push them together. By doing so, you're creating a connection point so the ribz can adhere together. As the ribz bake, they will expand and the adhesion will complete itself. This only needs to be done on one side; it's not necessary to flip the ribz over. Flatten the ribz until they are approximately ½-inch thick.

Fold the ribz in the foil to create a flattened package. Fold in the ends and crimp to seal shut. Place the package on the middle rack of the oven and bake for 45 minutes.

Remove the package from the oven to cool. Refrigerate the package for a minimum of 8 hours to firm and enhance the texture of the ribz.

Finishing the Ribz

Bring the refrigerated pan or package to room temperature about 1 hour before grilling or broiling. For Country-Style Ribz, flip the contents of the pan onto a work surface. Cut the slab in half down the center. With a knife, lightly score one segment to create 6 ribz. Avoid cutting all the way through. Repeat with the remaining segment. For Rack Ribz, cut the rack down the center to create 2 segments. Continue to follow the instructions for grilling or broiling.

Grill Method

Preheat an outdoor grill or indoor grill pan to medium-high heat. Brush or spray the ribz with cooking oil to discourage them from sticking to the grill surface. This is very important. Then brush them generously with sauce and grill for 3 to 5 minutes on each side or until the sauce is nicely caramelized and the ribz are heated through. Transfer to a serving platter. Pull the individual ribz apart to eat. Serve with additional sauce on the side if desired.

Broil Method

Line a baking sheet with foil and place the ribz onto the foil. Brush the ribz generously with sauce and broil for 3 to 5 minutes on each side or until the sauce is nicely caramelized and the ribz are heated through. Transfer to a serving platter. Pull the individual ribz apart to eat. Serve with additional sauce on the side if desired.

Smoky Brown Sugar Bacun

Bacon has a flavor and texture that many people miss when they transition to a plant-based diet. There are several steps to this recipe; however, don't be intimated because it's actually very easy to prepare and the results are well worth the effort. For the recipe, two batches of dough will be mixed to create the bacun. Dough 1 is for the light marble layer and Dough 2 is for the dark marble layer.

Dry Ingredients for Dough 1

- 1 cup (150 g) vital wheat gluten
- 1 T onion powder
- 2 tsp smoked paprika
- ¼ tsp ground white pepper

Liquid Ingredients for Dough 1

- ½ cup (120 ml) water
- 3 T tamari, soy sauce or Bragg Liquid Aminos™
- 2 T liquid hickory smoke
- 1 T dark brown sugar
- 1 T Worcestershire Sauce (pg. 25) or commercial vegan equivalent
- 1 T olive oil

Additional Item Needed

- 18-inch wide heavy-duty aluminum foil

Dry Ingredients for Dough 2

- ½ cup (75 g) vital wheat gluten
- 1 T garlic powder

Liquid Ingredients for Dough 2

- 6 T (90 ml) water
- 1 T olive oil
- ½ tsp fine sea salt or kosher salt

Rub Ingredients

- 2 T dark brown sugar
- optional: 1 tsp smoked black pepper or coarse ground black pepper

Warning! It is very important to use only heavy-duty aluminum foil for this recipe. Regular foil is not sturdy enough and can easily rupture from steam pressure which builds up inside the sealed package.

Preparing Dough 1

Preheat the oven to 325°F/170°F.

Combine the dry ingredients for Dough 1 in a large mixing bowl.

Whisk together the liquid ingredients for Dough 1 in a separate bowl or measuring cup until the brown sugar dissolves.

Pour the liquid ingredients into the dry ingredients and mix well to incorporate. "Knead" the dough with a spoon or spatula in the bowl until the dough offers some resistance to mixing. Divide the dough into 3 pieces. Set aside.

Preparing Dough 2

Combine the dry ingredients for Dough 2 in a small mixing bowl.

Stir together the liquid ingredients for Dough 2 in a separate bowl or measuring cup until the salt dissolves.

Pour the liquid ingredients into the dry ingredients and mix well to incorporate. Divide the dough in half.

Layering the Dough

Now you will begin the layering process which will create the marbling effect for the bacun.

Tear off a sheet of foil (about 18-inches) and place on your work surface. Take a piece of Dough 1 and flatten into a disc. Place the flattened dough onto the foil.

Next, repeat with a piece of Dough 2 and place on top of the first disc. Repeat with the remaining pieces of dough, alternating as you stack. Firmly press down on the stack until it is about 1-inch thick. Now, use your fingers to press and shape the dough into a compact, rectangular slab. Don't worry about being too precise; the dough will expand during baking to conform to the shape of the foil package.

Next, sprinkle the bacun with 1 tablespoon of brown sugar and ½ teaspoon of the optional black pepper. Gently rub the mixture over the surface of the bacun slab. Flip the slab over and repeat with the remaining brown sugar and optional pepper.

Fold the slab of bacun over in the foil several times (don't roll) to create a flat package. Fold in the sides of the foil, crimping to seal the foil as you fold. Rewrap in a second sheet of foil in the same manner. Place the package directly on the middle oven rack and bake for 90 minutes.

Cool the bacun in the foil and then refrigerate for a minimum of 8 hours. Chilling will firm and enhance the texture and make slicing easier - this is important. The bacun can be stored in the refrigerator for up to 1 week before slicing and finishing or in the freezer for up to 3 months.

For the best finished texture, use a very sharp knife and slice the bacun as thinly as possible. Of course, if you prefer a thicker cut, that's entirely up to you.

Finishing the Bacun

Finishing the bacun in the oven is my preferred method since heating is controlled and the bacun can be given a "rippled" appearance. To do this, preheat the oven to 350°F/180°C. Line a baking sheet with parchment paper and lay the slices on the paper. Mist or brush the slices with cooking oil. Use your fingers to "scrunch" the bacun slices, thus giving them a rippled appearance. Bake for 20 minutes. Let the bacun cool for about 5 minutes and then transfer to a serving plate. As the bacun cools it will crisp up a bit while still retaining a nice chewy texture. Transfer to a plate lined with paper towels to blot any excess oil.

Optionally, the bacun slices can be briefly fried in a non-stick skillet with a light layer of cooking oil over medium to medium-low heat. Frying "low and slow" is preferable to frying at a high temperature. The bacun will brown (and burn) quickly and the texture will become hard if the temperature is too high. Transfer to a plate lined with paper towels to blot any excess oil.

Serve warm; chop, dice or crumble in recipes; or layer on your favorite sandwich.

Sweet and Smoky Baco'bits

This recipe yields 1 cup of deliciously sweet, salty and smoky morsels, which are ideal for topping salads, sandwiches or eggless "egg" dishes just before serving. However, these crispy bits are not recommended for adding to soups or for cooking in moist foods such as casseroles or quiches because the coconut will rehydrate, lose its crispness and revert back to its chewy coconut texture. To retain crunch in moister applications, replace the coconut flakes with sliced almonds.

If using coconut for this recipe sounds peculiar to you, rest assured there is absolutely no undertone of coconut aroma or flavor in these crunchy bits (none that I perceive anyways).

Ingredients

- 1 cup dried unsweetened coconut flakes (such as Bob's Red Mill™ brand)
- 2 T tamari, soy sauce or Bragg Liquid Aminos™
- 1 T dark brown sugar or real maple syrup
- 2 tsp liquid smoke
- 1 tsp Worcestershire Sauce (pg. 25) or commercial vegan equivalent

Preparation

In a bowl, whisk together the seasoning ingredients until the sugar is dissolved. Add the coconut flakes and toss well to evenly distribute the seasoning. Cover and refrigerate for a minimum of several hours, and better overnight, to rehydrate the coconut flakes and absorb the flavors.

Preheat the oven to 350°F/180°C.

Line a baking sheet with parchment paper and distribute the seasoned coconut flakes on the parchment paper in a single layer. For a peppery bacun flavor, season with fine ground black pepper. Place the baking sheet in the oven on a middle rack and set a timer for 5 minutes.

Remove from the oven and stir the flakes, again redistributing them in a single layer. This process will need to be repeated every 5 minutes for a total of about 15 minutes for slightly chewy bacun bits, or 20 minutes for crispy bacun bits. Remove from the oven and let cool. Store the bacun bits in a food storage bag or a suitable covered container in the refrigerator until ready to use.

Country Garden Ham

Generously flavored with hickory smoke, brown sugar and warm spice, country garden ham is reminiscent of a natural uncured ham and can be served hot or cold. The ham can be finished with a savory tamari-black pepper glaze or a sweet and spicy brown sugar-mustard glaze included with the recipe, however any sweet, spicy or savory glaze can be used as desired. Spicy brown or Dijon mustard is the ideal condiment for enhancing the flavor of the sliced ham. This recipe yields about 2.5 lbs.

Aromatic Brine Ingredients

- 2 and ¼ cup (540 ml) water
- 3 T light brown sugar
- 2 T mild vegetable oil
- 2 T nutritional yeast flakes
- 2 T red miso paste*
- 2 T liquid hickory smoke
- 2 and ¼ tsp fine sea salt or kosher salt
- 1 T whole cloves
- ½ tsp ground ginger
- ½ tsp ground white pepper

Dry Ingredients

- 2 cups (300 g) vital wheat gluten
- ¼ cup all-purpose flour
- 2 T onion powder
- 1 T garlic powder

Pan-Browning Ingredient

- 2 T non-dairy butter or margarine

Additional Item Needed

- 18-inch wide heavy-duty aluminum foil

*If you cannot obtain red miso paste, substitute with 1 tablespoon tamari, soy sauce or Bragg Liquid Aminos™ and 1 tablespoon tomato paste, although this will alter the finished flavor to a degree.

Optional Tamari-Black Pepper Glaze Ingredients

- 2 T tamari, soy sauce or Bragg Liquid Aminos™
- coarse ground smoked black pepper or coarse ground black pepper, to taste

Optional Brown Sugar-Mustard Glaze Ingredients

- 2 T dark brown sugar
- 1 T prepared Dijon or spicy mustard
- 1 tsp tamari, soy sauce or Bragg Liquid Aminos™
- 1 tsp liquid hickory smoke

Preparing the Aromatic Brine

In a saucepan, bring the water to a brief boil and then remove from the heat. Add the remaining aromatic brine ingredients and stir until the sugar, yeast, miso and salt dissolves. Let the mixture cool to near room temperature (the mixture must cool before proceeding; do not add hot brine to the dry ingredients!)

Meanwhile, thoroughly mix together the dry ingredients in large mixing bowl; set aside.

Preparing the Dough

Warning! It is very important to use only heavy-duty aluminum foil for this recipe. Regular foil is not sturdy enough and can easily rupture from steam pressure which builds up inside the sealed package.

Preheat the oven to 350°F/180°C.

Strain the aromatic brine through a fine sieve into the dry ingredients in the mixing bowl and discard the strained solids (straining will remove any whole and undissolved seasoning sediment).

Combine thoroughly with a silicone spatula to develop the gluten. Let the dough rest 10 minutes to allow the dry ingredients to absorb as much liquid as possible.

Tear off a sheet of foil (about 18-inches) and place it on your work surface. Place the dough directly on top.

Form the dough into a round mass. The dough will be soft and have a tendency to spread out but try to keep it as compact as you can. Now, lift the edge of the foil over the dough and begin rolling into a cylinder, pinching the ends closed simultaneously while rolling. The goal is to create a thick, compact, cylindrical package. This may take practice, so be patient. Twist the ends tightly to seal, being careful not to tear the foil. Bend the twisted ends in half to lock them tight.

Wrap with an additional large sheet of foil and twist the ends tightly to completely seal the package. If the foil tears at any point while twisting the ends, rewrap in a third sheet of foil. Place directly on the middle rack of the oven and bake for 2 hours.

Remove from the oven and let cool to room temperature. Never attempt to open the package while it is hot or steam burns can result. Refrigerate the ham in the foil wrapper for a minimum of 8 hours before finishing, or for a maximum of 1 week. This will firm and enhance the texture. The ham can also be frozen for up to 3 months.

Place the foil package directly on the middle rack of the oven and bake for 2 hours.

After baking, let the ham cool in the foil wrapper and then refrigerate for a minimum of 8 hours before finishing. Chilling with enhance the texture. The ham can also be refrigerated in the foil wrapper for up to 1 week, or frozen for up to 3 months, before finishing.

Finishing the Ham

Tamari-Pepper Glaze Option

Let the wrapped ham come to room temperature for about 1 hour before finishing. Preheat the oven to 350°F/180°C.

In a skillet, lightly brown the ham on all sides in 2 tablespoons of non-dairy butter or margarine over medium heat. Add the tamari and continue to glaze the ham until nicely browned and then season with black pepper to taste. Transfer the ham to a baking dish, cover with foil and bake for 30 minutes. Transfer to a cutting board or serving platter for slicing.

Brown Sugar-Mustard Glaze Option

Let the wrapped ham come to room temperature for about 1 hour before finishing. Preheat the oven to 350°F/180°C.

Mix together the glaze ingredients in a small dish until the sugar dissolves; set aside.

In a skillet, brown the ham on all sides in 2 tablespoons of non-dairy butter or margarine over medium heat. Transfer the ham to baking dish and brush to coat evenly with the glaze. Cover with foil and bake for 30 minutes. Transfer to a cutting board or serving platter for slicing. Country garden ham is delicious served hot, cold or room temperature.

Split Pea Soup

with Country Garden Ham

Tender split peas, onions, carrots and potatoes merge together to create this classic soup. The garden ham adds a wonderful smoky flavor. This recipe yields about 6 servings.

Ingredients

- 8 cups porq simmering broth (pg. 106) or any seasoned vegetable broth
- 2 T olive oil
- 1 large onion, diced
- 3 cloves garlic, minced
- 2 large carrots, peeled and diced
- 1 large russet potato, peeled and diced
- 10 oz dried split green peas (1 and ¼ cup by volume)
- ½ tsp dried thyme leaves
- 1 cup small diced Country Garden Ham (pg. 122)
- ¼ tsp coarse ground black pepper, or more to taste
- sea salt or kosher salt, to taste

Preparation

Add the olive oil to a large cooking pot and place over medium heat. Add the onions and carrots and sauté until the onions are translucent. Add the garlic and sauté an additional minute.

Add the broth, potatoes, split peas, thyme and black pepper. Bring to a boil and then reduce heat to a gentle simmer. Cover the pot and cook for 1 hour and 30 minutes. Stir occasionally to prevent the solids from scorching and sticking to the bottom of the pot.

While the soup is cooking, mist a small skillet with cooking oil spray and lightly brown the garden ham. Add the diced garden ham the last 10 minutes of cooking time.

Season the soup with salt as needed and additional pepper as desired before serving.

Deli-Style Garden Ham

Generously flavored with hickory smoke, brown sugar and warm spice, these tasty luncheon slices remarkably capture the characteristic flavor and appearance of cured deli-style ham. An electric slicer is recommended for creating the uniformly thin slices. If you don't have an electric slicer, slice the ham as thinly as possible using a very sharp carving knife, since the coloring solution will not penetrate thicker slices evenly. This is a large roast, about 2.5 lbs.

Aromatic Brine Ingredients

- 2 cups (480 ml) water
- 3 T light brown sugar
- 2 T mild vegetable oil
- 2 T nutritional yeast flakes
- 2 T mellow white miso paste
- 2 T liquid hickory smoke
- 2 tsp fine sea salt or kosher salt
- 2 tsp whole cloves
- ½ tsp ground ginger
- ½ tsp ground white pepper

Dry Ingredients

- 2 cups (300 g) vital wheat gluten
- ¼ cup all-purpose flour
- 2 T onion powder
- 1 T garlic powder

Coloring Brine Ingredients

- ½ cup (120 ml) water
- ½ tsp beet powder
- ¼ tsp fine sea salt or kosher salt

Additional Item Needed

- 18-inch wide heavy-duty aluminum foil

Preparation

Warning! It is very important to use only heavy-duty aluminum foil for this recipe. Regular foil is not sturdy enough and can easily rupture from steam pressure which builds up inside the sealed package.

In a saucepan, bring the water to a brief boil and then remove from the heat. Add the remaining aromatic brine ingredients and stir until the sugar, yeast, miso and salt dissolves. Let the mixture cool to near room temperature (the mixture must cool before proceeding; do not add hot brine to the dry ingredients!)

Meanwhile, thoroughly mix together the dry ingredients in large mixing bowl; set aside. Preheat the oven to 350°F/180°C.

Strain the aromatic brine through a fine sieve into the dry ingredients in the mixing bowl and discard the strained solids (straining will remove any whole and undissolved seasoning sediment).

Combine thoroughly with a silicone spatula to develop the gluten. Let the dough rest 10 minutes to allow the dry ingredients to absorb as much liquid as possible.

Tear off a sheet of foil (about 18-inches) and place it on your work surface. Place the dough directly on top.

Form the dough into a round mass. The dough will be soft and have a tendency to spread out but try to keep it as compact as you can. Now, lift the edge of the foil over the dough and begin rolling into a cylinder, pinching the ends closed simultaneously while rolling. The goal is to create a thick, compact, cylindrical package. This may take practice, so be patient. Twist the ends tightly to seal, being careful not to tear the foil. Bend the twisted ends in half to lock them tight.

Wrap with an additional large sheet of foil and twist the ends tightly to completely seal the package. If the foil tears at any point while twisting the ends, rewrap in a third sheet of foil. Place directly on the middle rack of the oven and bake for 2 hours.

After baking, let the ham cool in the foil wrapper and then refrigerate for a minimum of 8 hours before finishing. Chilling with enhance the texture of the ham and make slicing easier.

Finishing the Ham

Combine the coloring brine ingredients in a small bowl and stir until the beet powder and salt is dissolved. Set aside.

Unwrap the ham and recycle the foil. Shave the ham as thin as possible using an electric slicer. Separate the slices as they will tend to stick together and place them into a food storage bag. Add the coloring brine, seal the bag (leave plenty of air in the bag) and toss gently but thoroughly to coat the slices with the coloring solution.

Open the bag and separate the slices and then seal and re-toss to ensure even coverage. Open the bag slightly and press out any air. Reseal and chill the sliced ham for a minimum of 1 hour or for up to 1 week. For longer storage, the slices can be frozen for up to 3 months.

To heat the slices, mist a non-stick skillet with cooking oil spray and place over medium-low heat. Gently toss the slices in the hot skillet until heated through. The slices can also be wrapped securely in foil and placed in an oven or steamer until heated through.

———————————————— ✕( )✕ ————————————————

Meatless Meat Specialties

Succulent Roast Turky

Succulent Roast Turky is created from a special blend of wheat protein, soy protein from tofu and select seasonings. The roast is prebaked until partially cooked, which seals in the ingredients and sets the texture. The roast will also create its own "skin" while prebaking.

The partially cooked roast is then simmered in a seasoned broth to complete the cooking process, infuse the roast with additional flavor and ensure that the roast remains moist and tender. After simmering the roast, the ample amount of remaining seasoned broth can be used for sauces, gravies, soups and stews.

The roast is finished by pan-glazing until golden brown before slicing and serving. This combination cooking method produces a tender, succulent, "white meat" roast with a superb texture that cannot be achieved by baking or simmering alone.

The roast requires a substantial amount of preparation time before finishing (including refrigeration in order to optimize its texture), so prepare at least the night before or up to 1 week ahead and then pan-glaze and reheat when ready to serve. This recipe yields an extra large roast, about 2.5 lbs.

Dry Ingredients

- 2 cups (300 g) vital wheat gluten
- ¼ cup all-purpose flour
- 4 tsp onion powder
- 2 tsp garlic powder

Blender Ingredients

- 10 oz (280 g) pressed extra-firm block tofu (see pg. 24 for instructions)
- 1 and ½ cup (360 ml) water
- 2 T mild vegetable oil
- 2 T mellow white miso paste
- 2 tsp fine sea salt or kosher salt
- 2 tsp nutritional yeast flakes
- 1 tsp poultry seasoning

Turk'y Simmering Broth

- 16 cups (4 quarts/1 gallon) water
- 4 large onions, peeled and quartered
- 4 ribs celery, chopped
- 2 carrots, unpeeled and chopped
- 1 handful parsley stems (leaves removed and saved for the pan-glaze and garnish)
- 8 cloves garlic, crushed
- ⅓ cup nutritional yeast flakes
- 2 tamari, soy sauce or Bragg Liquid Aminos™

- 4 tsp fine sea salt or kosher salt
- 2 tsp organic sugar
- 8 sprigs fresh thyme or 2 tsp dried thyme leaves
- 2 tsp dry rubbed sage
- 1 sprig fresh rosemary
- 2 bay leaves
- 1 and ½ tsp whole peppercorns

Notes: The fresh thyme, sage and rosemary can be replaced with 1 teaspoon commercial poultry seasoning if desired.

Fresh homemade broth is always best and is recommended for this recipe; however, for the sake of convenience the simmering broth can be made using commercial "no-chicken" broth cubes or bouillon paste.

Pan-Glaze Ingredients

- 3 T non-dairy butter or margarine
- 1 T tamari, soy sauce or Bragg Liquid Aminos™
- ¼ cup dry white wine or reserved simmering broth
- 1 tsp each minced fresh rosemary, sage and thyme*
- coarse ground black pepper, to taste

*The fresh herbs can be replaced with ¼ tsp commercial poultry seasoning if desired.

Preparation

Warning! It is very important to use only heavy-duty aluminum foil for this recipe. Regular foil is not sturdy enough and can easily rupture from steam pressure which builds up inside the sealed package.

Preheat the oven to 350°F/180°C.

Combine the dry ingredients in a large mixing bowl; set aside.

Crumble the pressed tofu into a blender and add the remaining blender ingredients. Process the contents until the tofu is completely liquefied and the mixture is smooth and creamy. This is essential! Stop the blender as necessary to scrape down the sides.

Scoop the tofu mixture into the dry ingredients (a small amount of the tofu mixture will remain in the blender; this is inconsequential) and combine with a sturdy silicone spatula until the tofu mixture is incorporated and a sticky ball of dough begins to form.

Place the dough into a food processor fitted with a dough blade and process for 1 full minute. Alternately, place the dough into a stand mixer fitted with a paddle and process on medium speed for 1 full minute.

If kneading by hand, knead the dough in the bowl vigorously for 3 full minutes. This is very important in order to develop the gluten. Test the dough by stretching it. If it tears easily, more kneading is required. The dough needs to exhibit a moderate degree of elasticity in order to produce the proper finished texture.

Tear off a large sheet of foil (about 24-inches) and place it on your work surface. Place the dough onto the foil and shape it into a round ball. Now, lift the edge of the foil over the dough and begin rolling into a cylinder, pinching the ends closed simultaneously while rolling. The goal is to create a compact cylindrical package. Twist the ends tightly to seal, being careful not to tear the foil. Bend the twisted ends in half to lock them tight.

Tip: While the ends need to be twisted tightly to seal the package, avoid twisting inwards so far as to tightly compress the dough. The dough will expand significantly as it bakes. Leaving room on each end for expansion will relieve pressure on the foil and thus discourage rupturing.

Wrap with a second sheet of foil and twist the ends tightly to completely seal the package. If the foil tears at any point while twisting the ends, rewrap in a third sheet of foil.

Place the package directly on the middle rack of the oven and bake for 1 hour and 30 minutes.

While the roast is prebaking, prepare the simmering broth. Add all of the broth ingredients to a large cooking pot and bring to a boil. Cover with a lid and reduce the heat to a gentle simmer. For quick broths, bring the water and bouillon paste, cubes or powder to a simmer in a large covered cooking pot after the roast has been removed from the oven.

Remove the roast from the oven and let cool for about 30 minutes. Unwrap the roast and with a fork, pierce the roast 4 times on the top and 4 times on the bottom.

If the broth was made from scratch, use a slotted spoon to remove and discard the large solid ingredients. It's not necessary to strain the broth completely. Bring the broth to a boil and carefully lower the roast into the broth. Reduce the heat to a simmer and cook for 1 hour. Turn the roast occasionally as it simmers. Monitor the pot frequently and adjust the heat as necessary to maintain the simmer. The broth should be gently bubbling. Do not boil, but do not let the roast merely poach in hot liquid either, as a gentle simmer is necessary to penetrate the roast and finish the cooking process.

Remove the pot from the heat, cover and let cool for several hours or until lukewarm. Remove the roast, seal in a food storage bag with ¼ cup broth and refrigerate for a minimum of 8 hours or for up to 1 week before finishing. To freeze the roast, place it into a freezer bag without the broth and freeze for up to 3 months. If the roast was frozen, thaw for several days in the refrigerator before finishing.

Finishing the Roast

Bring the roast to room temperature for about 2 hours before finishing. Preheat the oven to 350°F/180°C. Lightly blot the roast with a paper towel.

In a large, deep non-stick skillet or wok, melt the butter or margarine over medium heat. Add the roast and turn with 2 large spoons to coat the roast in the butter or margarine (wooden spoons are ideal, as they won't mar the surface of the roast). Continue to turn the roast occasionally until lightly browned. Add the tamari and continue to turn about 1 minute. Now add the wine or reserved broth, the herbs and a few pinches of black pepper. Continue to pan-glaze until the liquid has evaporated and the roast achieves a beautiful golden brown color.

Transfer to a shallow baking dish, cover with foil and bake for 30 minutes to heat through.

Transfer the roast to a serving platter, slice and serve immediately. Store any leftover roast in a food storage bag or sealable container in the refrigerator. Consume within 5 days or freeze.

Tip: Thinly sliced leftover cold roast makes superb hot or cold sandwiches. For hot sandwiches, slice the cold roast and then wrap the slices securely in foil. Place the foil package in a hot oven or in a steamer until heated through. The slices can also be gently reheated in the microwave.

Sage Dressing

with Mushrooms and Water Chestnuts

An artisanal bread dressing to serve with Succulent Roast Turky, consisting of root vegetables, mushrooms and chopped water chestnuts (or any nuts of your choice) flavored with sage and thyme.

Ingredients

- 1 loaf (about 16 oz) artisan white or whole grain bread
- olive oil
- 1 medium onion, diced
- 1 large leek, white and light green part, halved lengthwise and then sliced (be sure to rinse well to remove any sand)
- 2 ribs celery, diced
- 1 can (8 oz) water chestnuts, drained and chopped (or any nut of your choice)
- 3 cloves garlic, minced
- 1 T fresh chopped sage or 1 tsp dry rubbed sage, or more to taste
- leaves from 6 sprigs fresh thyme or 1 tsp dried thyme
- ½ tsp sea salt or kosher salt
- ½ tsp coarse ground black pepper
- ¼ cup (4 T) non-dairy butter or margarine
- 8 oz cremini mushrooms (baby portabellas), white button mushrooms or a blend of mushrooms of your choice, cut into quarters or bite-size pieces
- ¼ cup chopped parsley
- 1 cup turky simmering broth (pg. 127) or similar

Preparation

Preheat the oven to 200°F/100°C. Cut the bread into ½-inch cubes and place in a single layer on 2 baking sheets. Dry in the oven for 1 hour. Transfer to a large mixing bowl. This can be done the night before, if desired, and the bread left to sit out uncovered overnight.

When ready to prepare the dressing, preheat the oven to 350°F/180°C.

In a large skillet, add 2 tablespoons of olive oil and place over medium heat. Add the onions, leek and celery and sauté until the onions are translucent. Add the water chestnuts, garlic, sage, thyme, salt and pepper and continue to sauté an additional minute. Transfer to the mixing bowl.

In the same skillet, melt 2 tablespoons of the butter or margarine over medium heat. Add the mushrooms and sauté until golden brown. Add the remaining 2 tablespoons butter or margarine and stir just until melted. Transfer to the mixing bowl, add the parsley and toss all of the ingredients together thoroughly.

Drizzle in half of the broth and toss thoroughly. Drizzle in the remaining broth and toss until the dressing is evenly moistened. Spoon the dressing into a 'buttered" casserole dish and bake uncovered for 45 minutes or until a golden brown crust forms on top. Serve warm.

Amber Waves of Gravy

This recipe produces a velvety smooth and savory gravy that is superb for serving over slices of Succulent Roast Turky and/or mashed potatoes and dressing.

Ingredients

- 4 cups turky simmering broth (pg. 127) or similar
- 2 T olive oil
- 2 T non-dairy butter or margarine
- ¼ cup all-purpose flour or rice flour
- 1 tsp Worcestershire Sauce (pg. 25) or commercial vegan equivalent
- ½ tsp Browning Liquid (pg. 26) or commercial equivalent
- ¼ tsp poultry seasoning
- coarse ground black pepper, to taste
- sea salt or kosher salt, to taste (as needed)

Preparation

In a large saucepan, melt the butter or margarine in the oil over medium-low heat. Add the flour and whisk vigorously to create a paste (roux). Cook until the flour emits a nutty aroma, about 2 minutes.

Incorporate the broth in increments while whisking vigorously to eliminate lumps. Initially the mixture will be very thick and pasty and some of the flour may begin to brown and stick to the bottom of the saucepan. This is normal and will resolve as the broth continues to be added. When the mixture has thinned a bit and becomes very smooth, it's safe to pour in the remaining broth.

Add the Worcestershire, browning liquid and poultry seasoning. Continue to cook and stir until the mixture just begins to come to a boil. Reduce the heat to a gentle simmer and cook uncovered, stirring frequently, until the gravy is slightly thickened. For a thicker gravy simply simmer until the liquid reduces a bit. Season the gravy with pepper to taste and add salt as needed. Keep covered and warm over low heat until ready to serve. Stir occasionally.

Scaloppine/Escalope/Schnitzel

The Italian word "scaloppine" (and the American "scaloppini") refers to a thinly sliced cutlet of meat, usually pork or veal, which is sautéed or dredged in flour and/or breadcrumbs and then fried until golden brown.

In French, the term "escalope" (and the older usage "paillard") refers to a cutlet of meat that has been pounded until thin and tender and then sautéed or dredged in flour and/or breadcrumbs and fried. In German, the word "schnitzel" refers to the same as the French escalope. For the sake of this cookbook, all of these terms refer to a thin and tender meatless cutlet that can be used to replace thin veal or pork cutlets in any regional recipe.

The cutlets are prepared from gluten, soy protein from tofu and select seasonings. For this application, the seasoned dough is pressed and shaped into very thin cutlets, prebaked to set the texture and then gently simmered in a seasoned broth. For optimum texture, the cutlets require refrigeration for a minimum of 8 hours before finishing and serving, so plan accordingly. This recipe yields 8 thin cutlets.

Dry Ingredients

- 1 cup vital wheat gluten (150 g)
- 2 tsp onion powder
- 1 tsp garlic powder
- ¼ tsp ground white pepper

Simmering Broth

- 3 quarts (12 cups) porq simmering broth (pg. 106) or any seasoned vegetable broth

Additional Items Needed

- baking sheet
- stainless steel cooling rack (not required but recommended)
- parchment paper or silicone baking mat

Blender Ingredients

- 2.5 oz (70 g) pressed extra-firm block tofu (see pg. 24 for instructions)
- ½ cup water (160 ml)
- 1 T tamari, soy sauce or Bragg Liquid Aminos™
- 1 T mellow white miso paste
- 1 T mild vegetable oil

Preparation

Prepare the simmering broth in a large cooking pot, cover and simmer until the cutlets are prepared and prebaked. For homemade broth, use a slotted spoon to discard the larger solids before simmering the cutlets.

Place a stainless steel cooling rack on a baking sheet and line the rack with parchment paper or a silicone baking mat. The cooling rack is not required, but it is recommended, as it will prevent excessive browning which would occur from direct contact with the hot baking sheet.

Preheat the oven to 350°F/180°C.

Combine the dry ingredients in a large mixing bowl.

Crumble the pressed tofu into a blender and add the remaining blender ingredients. Process the contents until the tofu is completely liquefied and the mixture is smooth and creamy. This is essential! Stop the blender as necessary to scrape down the sides.

Scoop the tofu mixture into the dry ingredients (a small amount of the tofu mixture will remain in the blender; this is inconsequential) and stir with a sturdy silicone spatula until the tofu mixture is incorporated and a sticky dough begins to form.

Place the dough into a food processor fitted with a dough blade and process for 1 full minute. Alternately, place the dough into a stand mixer fitted with a paddle and process on medium speed for 1 full minute. Transfer the dough to a work surface.

If kneading by hand, knead the dough in the bowl vigorously for 3 full minutes. This is very important in order to develop the gluten. Test the dough by stretching it. If it tears easily, more kneading is required. The dough needs to exhibit a moderate degree of elasticity in order to produce the proper finished texture. Transfer the dough to a work surface.

Divide the dough into 8 roughly equal pieces. Press and stretch each piece against a work surface to create a very thin cutlet about ¼-inch thick. The dough will have a tendency to retract when stretched, so let it rest for a couple of minutes to relax the gluten and then press and stretch again.

Place the cutlets onto the parchment paper or baking mat. Bake uncovered on the middle rack of the oven for 20 minutes and then remove from the oven.

Bring the broth to a boil. If the broth was made from scratch, use a slotted spoon to remove and discard the larger solids. It's not necessary to strain the broth completely.

Lower the cutlets into the boiling broth and immediately reduce the heat to a gentle simmer. Leave the pot uncovered and set a timer for 20 minutes. Monitor the pot frequently to make sure the broth is maintained at a simmer. Do not boil. Carefully turn the cutlets occasionally once they float to the top of the pot to ensure even cooking. After simmering, remove the cooking pot from the heat, cover and let the cutlets cool in the broth for a few hours or until lukewarm.

Transfer the cutlets to a food storage bag and add ¼ cup of broth, or a desired marinade. Refrigerate for a minimum of 8 hours, or for up to 1 week, to firm and enhance their texture before finishing and serving. Chilling is very important so do not omit this step.

Strain the cooled broth into a sealable container and refrigerate. During this time, any seasoning sediment will settle on the bottom of the container. The broth can be refrigerated for up to 1 week or frozen for future use at your convenience. Decant the clear portion for preparing gravies or sauces that can be served with the finished cutlets; or use for other recipes as desired. Discard the sediment.

Season as desired and finish the cutlets by sautéing or breading and frying.

———————————————————×( )×———————————————————

Breading and Pan-Frying Technique

for Scaloppine/Escalope/Schnitzel

Ingredients

- ½ cup plain non-dairy milk
- 6 T rice flour or all-purpose flour
- 1 cup very fine plain dry breadcrumbs
- 1 tsp onion powder
- 1 tsp sweet paprika
- 1 tsp sea salt or kosher salt
- ½ tsp garlic powder
- ½ tsp coarse ground black pepper

Preparation

Whisk together the flour and milk in a bowl. Combine the remaining dry breading ingredients in a separate bowl. Dip each cutlet in the batter and then dredge in the breadcrumb mixture, coating evenly on both sides. Set aside on a plate to dry for about 10 minutes.

In a large skillet, add the cooking oil to ¼-inch depth and place over medium-high heat. When the oil begins to shimmer, add the cutlets and fry, turning frequently, until golden brown.

Watch carefully, as they will brown quickly. Transfer the cutlets to a plate lined with paper towels to drain for 1 minute and then to individual serving plates. Garnish as desired and serve immediately with a gravy or sauce of your choice.

Greek Gyro Roast

Tender slices of roast seitan are generously seasoned with aromatic Mediterranean herbs and spices. Sliced Gyro Roast (pronounced "year-row") is the primary component of the Classic Greek Gyro pita pocket sandwich (recipe follows). Döner is the Turkish variant of this roast.

Dry Ingredients

- 1 and ½ cup (225 g) vital wheat gluten
- 2 T porcini mushroom powder
- 1 T dried minced onion
- 1 T onion powder
- ½ tsp coarse ground black pepper

Blender Ingredients

- 1 and ½ cup (360 ml) water
- 3 T tamari, soy sauce or Bragg Liquid Aminos™
- 2 T olive oil
- ½ tsp Browning Liquid (pg. 26) or commercial equivalent
- 2 tsp ground cumin
- 2 tsp dried marjoram leaves
- 1 tsp dried oregano leaves
- ½ tsp dried ground rosemary

Additional Ingredient

- 2 T minced fresh garlic (about 6 large cloves)

Additional Item Needed

- 18-inch wide heavy-duty aluminum foil

Preparation

Warning! It is very important to use only heavy-duty aluminum foil for this recipe. Regular foil is not sturdy enough and can easily rupture from steam pressure which builds up inside the sealed package.

Preheat the oven to 350°F/180°C.

Combine the dry ingredients in a large mixing bowl. Process the blender ingredients until smooth. Stir the minced garlic into the blender ingredients but do not process.

Pour the blender mixture into the dry ingredients and combine thoroughly with a silicone spatula to develop the gluten. Let the dough rest 10 minutes to allow the dry ingredients to absorb as much liquid as possible.

Tear off a sheet of foil (about 18-inches) and place it on your work surface. Place the dough directly on top.

Form the dough into a round mass. The dough will be soft and have a tendency to spread out but try to keep it as compact as you can. Now, lift the edge of the foil over the dough and begin rolling into a cylinder, pinching the ends closed simultaneously while rolling. The goal is to create a thick, compact, cylindrical package. Due to the softness of the dough, this may take practice, so be patient. Twist the ends tightly to seal, being careful not to tear the foil. Bend the twisted ends in half to lock them tight.

Wrap with a second large sheet of foil and twist the ends tightly to completely seal the package. If the foil tears at any point while twisting the ends, rewrap in a third sheet of foil. Place directly on the middle rack of the oven and bake for 2 hours.

Remove from the oven and let cool to room temperature. Refrigerate the roast in its foil wrapper for a minimum of 8 hours before finishing, or for a maximum of 10 days. This will firm and enhance the texture.

Serving the Gyro Roast

Remove the foil and recycle. Stand the roast upright and shave thin slices with a sharp knife. Pan-sear the slices in a lightly oiled non-stick skillet or well-seasoned cast iron skillet until lightly browned. Serve warm on grilled pita bread with sliced onion, chopped tomatoes and Greek Tzatziki Sauce (pg. 207). Leftover roast can be frozen for up to 3 months.

———————————————)( )(———————————————

Classic Greek Gyro

Ingredients

- Greek Gyro Roast (see preceding recipe)
- olive oil
- pita bread or flatbread
- thinly sliced onion
- sliced or chopped tomatoes
- Greek Tzatziki Sauce (pg. 207)

Preparation

Shave thin slices from the roast with a sharp knife and pan-sear as directed in the recipe. Season the slices with ground sumac if desired.

Wrap in foil to keep warm and set aside. Brush the pita or flatbread with olive oil and place oiled-side down in the hot skillet to heat through.

Top the bread with the sliced gyro, sliced onion, chopped tomatoes and Greek Tzatziki sauce. Fold the bread to eat.

New-Fashioned Meatloaf

This is a new and original recipe created after many trials and disappointments with other plant-based meatloaf recipes. It's firm, yet tender and moist with a nice balance of seasonings. Leftovers make superb meatloaf sandwiches too!

Liquid Ingredients

- 2 cups water
- 3 T soy sauce, tamari or Bragg Liquid Aminos™
- 1 T tomato ketchup
- 2 tsp Worcestershire Sauce (pg. 25) or commercial vegan equivalent
- 1 and ½ tsp Browning Liquid (pg. 26) or commercial equivalent
- 1 tsp prepared Dijon, yellow or golden mustard

Dry Mix Ingredients

- ¾ cup vital wheat gluten
- ¼ cup garbanzo bean flour
- 2 tsp onion powder
- 1 tsp garlic powder
- 1 tsp dried oregano
- ½ tsp dried thyme
- ½ tsp coarse ground black pepper

Sauté Ingredients

- 2 T olive oil
- ½ cup onion, finely diced
- 1 large jalapeno or serrano pepper, seeded and finely diced (or ¼ cup finely diced red or green bell pepper if you prefer)
- 2 cloves minced garlic (2 tsp)
- 1 and ½ cup dry TVP/TSP granules (textured vegetable/soy protein)
- ½ cup fresh chopped parsley

Glaze Ingredients

- 3 T ketchup
- 1 T prepared Dijon, golden or yellow mustard
- 1 tsp Worcestershire Sauce (pg. 25) or commercial vegan equivalent

Additional Item Needed

- 9x5 standard metal loaf pan

Chef's tip: For a zesty flavor, replace the tomato ketchup in the meatloaf with BBQ sauce and also use the BBQ sauce as the glaze. For those who don't care for the traditional tomato-based glaze or BBQ sauce, or if you simply prefer something different, the meatloaf can be topped with brown gravy as a substitute for the glaze. Additional gravy can also be served on the side.

Preparation

Line the loaf pan with parchment paper leaving excess hanging over the sides. The excess will be used to cover the meatloaf before baking and will aid removal of the meatloaf from the pan after baking; set aside.

Combine the liquid ingredients in a large bowl or measuring cup and set aside. Don't worry about dispersing the mustard completely as this will take of itself later.

In a large mixing bowl, stir together the dry mix ingredients; set aside.

In a large skillet over medium heat, sauté the onion and jalapeno, serrano or bell pepper in the olive oil until the onion is translucent. Add the minced garlic and sauté just until the vegetables are lightly browned around the edges. Add the liquid ingredients and bring to a boil.

Add the dry vegetable/soy protein granules to the boiling liquid and stir well until completely moistened. Stir in the parsley and cover the skillet with a lid. Allow to rest for 30 minutes.

Preheat the oven to 350°F/180°C.

Scoop the skillet ingredients into the dry ingredients, including any liquid, and fold the contents until the dry mix is thoroughly and evenly combined with the wet mixture. This is important as the gluten needs to be evenly distributed in order for the meatloaf to hold together when slicing and serving.

Transfer the meatloaf mixture to the loaf pan and firmly pack the mixture into the pan while smoothing out the surface. Fold the excess parchment over the loaf and then seal the loaf pan securely with foil. Place in the oven and bake for 1 hour.

While the meatloaf is baking, mix together the glaze ingredients in a small bowl; set aside.

After 1 hour, remove the pan from the oven, remove the foil and fold back the parchment. Evenly spread the glaze mixture over the surface; return to the oven and bake uncovered for 15 minutes.

Remove the meatloaf from the oven and let cool for about 15 minutes before lifting the meatloaf from the pan and transferring to a work surface for slicing. Leftovers can be reheated in the microwave or by wrapping securely in foil and heating in a 350°F/180°C oven for 15 to 20 minutes.

Grillin' Burgers

At last! Homemade plant-based burgers with the appearance, taste and texture of real ground beef hamburgers; and the best part is they're 100% cruelty-free! This recipe yields 4 to 6 burgers, depending upon how thick or thin you like them. A 4-inch ring mold is helpful for shaping the burgers but not essential.

Wet Ingredients

- 2 T dry TVP/TSP granules (textured vegetable/soy protein)
- 2 T boiling water (to reconstitute the TVP/TSP granules)
- ¾ cup (180 ml) water
- 2 T tamari, soy sauce or Bragg Liquid Aminos™
- 2 tsp Worcestershire Sauce (pg. 25) or commercial vegan equivalent
- 1 T olive oil
- ½ tsp Browning Liquid (pg. 26) or commercial equivalent

Dry Ingredients

- 1 cup (150 g) vital wheat gluten
- 1 T porcini mushroom powder or garbanzo bean flour
- 1 T dried minced onion
- 2 tsp onion powder
- 1 and ½ tsp garlic powder
- ½ tsp coarse ground black pepper
- ¼ tsp ground dried rosemary

Additional Items Needed

- baking sheet
- stainless steel cooling rack (not required but recommended)
- parchment paper or silicone baking mat

Finishing Marinade

- ¼ cup water
- 1 T liquid smoke, or less to taste
- 1 tsp Worcestershire Sauce (pg. 25) or commercial vegan equivalent

Preparation

In a small bowl, add 2 tablespoons boiling water to the TVP/TSP granules and let reconstitute for 10 minutes.

In another bowl, combine ¾ cup water with the remaining wet ingredients. Stir the reconstituted TVP/TSP granules into the wet mixture. Set aside.

Place a stainless steel cooling rack on a baking sheet and line the rack with parchment paper or a silicone baking mat. The cooling rack is not required, but it is recommended, as it will prevent excessive browning which would occur from direct contact with the hot baking sheet.

Preheat the oven to 350°F/180°C.

Thoroughly stir together the dry ingredients in a large mixing bowl. Give the wet ingredients a quick stir and then pour all at once into the dry ingredients.

Fold the mixture together with a silicone spatula just until all ingredients are incorporated and a soft dough begins to form. Do not knead the dough as this will make the dough elastic and difficult to shape into patties.

Flatten the dough evenly in the bottom of the mixing bowl and divide into 6 roughly equal portions with the edge of the spatula.

Pick up a piece of dough, form into a ball and then press flat in the palm of your hand. Place the ring mold on the lined baking sheet and place the flattened dough inside the ring mold. With your fingers, press the dough to fill the ring. Remove the ring and repeat with the additional pieces of dough. If you don't have a ring mold, form the dough into a ball, press flat on the baking sheet and then continue to press and shape the burgers with your fingers.

Drape a large sheet of foil over the baking sheet and crimp the edges to seal the foil. Place on the middle rack of the oven and bake for 45 minutes.

Remove the baking sheet and let the burgers cool for about 30 minutes with the foil cover in place. When cool enough to handle, but still warm, remove the foil and transfer the burgers to a food storage bag. Add the finishing marinade (or plain water if you don't care for smoke seasoning), press out as much air as possible and seal the bag. Refrigerate until well-chilled and most of the marinade has been absorbed before grilling (the burgers can remain stored in this bag in the refrigerator for up to 10 days before grilling). Once the burgers have absorbed the marinade, they can also be frozen for up to 3 months. Simply wrap them between layers of wax paper or parchment paper and place them in a freezer storage bag. Be sure to thaw them completely before grilling.

Grilling the Burgers

To grill the burgers on the stove, oil a non-stick skillet or grill pan and place over medium heat. Pan-sear the burgers until nicely browned on both sides. For outdoor grilling, brush the burgers with cooking oil. Grill over hot embers or a medium gas flame until grill marks appear (avoid overcooking since they are already precooked). Serve with your favorite condiments.

Meatballs

These tender and delicious meatless meatballs are perfect for using in your favorite pasta sauce, soup, stew or for meatball sandwiches. They hold up very well to prolonged simmering in sauces, soups and stews, unlike many commercial plant-based meatballs which tend to break down. The prepared meatballs require several hours of refrigeration before using in recipes to firm and enhance their texture, so plan accordingly. This recipe yields approximately 10 large meatballs, 20 medium meatballs or 25 small meatballs.

Wet Ingredients

- 2 T dry TVP/TSP granules (textured vegetable/soy protein)
- 2 T boiling water (to reconstitute the TVP/TSP granules)

Liquid Ingredients

- ½ cup water
- 3 T tamari, soy sauce or Bragg Liquid Aminos™
- 1 T olive oil
- ½ tsp Browning Liquid (pg. 26) or commercial equivalent

Dry Ingredients

- 1 cup vital wheat gluten (150 g)
- 1 T garbanzo bean flour
- 1 T dried minced onion
- 2 tsp onion powder
- 2 tsp dried parsley
- 1 and ½ tsp garlic powder
- ½ tsp coarse ground black pepper

Seasoning Variations

- ❖ *For Italian meatballs omit the dried parsley from the dry ingredients and add 1 tsp dried basil leaves, 1 tsp dried oregano leaves and ¼ tsp crushed red pepper.*
- ❖ *For Swedish meatballs omit the dried parsley from the dry ingredients and add ½ tsp ground nutmeg and ½ tsp ground allspice.*
- ❖ *For Mexican meatballs omit the dried parsley from the dry ingredients and add 1 tsp dried oregano leaves, ½ tsp ground cumin, ½ tsp ground coriander and ¼ tsp ground red pepper.*
- ❖ *For Mediterranean meatballs add 1 tsp dried oregano leaves and ½ tsp ground cumin to the dry ingredients.*
- ❖ *For Moroccan meatballs add ½ tsp ground cumin, ½ tsp ground allspice and ¼ tsp ground red pepper to the dry ingredients.*

Simmering Broth

- 3 quarts (12 cups) porq simmering broth (pg. 106) or any seasoned vegetable broth

Preparation

Prepare the simmering broth in a large cooking pot prior to preparing the meatballs. If the broth was made from scratch, cover and allow it to simmer for one hour.

Stir together the dry ingredients in a large mixing bowl. Set aside.

In a small bowl, add 2 tablespoons boiling water to the TVP/TSP granules to reconstitute. In a larger bowl, combine ½ cup water with the remaining liquid ingredients.

Mince the reconstituted granules and then stir them into the liquid mixture.

Pour the liquid ingredients into the dry ingredients. Mix just until the liquid is incorporated and the dry ingredients are moistened; the mixture may seem a bit dry. Do not knead the dough or the meatballs will be difficult to roll.

Pinch off a piece of dough and compress the dough in your hands. Roll the dough into a round meatball shape between your palms, about ¾-inch diameter for small meatballs, 1-inch diameter for medium meatballs or 1 and ½-inch diameter for large meatballs and set aside on your work surface. Repeat with the remaining dough. Try to work quickly when rolling; the gluten in the dough becomes more elastic the longer the dough sits, and this will make rolling more difficult.

Bring the broth to a boil. If the broth was made from scratch, use a slotted spoon to remove and discard the larger solids. It's not necessary to strain the broth completely.

Roll each meatball again briefly between the palms of your hands before adding to the boiling broth. This will remove the flat dent created from sitting on the work surface. Add the meatballs to the boiling broth and immediately reduce the heat to a gentle simmer. Cook uncovered 25 minutes for large meatballs, 20 minutes for medium meatballs and 15 minutes for small meatballs.

Check frequently to maintain the broth at a very gentle simmer. Do not boil! Turn occasionally once the meatballs float to the top of the pot. When simmering is complete, remove the pot from the heat and let the meatballs cool in the broth for several hours or until lukewarm. Transfer the meatballs to a food storage bag with ¼ cup of broth and refrigerate for a minimum of 8 hours, or for up to 1 week, before browning in the skillet. This will firm and enhance their texture. You can also freeze them for up to 3 months without the broth.

Be sure to reserve the simmering broth. The broth can be strained and used immediately for soups, stews, sauces or gravies. Be sure to add back a little water as necessary before using, since the seasoning will have become concentrated from evaporation during simmering.

If the broth won't be used immediately, strain into a sealable container and refrigerate. During this time, any seasoning sediment will settle on the bottom of the container. Simply decant the clear portion for use in other recipes. The broth can be refrigerated for up to 10 days or frozen for future use at your convenience.

Browning the Meatballs

Brown the meatballs in a non-stick skillet with 2 tablespoons of cooking oil over medium heat. Add them to your favorite sauce, soup or stew the last 15 minutes of cooking time before serving.

Kebabi

Kebabi consists of aromatically seasoned "minced meat" formed around mini bamboo skewers. The kebabi is seasoned with herbs and spices commonly used in a variety of Middle Eastern and Eastern Mediterranean cuisines, rather than from one specific country, since each country has its own version of kebab or kabob. Grilling over charcoal imparts an authentic smoky flavor but the kebabi can be finished on a gas grill or indoor grill pan too. This recipe yields 8 kebabi.

Wet Ingredients

- 2 T dry TVP/TSP granules (textured vegetable/soy protein)
- 2 T boiling water (to reconstitute the TVP/TSP granules)

Liquid Ingredients

- ¾ cup (180 ml) water
- 2 T tamari, soy sauce or Bragg Liquid Aminos™
- 2 tsp Worcestershire Sauce (pg. 25) or commercial vegan equivalent
- 1 T olive oil, plus additional for grilling
- ½ tsp Browning Liquid (pg. 26) or commercial equivalent

Dry Ingredients

- 1 cup (150 g) vital wheat gluten
- 1 T porcini mushroom powder
- 1 T dried minced onion
- 1 T dried parsley
- 2 tsp garlic powder
- 2 tsp onion powder
- 1 tsp ground cumin
- 1 tsp smoked or sweet paprika
- 1 tsp dried mint or oregano
- ½ tsp ground coriander
- ½ tsp coarse ground black pepper
- ¼ tsp ground allspice

Finishing Marinade

- ¼ cup water
- 1 T liquid smoke
- 1 tsp Worcestershire Sauce (pg. 25) or commercial vegan equivalent

Additional Items Needed

- 8 six-inch bamboo skewers
- baking sheet
- stainless steel cooling rack (not required but recommended)
- parchment paper or silicone baking mat

Preparation

In a small bowl, add 2 tablespoons boiling water to the TVP/TSP granules and let reconstitute for 10 minutes. Finely mince the reconstituted granules.

In another bowl, combine the liquid ingredients. Stir the finely minced TVP/TSP granules into the liquid mixture. Set aside.

Place a stainless steel cooling rack on a baking sheet and line the rack with parchment paper or a silicone baking mat. The cooling rack is not required, but it is recommended, as it will prevent excessive browning which would occur from direct contact with the hot baking sheet.

Preheat the oven to 350°F/180°C.

Thoroughly stir together the dry ingredients in a large mixing bowl. Give the liquid mixture a quick stir and then pour all at once into the dry ingredients.

Fold the mixture together with a silicone spatula just until all ingredients are incorporated and a soft dough begins to form. Do not knead the dough as this will make the dough elastic and difficult to shape around the skewers.

Flatten the dough evenly in the bottom of the mixing bowl and divide into 6 roughly equal portions with the edge of the spatula.

Pick up a piece of dough, form into a ball and then roll it into a sausage shape. Skewer the dough and continue to shape the dough around the skewer with your fingers. Pinch the ends to taper the kebabi. Place the skewer on the baking sheet and repeat with the remaining dough.

Drape a large sheet of foil over the baking sheet and crimp the edges to seal the foil. Place on the middle rack of the oven and bake for 45 minutes.

Remove the baking sheet and let the kebabi cool for about 30 minutes with the foil cover in place. When cool enough to handle, but still warm, remove the foil and transfer the kebabi to a food storage bag. Add the finishing marinade, press out as much air as possible and seal the bag. Exercise caution so the sharp points of the skewers do not puncture the bag.

Refrigerate for a minimum of 8 hours, or for up to 10 days, before grilling. Once the kebabi have absorbed the marinade, they can also be frozen for up to 3 months. Simply wrap them between layers of wax paper or parchment paper and place a freezer storage bag. Be sure to thaw them completely before grilling.

Grilling the Kebabi

Rub a barbecue grill rack with oil and light the charcoal; optionally, season a grill pan with oil and place over medium-high heat.

Brush the kebabi with olive oil and place on the hot grill over glowing embers (no flames) or the hot grill pan. Turn occasionally, brushing with olive oil every few minutes to avoid drying out. Sprinkle with a little ground sumac if desired. Grill until nicely browned. Serve with rice or couscous. Greek Tzatziki sauce (pg. 207), a Mediterranean condiment, nicely compliments the flavor of the kebabi.

Sausages

Individual Hand-Rolled Sausages

For the individual hand-rolled sausages, the seasoned dough is divided into individual portions. The portions are rolled and sealed in aluminum foil and then steamed. After steaming, the sausages are chilled to firm and enhance their texture before browning in a skillet or on the grill.

Pop-up aluminum foil (9"x 10¾") is recommended for wrapping the sausages prior to steaming. Pop-up foil is commonly used in the restaurant industry for wrapping baked potatoes. It's very convenient because cutting foil to create wrappers is not required. While pop-up foil is not available in all supermarkets, it is commonly used in hair salons for hair coloring and can be found in beauty supply stores. It can also be purchased online. Pop-up foil is very thin and flimsy, so double wrapping the sausages is required so they do not burst open while steaming.

If you don't have pop-up foil, standard and heavy-duty aluminum foil can be used; however, the foil will need to be cut with scissors to create six 8"x10" wrappers. For the Maple Sage Sausage Links, cut the foil to create ten 6"x8" wrappers. The sausages only need to be wrapped once when using standard or heavy-duty foil (unless the foil tears when twisting the ends).

You may be wondering why the individual sausages are steamed rather than baked. When working with smaller portions of dough, such as with the individual hand-rolled sausages, the moist steam heat cooks the dough evenly and prevents overcooking and excessive browning. The steam pressure inside the cooking pot also helps equalize the steam pressure inside the foil packages thus discouraging the moisture from leaking out, which would contribute to an excessively dry and bread-like texture. For other sausages and meat analogues requiring large portions of dough, baking is more practical and effective, since longer cooking times are required at a steady high temperature.

For steaming, you will need a large cooking pot with a lid and a steamer insert. Add enough water to the pot to just reach the bottom of the steamer insert. Do not overfill or the foil packages will be sitting in water.

The sausage recipes are formulated with as much liquid as possible, beyond the point of saturation. This saturation is necessary for creating a juicy and meaty sausage. It's not uncommon to have a small amount of excess liquid remaining in the bottom of the mixing bowl after mixing the dough. Resist the urge to add more gluten or garbanzo bean flour to absorb the extra liquid - we're making sausages, not bread. However, handling and rolling the soft, wet dough in foil can be a little tricky, at least initially. So be patient when learning to wrap the sausages. Like any skill, it takes a little practice.

Meat-based sausages use a casing to contain the meat and give the sausage its shape. Plant-based sausages on the other hand, have no casing and since they are hand-rolled in aluminum foil, imperfections in their appearance are to be expected. However, these surface imperfections will not detract from their excellent taste and texture. Browning the sausages before serving actually creates a light "casing", so to speak, that significantly improves their appearance and minimizes these imperfections.

Steamed sausages require cooling to room temperature and then refrigeration for a minimum of 8 hours before browning and serving, so plan accordingly. Chilling changes the gluten structure and will firm and enhance the sausage texture. The sausages will be soft and fragile after steaming, so refrigerate them in their foil wrappers until they have firmed up.

The prepared sausages are at their best when browned in the skillet with cooking oil before serving, but they are ideal for grilling too. Just be sure to brush them with cooking oil to keep them moist while grilling. Do not grill the sausages over open flames - hot embers are best; and avoid overcooking as this can cause excessive dryness.

General Sausage Preparation Instructions

Preparing the Dough

Add enough water to your steam cooking pot to just reach the bottom of the steamer insert.

Combine the dry ingredients in a large mixing bowl.

Process the blender ingredients until any seasonings are finely ground. For the Chikun Apple Sausages, stir the chopped dried apple into the blender ingredients after processing. Do not process once the apple has been added.

Pour the blender mixture into the dry ingredients and combine thoroughly with a silicone spatula to develop the gluten. The dough will be soft and wet. Let the dough rest for 5 minutes to allow the dry ingredients to absorb as much liquid as possible.

Flatten the dough evenly in the mixing bowl and divide with the edge of the spatula into 6 roughly equal portions (or 10 portions for Maple Sage Sausage Links).

Foil Wrapping the Dough

Place a portion of dough onto a foil square and with your fingers shape the dough into a rough sausage shape. The dough will be very wet, so keep a moist paper towel on hand to wipe your fingers as you work. Don't worry too much about shaping perfection, as the dough will expand to conform to the cylindrical shape of the foil package when steamed.

Roll the dough inside the foil to create a small cylinder while simultaneously pinching the ends closed. Twist the ends tightly to seal. When using pop-up foil, roll again in a second foil wrapper. If the foil should tear while twisting the ends, roll again in additional foil. The dough needs to be securely sealed in the foil to prevent moisture from leaking out but also to prevent steam moisture from entering the packages.

Repeat with the remaining pieces of dough and set aside while the water in the cooking pot is brought to a full boil. The water must be boiling to generate the proper amount of steam heat to cook the sausages thoroughly and evenly.

Steaming the Sausages

Once the water in the cooking pot has come to a full boil, add the foil packages. Depending upon the size of your steamer insert, the twisted ends may need to be bent inwards to allow the packages to fit.

Cover and set the timer for 45 minutes, except for the Maple Sage Sausage Links which require only 30 minutes. Check the pot at 15 to 20 minute intervals to monitor water loss (use an oven mitt to avoid steam burns) and add HOT water to replace water lost to steam evaporation. DO NOT let the pot boil dry. If you're steaming in a smaller cooking pot with a shallow volume of water, it's not unusual to replace several cups of water during steaming. Replacing water should be unnecessary in larger steamers that hold a large volume of water.

When the sausages have finished steaming, remove the foil packages from the pot with cooking tongs and let them cool to room temperature. Refrigerate the sausages in their foil wrappers for a minimum of 8 hours to firm and enhance their texture (or for up to 10 days) before browning and serving. The foil-wrapped packages can also be frozen for up to 3 months.

Browning the Sausages

Bring the foil packages to room temperature, about 30 minutes.

Remove the foil and recycle. In a non-stick skillet or well-seasoned cast iron skillet, brown the sausages in two tablespoons of cooking oil over medium heat. A teaspoon of tamari, soy sauce or Bragg Liquid Aminos™ will encourage browning, but this is optional. Transfer to a plate lined with paper towels to blot any excess oil. The sausages are ready to eat or use in your favorite recipe.

For grilling, brush the sausages with cooking oil and grill over hot embers until lightly browned, or until grill marks appear. Avoid direct flames and do not overcook.

Italian Sausages

"Sweet" or "Hot"

Classic Italian seasonings give these sausages their characteristic flavor. The seasoning blend offers options for "sweet" (mild) sausages or "hot" and spicy sausages. Please review the sausage introduction on pg. 145 and then refer to the instructions on pg. 146 for preparation. This recipe yields 6 sausages.

Dry Ingredients

- 1 cup (150 g) vital wheat gluten
- 1 T garbanzo bean flour or soy flour
- 1 T dried minced onion
- 2 tsp onion powder
- 1 tsp whole fennel seeds*

Blender Ingredients

- 1 and ¼ cup (300 ml) water
- 2 T tamari, soy sauce or Bragg Liquid Aminos™
- 1 T minced fresh garlic (about 3 large cloves)
- 1 T olive oil
- 1 tsp whole fennel seeds*
- 1 tsp dried oregano leaves
- 1 tsp dried basil leaves
- 1 tsp liquid smoke
- ¼ tsp ground white pepper for "sweet" (mild) sausages
  or 2 tsp crushed red pepper flakes for "hot" (spicy) sausages

Note: Some of the fennel seeds are left whole, while some are finely ground with the blender ingredients. This is not a misprint.

Bavarian Bratwurst

These flavorful meatless sausages are perfect for celebrating Oktoberfest, but are delicious any time of the year. This recipe is made with my special blend of German-inspired seasonings and yields 6 bratwursts. Please review the sausage introduction on pg. 145 and then refer to the instructions on pg. 146 for preparation.

Dry Ingredients

- 1 cup (150 g) vital wheat gluten
- 1 T garbanzo bean flour or soy flour
- 1 T dried minced onion
- 2 tsp onion powder

Blender Ingredients

- 1 and ⅓ cup (320 ml) water
- 2 T mellow white miso paste
- 1 T mild vegetable oil
- 1 T minced fresh garlic (about 3 large cloves)
- ½ tsp fine sea salt or kosher salt
- ½ tsp poultry seasoning
- ¼ tsp caraway seed
- ¼ tsp ground ginger
- ¼ tsp ground allspice
- ¼ tsp ground nutmeg
- ¼ tsp ground white pepper

Frankfurts

My special blend of seasonings gives these plump, tasty franks their characteristic flavor. Because they're hand-rolled, they're a bit rustic in appearance but delicious nonetheless. Garnish with your favorite accoutrements, such as diced onion, relish, ketchup and/or prepared mustard. Try topping with veggie chili for chili dogs. Please review the sausage introduction on pg. 145 and then refer to the instructions on pg. 146 for preparation. This recipe yields 6 jumbo franks.

Dry Ingredients

- 1 cup (150 g) vital wheat gluten
- 1 T onion powder

Blender Ingredients

- 1 and ¼ cup (300 ml) water
- 1 T minced fresh garlic (about 3 large cloves)
- 1 T mellow white miso paste
- 1 T tamari, soy sauce or Bragg Liquid Aminos™
- 1 T mild vegetable oil

Blender Ingredients (cont'd.)

- ¾ tsp smoked paprika
- ½ tsp dry ground mustard
- ½ tsp ground coriander
- ½ tsp poultry seasoning
- ½ tsp ground nutmeg
- ½ tsp Browning Liquid (pg. 26) or commercial equivalent
- ¼ tsp ground white pepper
- ¼ tsp fine sea salt or kosher salt

Andouille Sausage

Andouille sausage is French in origin and was later brought to Louisiana by French immigrants. In the United States, the sausage is most often associated with Cajun cooking. Andouille sausages, which are heavily seasoned with garlic and cayenne pepper, are sometimes referred to as "hot link" sausages. I offer you a compassionate and healthier version of this flavorful sausage. Please review the sausage introduction on pg. 145 and then refer to the instructions on pg. 146 for preparation. This recipe yields 6 sausages. Bon appétit!

Dry Ingredients

- 1 cup (150 g) vital wheat gluten
- 1 T garbanzo bean flour or soy flour
- 1 T dried minced onion
- 1 tsp onion powder
- 1 tsp garlic powder

Blender Ingredients

- 1 and ¼ cup (300 ml) water
- 2 T tamari, soy sauce or Bragg Liquid Aminos™
- 1 T minced fresh garlic (about 3 large cloves)
- 1 T mild vegetable oil
- 1 tsp liquid smoke
- 1 tsp organic sugar
- ½ tsp cayenne pepper (or 1 tsp for fiery sausage)
- ½ tsp poultry seasoning
- ½ tsp sweet paprika

Maple Sage Sausage Links

The wonderful flavors of rubbed sage and maple syrup complement these tasty breakfast sausages. They're perfect served alongside scrambles, pancakes or French toast. Please review the sausage introduction on pg. 145 and then refer to the instructions on pg. 146 for preparation. This recipe yields 10 sausage links.

Dry Ingredients

- 1 cup (150 g) vital wheat gluten
- 1 T garbanzo bean flour or soy flour
- 1 T dried minced onion
- 2 tsp onion powder
- ¼ tsp coarse ground black pepper

Blender Ingredients

- 1 cup plus 2 T (270 ml) water
- 2 T tamari, soy sauce or Bragg Liquid Aminos™
- 2 T real maple syrup
- 1 T minced fresh garlic (about 3 large cloves)
- 1 T mild vegetable oil
- 2 tsp dry rubbed sage
- ½ tsp poultry seasoning
- ½ tsp sweet paprika
- ½ tsp ground nutmeg
- ⅛ tsp ground red pepper or cayenne pepper

British "Bangers"

Bangers are a type of short, plump sausage common to the United Kingdom. Bangers are often an essential part of pub food, as they are quick to prepare and Bangers and Mash is the traditional British Isles favorite (sausages with mashed potatoes and onion gravy). The term "bangers" is attributed to the fact that sausages, particularly the kind made during World War II under rationing, were made with water so they were more likely to explode under high heat if not cooked carefully. Fortunately, this isn't an issue with their plant-based counterparts. Please review the sausage introduction on pg. 145 and then refer to the instructions on pg. 146 for preparation. This recipe yields 8 plump sausages. The recipe for Savory Onion Gravy can be found on pg. 185.

Dry Ingredients

- 1 cup (150 g) vital wheat gluten
- 1 T garbanzo bean flour or soy flour
- 1 T dried minced onion
- 2 tsp onion powder
- ½ tsp coarse ground black pepper

Blender Ingredients

- 1 and ¼ cup (300 ml) water
- 1 T minced fresh garlic (about 3 large cloves)

Blender Ingredients (cont'd.)

- 1 T tamari, soy sauce or Bragg Liquid Aminos™
- 1 T mellow white miso paste
- 1 T mild vegetable oil
- 2 tsp dry rubbed sage
- 1 tsp fresh grated lemon zest, loosely packed
- 1 tsp liquid smoke
- ½ tsp ground ginger
- ½ tsp ground nutmeg
- ¼ tsp fine sea salt or kosher salt

Chikun Apple Sausage

Sweet apple and savory seasonings flavor these superb sausages. Please review the sausage introduction on pg. 145 and then refer to the instructions on pg. 146 for preparation. This recipe yields 6 sausages.

Dry Ingredients

- 1 cup (150 g) vital wheat gluten
- 1 T garbanzo bean flour or soy flour
- 2 tsp onion powder

Special Ingredient

- 2 T finely chopped dried apple (preferably unsulfured)

Blender Ingredients

- 1 and ⅓ cup (320 ml) water
- 1 T minced fresh garlic (about 3 large cloves)
- 1 T mellow white miso paste
- 1 T mild vegetable oil
- 1 tsp nutritional yeast flakes
- 1 tsp organic sugar
- ¾ tsp fine sea salt or kosher salt
- ½ tsp poultry seasoning

Polska Kiełbasa

(Polish Sausage)

Kiełbasa is the Polish word for "sausage". In Poland, many varieties of kielbasa exist and are seasoned differently according to region and even family. They're seasoned with my own special blend of onion, black and white pepper, an abundance of fresh garlic, and other select herbs and spices. Spicy golden mustard, horseradish mustard or Dijon mustard are ideal condiments to serve with kielbasa sausage. Please review the sausage introduction on pg. 145 and then refer to the instructions on pg. 146 for preparation. This recipe yields 6 sausages.

Dry Ingredients

- 1 cup (150 g) vital wheat gluten
- 1 T garbanzo bean flour or soy flour
- 1 T dried minced onion
- 2 tsp onion powder
- 1 tsp garlic powder
- ½ tsp coarse ground black pepper

Blender Ingredients

- 1 and ¼ cup (300 ml) water
- 1 T minced fresh garlic (about 3 large cloves)
- 1 T tamari, soy sauce or Bragg Liquid Aminos™
- 1 T mellow white miso paste
- 1 T mild vegetable oil
- 2 tsp liquid smoke
- 1 tsp dried marjoram or summer savory
- ½ tsp ground white pepper
- ¼ tsp ground nutmeg
- ¼ tsp ground allspice
- ¼ tsp fine sea salt or kosher salt

Sausage Rolls

Country Breakfast Sausage Patties

For this recipe, the sausage roll is baked rather than steamed, refrigerated for a minimum of 8 hours to firm and enhance its texture, and then sliced into patties and browned in a skillet. The sausage roll can also be broken into crumbles or ground in a food processor, browned in a skillet and used in your favorite recipes as desired.

Dry Ingredients

- 1 cup (150 g) vital wheat gluten
- 1 T garbanzo bean flour or soy flour
- 1 T dried minced onion
- 2 tsp onion powder
- ¼ tsp coarse ground black pepper

Blender Ingredients

- 1 and ¼ cup (300 ml) water
- 2 T tamari, soy sauce or Bragg Liquid Aminos™
- 1 T minced fresh garlic (about 3 large cloves)
- 1 T mild vegetable oil
- 2 tsp dry rubbed sage
- ½ tsp poultry seasoning
- ½ tsp sweet paprika
- ½ tsp ground nutmeg
- ¼ tsp ground red pepper or cayenne pepper

Additional Item Needed

- 18-inch wide heavy-duty aluminum foil

Preparation

Warning! It is very important to use only heavy-duty aluminum foil for this recipe. Regular foil is not sturdy enough and can easily rupture from steam pressure which builds up inside the sealed package.

Preheat the oven to 350°F/180°C.

Combine the dry ingredients in a large mixing bowl. Process the blender ingredients until the seasonings are finely ground.

Pour the blender mixture into the dry ingredients and combine thoroughly with a silicone spatula to develop the gluten. The dough will be very soft and wet. Let the dough rest for 10 minutes to allow the dry ingredients to absorb as much liquid as possible.

Tear off a sheet of foil (about 18-inches) and place it on your work surface. Place the dough directly on top.

Form the dough into a round mass. The dough will be soft and wet and have a tendency to spread out but try to keep it as compact as you can. Now, lift the edge of the foil over the dough and begin rolling into a cylinder, pinching the ends closed simultaneously while rolling. The goal is to create a compact cylindrical package - not a thin sausage shape. This may take practice, so be patient. Twist the ends tightly to seal, being careful not to tear the foil. Bend the twisted ends in half to lock them tight.

Wrap with an additional large sheet of foil and twist the ends tightly to completely seal the package. If the foil tears at any point while twisting the ends, rewrap in a third sheet of foil. Place directly on the middle rack of the oven and bake for 1 hour and 30 minutes.

Remove from the oven and let cool to room temperature. Never attempt to open the package while it is hot or steam burns can result. Refrigerate the sausage roll in its foil wrapper for a minimum of 8 hours before finishing, or for a maximum of 10 days. This will firm and enhance the sausage texture. The sausage can also be frozen for up to 3 months.

Slicing and Browning the Sausage

Remove the foil and recycle. Slice the sausage roll into ¼-inch thick patties. In a non-stick skillet or well-seasoned cast iron skillet, brown the patties in two tablespoons of cooking oil over medium heat. Transfer to a plate lined with paper towels to blot any excess oil before serving.

For sausage crumbles, remove the foil and recycle. Slice into 1-inch chunks. Place the chunks into a food processor and pulse to grind to desired texture. For larger crumbles, break the chunks apart with your fingers. In a skillet over medium heat, lightly brown the sausage crumbles in two tablespoons of cooking oil. Use in your favorite recipe as desired.

Italian Sausage Roll and Crumbles
("Sweet" or "Hot")

Classic Italian seasonings give this sausage roll its characteristic flavor. The seasoning blend offers options for a "sweet" (mild) sausage or "hot" and spicy sausage. For this Italian sausage variation, the sausage roll is baked rather than steamed, refrigerated for a minimum of 8 hours to firm and enhance its texture, and then sliced into patties and browned in a skillet. The sausage roll can also be broken into crumbles or ground in a food processor, browned in a skillet and used in your favorite recipes as desired. As a pizza topping, simply add the crumbles with your other favorite toppings before baking - no skillet browning required.

Dry Ingredients

- 1 cup (150 g) vital wheat gluten
- 1 T garbanzo bean flour or soy flour
- 1 T dried minced onion
- 2 tsp onion powder
- 1 tsp whole fennel seeds*

Blender Ingredients

- 1 and ¼ cup (300 ml) water
- 2 T tamari, soy sauce or Bragg Liquid Aminos™
- 1 T minced fresh garlic (about 3 large cloves)
- 1 T olive oil
- 1 tsp whole fennel seeds*
- 1 tsp dried oregano leaves
- 1 tsp dried basil leaves
- ¼ tsp ground white pepper for "sweet" (mild) sausage or
  2 tsp crushed red pepper flakes for "hot" (spicy) sausage

Additional Item Needed

- 18-inch wide heavy-duty aluminum foil

Note: Some of the fennel seeds are left whole, while some are finely ground with the blender ingredients. This is not a misprint.

Preparation

Warning! It is very important to use only heavy-duty aluminum foil for this recipe. Regular foil is not sturdy enough and can easily rupture from steam pressure which builds up inside the sealed package.

Preheat the oven to 350°F/180°C. Combine the dry ingredients in a large mixing bowl. Process the blender ingredients until the seasonings are finely ground.

Pour the blender mixture into the dry ingredients and combine thoroughly with a silicone spatula to develop the gluten. The dough will be very soft and wet. Let the dough rest for 10 minutes to allow the dry ingredients to absorb as much liquid as possible.

Tear off a sheet of foil (about 18-inches) and place it on your work surface. Place the dough directly on top.

Form the dough into a round mass. The dough will be soft and wet and have a tendency to spread out but try to keep it as compact as you can. Now, lift the edge of the foil over the dough and begin rolling into a cylinder, pinching the ends closed simultaneously while rolling. The goal is to create a compact cylindrical package - not a thin sausage shape. This may take practice, so be patient. Twist the ends tightly to seal, being careful not to tear the foil. Bend the twisted ends in half to lock them tight.

Wrap with an additional large sheet of foil and twist the ends tightly to completely seal the package. If the foil tears at any point while twisting the ends, rewrap in a third sheet of foil. Place directly on the middle rack of the oven and bake for 1 hour and 30 minutes.

Remove from the oven and let cool to room temperature. Never attempt to open the package while it is hot or steam burns can result. Refrigerate the sausage roll in its foil wrapper for a minimum of 8 hours before finishing, or for a maximum of 10 days. This will firm and enhance the sausage texture. The sausage can also be frozen for up to 3 months.

Slicing and Browning the Sausage

Remove the foil and recycle. Slice the sausage roll into ¼-inch thick patties. In a non-stick skillet or well-seasoned cast iron skillet, brown the patties in two tablespoons of cooking oil over medium heat. Transfer to a plate lined with paper towels to blot any excess oil before serving.

For sausage crumbles, remove the foil and recycle. Slice into 1-inch chunks. Place the chunks into a food processor and pulse to grind to desired texture. For larger crumbles, break the chunks apart with your fingers. In a skillet over medium heat, lightly brown the sausage crumbles in two tablespoons of cooking oil. Use in your favorite recipe as desired. As a pizza topping, simply add the crumbles with your other favorite toppings before baking - no skillet browning required.

Hard Sausages

Pepperoni

I was a big fan of pepperoni before I embraced veganism, so my taste for it has never waned. I can say that the flavor of this plant-based pepperoni rivals the best of its meat-based counterpart. It took a few years of experimentation to get the recipe formulated just right, but I feel the finished product is a great success. Unlike the individual hand-rolled sausage recipes which utilize steam for cooking, this recipe requires oven baking. Buon Appetito!

Dry Ingredients

- 1 cup (150 g) vital wheat gluten
- 1 T onion powder

Blender Ingredients

- ½ cup (120 ml) water
- 3 T olive oil
- 2 T tamari, soy sauce or Bragg Liquid Aminos™
- 2 T tomato paste
- 2 tsp smoked paprika
- 2 tsp red wine vinegar or raw apple cider vinegar
- 2 tsp organic sugar
- 2 tsp whole fennel seeds
- 1 tsp crushed red pepper flakes (or more or less to taste)
- 1 tsp dry ground mustard

Additional Wet Ingredient

- 1 T minced fresh garlic (about 3 large cloves)

Additional Item Needed

- 18-inch wide heavy-duty aluminum foil

Preparation

Warning! It is very important to use only heavy-duty aluminum foil for this recipe. Regular foil is not sturdy enough and can easily rupture from steam pressure which builds up inside the sealed package.

Preheat the oven to 325°F/170°F.

Combine the dry ingredients in a large mixing bowl. Process the blender ingredients until the spices are finely ground. Small flecks of spice are okay. Stir the minced garlic into the blender mixture. Do not process once the garlic has been added.

Pour the blender mixture into the dry ingredients and combine thoroughly with a silicone spatula. Knead the dough in the bowl with one hand until it exhibits some elasticity, about 1 minute.

Tear off a large sheet of foil (about 24-inches) and place it horizontally on your work surface. Shape the dough into a slender log about 10 to 12-inches long, depending on the desired diameter of the pepperoni when sliced, and place it near the edge of the foil.

Lift the edge of the foil over the dough and begin rolling into a tight cylinder, pinching the ends closed simultaneously while rolling. The goal is to create a slender cylindrical package. Twist the ends tightly to seal, being careful not to tear the foil. Bend the twisted ends in half to lock them tight.

Wrap with an additional large sheet of foil and twist the ends tightly to completely seal the package. If the foil tears at any point while twisting the ends, rewrap in a third sheet of foil. With the hard sausages, it is better to use extra foil rather than not enough. Place directly on the middle rack of the oven and bake for 1 hour and 30 minutes.

Remove from the oven and let cool to room temperature. Never attempt to open the package while it is hot or steam burns can result. Refrigerate the pepperoni in its foil wrapper for a minimum of 8 hours before finishing, or a maximum of 10 days. This will firm and enhance the sausage texture and make thin slicing easier.

After chilling, remove the foil and recycle. The pepperoni is ready to eat or use in recipes; it does not require any additional finishing. Simply slice thick or thin and use as needed. Store the pepperoni sealed tightly in plastic wrap in the refrigerator and consume within 10 days or freeze for up to 3 months.

Variation: For individual snack-size pepperoni sausages, or "pepperettes", divide the dough into six roughly equal portions. Wrap and steam the dough for 45 minutes according to the Individual Hand-Rolled Sausage instructions on pg. 146.

Hard Salami

Traditional meat-based salami is a cured, fermented and air-dried sausage. This presented some fundamental problems in creating a plant-based version. In spite of these challenges, and the few extra steps involved in preparation, I feel this recipe offers a very satisfying plant-based version of traditional meat salami.

Dry Ingredients for Light Marbling

- ⅓ cup (50 g) vital wheat gluten
- 1 tsp onion powder
- 1 tsp garlic powder

Wet Ingredients for Light Marbling

- ¼ cup (60 ml) water
- 2 tsp olive oil
- ½ tsp fine sea salt or kosher salt

Dry Ingredients for Dark Marbling

- 1 cup (150 g) vital wheat gluten
- 2 tsp onion powder
- 2 tsp garlic powder
- 2 tsp cracked black pepper

Blender Ingredients for Dark Marbling

- ½ cup (120 ml) water
- 2 T tamari, soy sauce or Bragg Liquid Aminos™
- 2 T olive oil
- 2 T tomato paste
- 1 T red miso paste
- 1 tsp organic sugar
- 2 tsp red wine vinegar or raw apple cider vinegar
- 1 tsp liquid smoke
- ½ tsp Browning Liquid (pg. 26) or commercial equivalent

Additional Ingredient for "Mold Bloom"

- tapioca starch, unmodified modified potato starch, cornstarch or arrowroot powder

Additional Item Needed

- 18-inch wide heavy-duty aluminum foil

Warning! It is very important to use only heavy-duty aluminum foil for this recipe. Regular foil is not sturdy enough and can easily rupture from steam pressure which builds up inside the sealed package.

Preparing the Dough for the Light Marbling

Combine the dry ingredients for the light marbling in a small mixing bowl. Stir together the wet ingredients for the light marbling in a separate bowl or measuring cup until the salt has dissolved.

Pour the wet mixture into the dry ingredients and mix with a silicone spatula to form the light marbling dough.

Wrap the dough securely in a sheet of aluminum foil and place in a steamer over high heat for 30 minutes. Remove to cool for about 20 minutes. Remove the foil and finely mince the cooked gluten. Set the minced gluten aside while the dough for the dark marbling is prepared.

Preparing the Dough for the Dark Marbling

Preheat the oven to 350°F/180°C.

Combine the dry ingredients for the dark marbling in a large mixing bowl. Whisk together the wet ingredients for the dark marbling in a separate bowl or measuring cup until the tomato paste, miso and sugar are dissolved.

Stir the cooked light marble minced gluten into the wet ingredients.

Pour the wet mixture into the dry ingredients and combine thoroughly with a silicone spatula. Knead the dough in the bowl with one hand until it exhibits some elasticity, about 1 minute.

Wrapping and Baking the Dough

Tear off a sheet of foil (about 18-inches) and place it on your work surface. Shape the dough into an 8-inch log and place it near the edge of the foil.

Lift the edge of the foil over the dough and begin rolling into a tight cylinder, pinching the ends closed simultaneously while rolling. The goal is to create a cylindrical package. Twist the ends tightly to seal, being careful not to tear the foil. Bend the twisted ends in half to lock them tight.

Wrap with an additional large sheet of foil and twist the ends tightly to completely seal the package. If the foil tears at any point while twisting the ends, rewrap in a third sheet of foil. With the hard sausages, it is better to use extra foil rather than not enough. Place directly on the middle rack of the oven and bake for 1 hour and 30 minutes.

Remove from the oven and let cool to room temperature. Never attempt to open the package while it is hot or steam burns can result. Refrigerate the salami in its foil wrapper for a minimum of 8 hours before finishing, or a maximum of 10 days. This will firm and enhance the sausage texture and make thin slicing easier.

Finishing the Salami

After chilling, remove the foil and recycle. Sprinkle some starch on a plate or work surface and roll the salami in the starch thoroughly and evenly, shaking off any excess. The salami is now ready to be sliced. Ultra-thin slicing is recommended (an electric slicer is ideal for this, if you have one).

Store the salami sealed tightly in plastic wrap in the refrigerator and consume within 10 days or freeze for up to 3 months.

Chorizo

Chorizo is a popular Latin American sausage with origins in Spain and Portugal. My compassionate version is seasoned with ancho and chipotle chili powder, onion, fresh garlic, smoked paprika and other select spices and flavorings. Chorizo can be sliced and browned in the skillet; or it can be ground in a food processor and lightly browned in the skillet as a spicy addition to your favorite recipe. Unlike the individual hand-rolled sausage recipes which utilize steam for cooking, this recipe requires oven baking.

Dry Ingredients

- 1 cup (150 g) vital wheat gluten
- 1 T dried minced onion
- 2 tsp onion powder
- 1 tsp garlic powder

Blender Ingredients

- ½ cup (120 ml) water
- 3 T olive oil
- 2 T tamari, soy sauce or Bragg Liquid Aminos™
- 2 T organic tomato paste
- 2 tsp red wine vinegar or raw apple cider vinegar
- 1 tsp liquid smoke
- 1 tsp ancho chili powder
- 1 tsp chipotle chili powder*
- 1 tsp smoked paprika
- 1 tsp dried oregano
- ½ tsp ground cumin
- ½ tsp ground coriander

Additional Wet Ingredient

- 1 T minced fresh garlic (about 3 large cloves)

Additional Item Needed

- 18-inch wide heavy-duty aluminum foil

*For milder chorizo, substitute the chipotle chili powder with additional ancho chili powder. Ancho chili powder is made from milder poblano chilies, whereas chipotle chili powder is made from ripe jalapenos which have a fiery flavor.

Preparation

Warning! It is very important to use only heavy-duty aluminum foil for this recipe. Regular foil is not sturdy enough and can easily rupture from steam pressure which builds up inside the sealed package.

Preheat the oven to 325°F/170°F.

Combine the dry ingredients in a large mixing bowl. Process the blender ingredients until smooth. Stir the minced garlic into the blender mixture. Do not process once the garlic has been added.

Pour the blender mixture into the dry ingredients and combine thoroughly with a silicone spatula. Knead the dough in the bowl with one hand until it exhibits some elasticity, about 1 minute.

Tear off a large sheet of foil (about 24-inches) and place it horizontally on your work surface. Shape the dough into a slender log about 12-inches long and place it near the edge of the foil.

Lift the edge of the foil over the dough and begin rolling into a tight cylinder, pinching the ends closed simultaneously while rolling. The goal is to create a slender cylindrical package. Twist the ends tightly to seal, being careful not to tear the foil. Bend the twisted ends in half to lock them tight.

Wrap with an additional large sheet of foil and twist the ends tightly to completely seal the package. If the foil tears at any point while twisting the ends, rewrap in a third sheet of foil. With the hard sausages, it is better to use extra foil rather than not enough. Place directly on the middle rack of the oven and bake for 1 hour and 30 minutes.

Remove from the oven and let cool to room temperature. Never attempt to open the package while it is hot or steam burns can result. If you plan to grind the chorizo before using in recipes (ground chorizo is superb when mixed with egg-free scrambles), slice and grind the sausage in a food processor while the chorizo is still slightly warm. Place the ground sausage into a food storage bag, seal and refrigerate for a minimum of 8 hours, or for a maximum of 10 days, before using in recipes. This will firm and enhance the sausage texture. The sausage can also be frozen for up to 3 months.

Otherwise, refrigerate the foil package for a minimum of 8 hours before slicing and browning the chorizo, or for a maximum of 10 days.

Browning the Chorizo

Brown the sliced or ground chorizo with two tablespoons of cooking oil over medium heat in a non-stick skillet or well-seasoned cast iron skillet. Serve or use in your favorite recipes as desired.

Surf

Tunada

Tunada is a plant-based alternative to canned tuna fish. It has a flaky texture that works well for mock tuna salad, tuna melts or tuna casserole recipes. This recipe yields about 8 ounces of tunada.

Seaweed Infusion Ingredients

- ¾ cup (180 ml) boiling water
- 1 T (2 g) dried wakame flakes

Dry Ingredients

- ⅔ cup (100 g) vital wheat gluten
- 2 T garbanzo bean flour

Blender Ingredients

- strained sea weed infusion (details are provided in the preparation instructions)
- 5 oz (140 g) pressed extra-firm block tofu (see pg. 24 for instructions)
- 1 T mellow white miso paste
- 1 tsp dried kelp powder
- ½ tsp fine sea salt or kosher salt
- ¼ tsp ground white pepper
- 1 T mild vegetable oil

Additional Item Needed

- 18-inch wide heavy-duty aluminum foil

Preparation

Warning! It is very important to use only heavy-duty aluminum foil for this recipe. Regular foil is not sturdy enough and can easily rupture from steam pressure which builds up inside the sealed package.

Create the seaweed infusion by steeping the wakame flakes in the boiling water in a heatproof cup. Let cool completely and then strain, reserving the liquid. Use the back of a spoon to extract as much liquid as possible when straining. Discard the seaweed or save for use in miso soup or mock seafood recipes.

Preheat the oven to 350°F/180°C.

Combine the dry ingredients in a large mixing bowl.

Crumble the pressed tofu into a blender and add the remaining blender ingredients including the seaweed infusion. Process the contents until the tofu is completely liquefied and the mixture is smooth and creamy. This is essential! Stop the blender as necessary to scrape down the sides.

Scoop the tofu mixture into the dry ingredients (a small amount of the tofu mixture will remain in the blender; this is inconsequential) and combine with a sturdy silicone spatula until the tofu mixture is incorporated and a sticky ball of dough begins to form. Let the dough rest about 5 minutes. This will give the gluten a chance to absorb the liquid and help reduce stickiness. Do not add additional gluten to the dough to reduce stickiness!

Place the dough into a food processor fitted with a dough blade and process for 1 full minute. Alternately, place the dough into a stand mixer fitted with a paddle and process on medium speed for 1 full minute. Transfer the dough back to the mixing bowl.

If a food processor or stand mixer is unavailable, "knead" the dough with the spatula in the bowl until some resistance is felt, about 3 full minutes. The dough will remain very sticky.

Tear off a sheet of foil (about 18-inches) and place it on your work surface. Scoop the dough onto the foil. Using the spatula or your fingers, shape the dough into a compact rectangular slab about 2-inches thick. Shaping perfection is unnecessary. Fold the slab of dough in the foil (don't roll), creating a semi-flat package. Fold in the ends but leave a little room (about 1-inch on each side) to allow the dough to expand as it bakes. This is very important! Crimp the folded ends to seal the package.

Rewrap the package in a second sheet of foil and place the package directly on the middle rack of the oven. Bake for 1 hour and 30 minutes.

Let the tunada cool in the foil to room temperature and then refrigerate for a minimum of 8 hours to firm and enhance its texture, or for up to 1 week, before flaking and using in recipes. You can also store the tunada in the freezer wrapped in the foil for up to 3 months.

Remove the foil and recycle. With a sharp knife, trim away the thin crust or "skin" and discard. Flake the tunada using a scraping motion with the edge of a fork or a sharp knife; or use a combination of both. The knife will create smoother textured flakes and the fork will create rougher textured flakes and the combination of textures is very nice. Use in your favorite recipe as desired.

Mock Tuna Sashimi

The texture of seedless watermelon is remarkably transformed to create this amazing "tuna" sashimi. Typically, modern gastronomists use a vacuum chamber called a Cryovac™ to produce this effect, but the equipment is very expensive and not practical for most household budgets. With some experimentation, I discovered a simple and inexpensive way to create this same effect at home.

Watermelon that is not quite in season works best, since it has a lower sugar content than ripe summer watermelon. Also, the flesh needs to be firm and crisp. Purchase a watermelon that has already been cut in half at the market, that way you can make sure the flesh isn't mealy or mushy. Mock tuna sashimi is wonderful when used for sushi too. Please note: Since the sashimi is not meat and contains no protein, it will not pan-sear like real tuna.

Ingredients

- ½ large seedless watermelon
- 4 tsp sea salt or kosher salt

Marinade Ingredients

- ½ cup tamari, soy sauce or Bragg Liquid Aminos™
- ¼ cup water
- 2 T mirin (Japanese sweet rice wine)
- 1 T (2 g) dried wakame flakes
- 1 tsp sesame oil

Preparation

Cut 2 or 3 rectangular blocks from the center of the watermelon. Each block should be about 4-inches long and no more than 1 and ½-inch thick. Keep in mind that even seedless watermelon contains some pale, soft seeds and there's simply no way to remove them completely.

Bring 2 quarts of water to a boil in a 3-quart cooking pot. Add 4 teaspoons of salt. Add the blocks of watermelon and boil for 15 minutes. Gently turn the blocks occasionally as they cook.

While the watermelon boils, add the marinade ingredients to a small saucepan and bring to a brief boil. Remove from the heat to cool.

Transfer the blocks of watermelon to a plate lined with several layers of paper towels or a lint-free kitchen towel to drain. As the watermelon cools and drains, the texture will change and become uncannily similar to the texture of raw tuna (boiling ruptures the cells of the watermelon and draining on the towel(s) pulls water from the ruptured cells by absorption). Change the towel(s) occasionally as a substantial amount of water will be absorbed.

When the watermelon has drained sufficiently and the marinade has cooled, place the watermelon in a food storage bag or sealable container, add the marinade and seal and refrigerate for several hours.

When ready to use, drain the sashimi on a few paper towels to absorb the excess marinade. Gently press the "filets" in lightly toasted sesame seeds if desired. Slice and serve with your favorite Asian condiments, such as pickled ginger and wasabi; or use for making sushi.

Carrot Caviar

Carrot caviar makes a lovely garnish for appetizers and plated entrées. For this recipe, you will need two ingredients common in molecular gastronomy: sodium alginate (a derivative of red algae) and calcium chloride. The caviar is created through a simple process known as "spherification", in which a solution containing alginate is placed by droplets into a calcium chloride bath. A molecular reaction occurs creating a thin membrane around the droplets of juice.

Sodium alginate and calcium chloride powder, as well as many other ingredients used in modernist cuisine, can be purchased in economical small packages from ModernistPantry.com. Modernist Pantry also offers kits especially devoted to making the caviar.

The prepared caviar has a very brief shelf life, so prepare the caviar no more than a few hours before serving.

Ingredients

- 1 cup carrot juice
- ¾ tsp sodium alginate
- ½ tsp fine sea salt or kosher salt
- 1 quart (4 cups) ice water
- 1 tsp calcium chloride

Preparation

In a bowl or measuring cup, whisk together the carrot juice, alginate and salt until dissolved (an immersion blender is helpful).

Add the calcium chloride to the ice water in a separate large bowl and stir until dissolved.

Using a needleless syringe or eye dropper, add droplets of the juice solution to the calcium chloride bath. Wait two minutes and then lift the caviar with a small strainer and transfer to a cold fresh water bath.

Lift again with the strainer to drain and transfer to a sealable container to chill until ready to serve.

Ceviche

Ceviche (pronounced "seh-VEE-chay") is a Latin American dish which traditionally consists of raw fish or shellfish marinated in citrus juice (usually lime and/or lemon juice). The acid in the citrus juice coagulates (denatures) the proteins in the seafood, effectively cooking it. Since no heat is used, the dish is served cold. There are many recipe variations combining the marinated fish/shellfish with a wide variety of other fresh ingredients such as onion, tomato, cilantro, chili peppers and avocado.

My plant-based version relies upon cooked unripe green jackfruit as a replacement for the fish/shellfish, since it has a neutral flavor which takes on the flavor of the marinade and a flaky texture reminiscent of cooked crab. The dish is essentially a zesty, marinated plant-based salad which is served cold as a refreshing appetizer with crispy corn tortilla chips. This recipe yields enough ceviche for 2 to 3 guests; for more simply multiply the recipe.

Ingredients

- 1 can (17 to 20 oz) green jackfruit in water or brine*
- ½ cup peeled and small diced tomato
- ½ cup peeled, seeded and small diced cucumber
- ¼ cup small diced onion
- ¼ cup chopped cilantro
- 1 clove garlic, minced
- 1 small Serrano chili, seeded and finely minced
- juice of 1 lime
- 1 T mild olive oil
- ½ tsp fine sea salt or kosher salt, or more to taste
- ¼ tsp coarse ground black pepper
- ¼ tsp ground cumin
- ½ ripe but firm avocado, diced

*Canned green jackfruit bears a resemblance to flaked crabmeat. It can be found in Indian and Asian markets or purchased through the internet. Look for the label "Green Jackfruit" or "Young Green Jackfruit" and be sure that it's packed in water or brine and not syrup. Cans of ripe jackfruit packed in syrup may be stocked nearby, but don't be tempted to substitute as the ripe fruit will be too sweet for this application.

Chef's note: Ceviche made with fresh animal-based seafood has a fresh, clean flavor and should not be fishy. However, if you wish to add an ocean flavor to this plant-based version add some flaked wakame that has been rehydrated in water and then drained well.

Preparation

Drain the jackfruit and lightly rinse. If the jackfruit was canned in brine, rinse thoroughly. Add the chunks of jackfruit to 1 quart salted boiling water. Reduce the heat to a slow boil and cook for 15 minutes. Drain in a colander and let cool. When cool enough to handle, remove the tough core from each chunk of jackfruit with a sharp knife and discard. Break the chunks apart with your fingers and remove the soft seeds and seed membranes and discard. The remaining flaky pulp is the only portion you will want to use in the dish, so sort through the chunks carefully (there will be a significant amount of unusable material). Wrap the pulp in a lint-free kitchen towel and squeeze to remove excess water. Coarsely chop the pulp and place in a mixing bowl.

Add the remaining ingredients except for the avocado and toss well to combine. Refrigerate for several hours to marinate the ingredients and blend the flavors. Add the diced avocado just before serving and toss well. The avocado can also be placed into a ring mold and the ceviche layered on top for a lovely presentation. Season the ceviche with additional salt as desired and to taste. Serve with crunchy tortilla chips.

Chef's tip: Strips of flour or corn tortilla that have been flash-fried in cooking oil make an interesting and crunchy garnish.

Clamz

Clamz are a gluten-based alternative to clams. They're tender and yet slightly chewy with a subtle hint of sweetness. They can be used in any recipe calling for minced clams, diced clams or clam strips. The reserved simmering broth can be used in any recipe calling for clam broth. This recipe yields about 8 oz.

Clamz Simmering Broth Ingredients

- 6 cups water
- 1 medium onion, peeled and quartered
- 1 rib celery, chopped
- 1 carrot, unpeeled and chopped
- 3 T (6 g) dried wakame flakes, lightly rinsed and drained
- 3 cloves garlic, crushed
- ¼ cup mellow white miso paste
- 1 bay leaf
- ½ tsp whole peppercorns
- sea salt or kosher salt, to taste

Dry Ingredients

- ½ cup vital wheat gluten
- 1 T garbanzo bean flour

Liquid Ingredients

- ½ cup water
- 1 and ½ tsp organic sugar
- ½ tsp sea salt or kosher salt

Preparation

Combine the simmering broth ingredients in a large cooking pot, cover and simmer for a minimum of 1 hour. Strain into another cooking pot and discard the solids. Cover and bring back to a simmer while the dough is prepared.

Combine the dry ingredients in a large mixing bowl. Combine the liquid ingredients in a separate bowl or measuring cup and stir until the sugar and salt dissolves.

Pour the liquid mixture (not the simmering broth) into the dry ingredients and combine thoroughly with a sturdy silicone spatula to form the dough and begin developing the gluten.

Transfer the dough to a work surface and knead vigorously until elastic. Cut thin, narrow fragments from the dough, about 1 and ½ to 2-inches long (the dough will expand while simmering, so if the clamz become too large, they can always be cut into smaller sizes later).

Remove the lid from the pot and bring the broth to a boil. Add the dough fragments and immediately reduce the heat to a gentle simmer for 10 minutes. Do not boil the clamz!

Remove the pot from the heat, cover and let the clamz cool in the pot for a few hours or until lukewarm. Using a spider or slotted spoon, transfer the clamz to a food storage bag with ¼ cup of the broth and refrigerate for a minimum of 4 hours to firm and enhance their texture before using in recipes.

Transfer the cooled broth to a sealable container and refrigerate for up to 10 days. Use in any recipe calling for clam broth. If necessary, cut the clamz to an appropriate size before using in recipes.

——)( )(——

Linguini with Clamz Sauce

An Italian-American classic reinvented with plant-based diced clamz and non-dairy butter. This recipe yields 4 to 6 servings.

Ingredients

- 1 pound dry linguine
- 1 T olive oil
- 6 cloves garlic, finely chopped
- 1 cup diced Clamz (see preceding recipe)
- 1 shallot, minced
- ½ cup non-dairy butter or margarine
- ½ cup Clamz Broth (reserved from simmering the Clamz; see preceding recipe)
- ½ cup dry white wine such as Chardonnay, Pinot Grigio, Riesling or Sauvignon Blanc
- sea salt or kosher salt and coarse ground black pepper, to taste
- 2 T chopped parsley

Preparation

Bring a large pot of salted water to a boil and cook the pasta, following the package instructions, until al dente.

Meanwhile, add the olive oil to a skillet and place over medium heat. Add the shallot and sauté until softened, about 2 to 3 minutes. Add the garlic and sauté an additional 2 minutes. Add the wine, bring it to a simmer and allow it to cook about 1 minute to eliminate some of the alcohol. Add the butter or margarine and stir until melted. Add the clamz and broth and bring back to a simmer. Cook until the sauce reduces and thickens a bit, about 5 minutes; season with salt and pepper to taste. Remove from the heat and stir in the parsley.

Drain the pasta, place back in the cooking pot and add a ladle of the sauce. Toss the pasta in the pot (tossing with small amount of sauce will discourage the pasta from sticking). Distribute the pasta on serving plates and top with the sauce; serve immediately.

——)( )(——

Fried Clamz

Tender sweet clamz are battered and fried and served with your choice of Tartar Sauce or Cocktail Sauce; or try the Fire-Roasted Jalapeno and Lime Tartar Sauce (sauce recipes follow).

Preparation

Prepare your choice of dipping sauce and keep refrigerated until ready to use.

Combine ¼ cup rice flour or all-purpose flour with the breadcrumbs in a bowl. Mix in the salt, paprika and white pepper; set aside.

Place the clamz into a food storage bag and add the remaining ¼ cup flour. Seal and shake well to coat. Add the milk to the food storage bag, seal and shake until the clamz are coated.

Ingredients

- 1 recipe Clamz (pg. 169)
- ¼ cup plain unsweetened non-dairy milk
- ½ cup fine dry breadcrumbs combined with ¼ cup rice flour or all-purpose flour
- 1 tsp sea salt or kosher salt
- ½ tsp sweet paprika
- ½ tsp ground white pepper
- ¼ cup all-purpose flour
- high-heat cooking oil for frying

Dredge the clamz in the breadcrumb mixture until well-coated. Set aside to dry on a plate while the oil is heating.

In a deep wok or skillet, heat about ½-inch of oil over medium-high heat until the oil begins to shimmer. Fry the clams until golden. They will cook quickly, about 45 seconds to 1 minute, so watch them carefully. Remove with a spider or slotted spoon and drain on a plate lined with paper towels. Serve hot with lemon wedges and the sauce of your choice for dipping.

Fire-Roasted Jalapeno and Lime Tartar Sauce

Ingredients

- 1 large jalapeno pepper
- ½ cup No-Eggy Mayo (pg. 202) or commercial egg-free mayonnaise
- 2 T minced fresh onion
- 1 tsp fresh grated lime zest and a squeeze of fresh lime juice
- sea salt or kosher salt to taste

Preparation

Place the jalapeno directly on the stove burner over medium heat. Turn frequently with tongs until the pepper is blistered and blackened. Place the pepper on a plate and cover with foil to hold in the steam. Let cool. The skin should slip off easily. Cut off the stem end, split the jalapeno lengthwise and remove the seeds and membrane. Finely mince the pepper and place in a small bowl.

Stir in the mayonnaise, onion, the lime zest and a squeeze of lime juice, mix well and season with salt to taste. Refrigerate to blend the flavors and until ready to serve.

New England Clamz Chowdah

Tender diced potatoes, celery, onions and diced Clamz are combined together in this creamy and satisfying chowder. This recipe yields 4 to 6 servings.

Ingredients

- ¼ cup olive oil
- 1 large onion, diced
- 2 ribs celery, diced
- 2 cloves garlic, minced
- 1 recipe Clamz (pg. 169), diced
- ¼ cup all-purpose flour or rice flour
- 4 cups Clamz Broth (reserved from preparing the Clamz)
- 2 russet potatoes, peeled and diced into ½-inch cubes
- 1 bay leaf
- ¼ tsp coarse ground black pepper, or more to taste
- 2 cups plain non-dairy milk
- sea salt or kosher salt, to taste

Preparation

Add the olive oil to a 3-quart cooking pot and place over medium heat. Add the onions and celery and sauté until the onions are translucent. Add the garlic and sauté an additional minute.

Sprinkle in the flour, stir until blended and cook until the flour emits a nutty aroma, about 1 minute.

Incorporate the broth in small increments while vigorously stirring. Add the diced Clamz, potatoes, bay leaf and black pepper. Bring the chowder to a gentle simmer. Cover the pot and cook about 30 minutes, stirring occasionally, or until the potatoes are very tender.

Add the milk and stir until heated through. Season the chowder with salt and pepper to taste.

Maryland Crab'less Cakes

Maryland Crab'less Cakes have an amazing crab-like texture and authentic seafood flavor, which makes them an impressive plant-based surf appetizer or first course. The cakes are baked first which ensures that they are cooked through evenly, and then briefly fried in a skillet with a small amount of cooking oil until golden brown. The cakes can be served with a squeeze of fresh lemon, Fire-Roasted Jalapeno and Lime Tartar Sauce (pg. 171), Creamy Horseradish Sauce (pg. 195), or another sauce of your choice. This recipe yields 8 crab'less cakes.

Ingredients

- 1 carton (12 oz/340 g) Mori-Nu™ extra-firm silken tofu, or equivalent
- 2 cans (17 to 20 oz each) green jackfruit in water or brine
- 1 T (2 g) dried wakame flakes
- 1 T olive oil
- ¼ cup finely chopped green onion, white and light green parts only
- ¼ cup seeded and finely diced red bell pepper or sweet red pepper
- 2 cloves garlic, minced (2 tsp)
- ¼ cup No-Eggy Mayo (pg. 202) or commercial egg-free mayonnaise
- 3 T unmodified potato starch, cornstarch or arrowroot powder
- 1 T Chesapeake Bay™ or Old Bay™ seasoning
- 1 tsp Worcestershire Sauce (pg. 25) or commercial vegan equivalent
- 1 cup panko bread crumbs
- cooking oil for pan-browning the cakes

Additional Items Needed

- baking sheet
- parchment paper or silicone baking mat

*Canned green jackfruit bears a resemblance to flaked crabmeat. It can be found in Indian and Asian markets or purchased through the internet. Look for the label "Green Jackfruit" or "Young Green Jackfruit" and be sure that it's packed in water or brine and not syrup. Cans of ripe jackfruit packed in syrup may be stocked nearby, but don't be tempted to substitute as the ripe fruit will be too sweet for this application.

Preparation

Remove the silken tofu from the carton. Slice the tofu into 4 slabs and place the slabs on a plate lined with several layers of paper towels or a lint-free kitchen towel to drain for a minimum of 30 minutes. Firmly blot the tofu with additional towels to remove as much moisture as possible.

Drain the jackfruit, lightly rinse and drain again. If the jackfruit was canned in brine, rinse thoroughly and drain. Remove the tough core from each chunk of jackfruit with a sharp knife and discard. Break the chunks apart with your fingers and remove the soft seeds and discard. The remaining flaky pulp is the only portion you will want to use in the dish, so sort through the chunks carefully (there will be a significant amount of unusable material). Wrap the pulp in a lint-free kitchen towel and squeeze firmly to remove excess water. The squeezed pulp should be lightly moist. Coarsely chop the pulp and set aside in a large mixing bowl.

In a small dish, cover the wakame with water and let soak for 10 minutes to rehydrate. Squeeze the seaweed in your hand to remove the excess water. Finely chop and set aside.

Preheat the oven to 375°F/190°C. Line a baking sheet with parchment paper or a silicone baking mat; set aside.

Add the olive oil to a small skillet and sweat the green onion, bell pepper and garlic over medium-low heat about 10 minutes. If you hear a loud sizzle, the heat is too high; reduce the heat. The goal of sweating vegetables is to bring out their flavor, eliminate moisture and render them tender without browning. Add the chopped seaweed and stir an additional minute. Transfer the vegetables to the large mixing bowl.

Crumble the pressed silken tofu into a separate mixing bowl. Mash the tofu with the back of a fork until a "ricotta-like" texture is achieved. Add the starch, mayonnaise, Chesapeake Bay™ or Old Bay™ seasoning and Worcestershire sauce and continue to mash thoroughly into a smooth paste (as smooth as you can achieve). This can also be done in a food processor for ease, expediency and efficiency.

Scoop the seasoned tofu into the mixing bowl with the sautéed vegetables and jackfruit. Add the panko crumbs and fold to combine the ingredients with a sturdy silicone spatula until the mixture begins to hold together. Press the mixture evenly into the bottom of the bowl and divide into 8 roughly equal portions using the edge of the spatula.

Form 8 patties from the mixture, about 3-inches in diameter and ½-inch thick and place them on the parchment paper or baking mat. Working with the mixture is a messy affair so keep a damp towel nearby to wipe your hands. Bake uncovered on the middle rack of the oven for 20 minutes and remove to cool and "set" for 20 minutes before proceeding.

At this point, the cakes can finished immediately or chilled for up to 1 week until ready to finish and serve. The prebaked cakes can also be frozen between layers of wax paper for up to 3 months, thawed and then finished at a later date.

Finishing and Serving

If the cakes were previously chilled, bring them to room temperature before pan-browning to ensure that they heat through completely. Generously coat the bottom of a large non-stick skillet with cooking oil and place over medium heat. When the oil is hot, add the cakes and fry until golden brown on both sides (don't crowd the skillet; fry in 2 batches if necessary). Transfer to a plate lined with a paper towel. If necessary, keep the cakes warm in a low oven on a heat-proof plate until ready to serve.

Serve immediately with a squeeze of lemon or the garnish or sauce of your choice.

Chef's tip: Use good oil when cooking. Smell it and taste it: If it doesn't taste good alone, it won't taste good in your food.

Breaded Jackfysh Filets

This is my signature recipe for creating a delicious alternative to moist, flaky fish. The filets are breaded and baked to cook them through and then lightly fried in the skillet for a crispy texture.

To spice things up, try adding Chesapeake Bay™, Old Bay™, Cajun/Creole or Southwestern seasonings to the breading; the possibilities of seasoning combinations are endless. The filets can also coated with finely crushed nuts (finely crushed macadamia nuts are superb for this purpose).

Canned green jackfruit provides the amazingly moist and flaky texture in these filets. Canned green jackfruit can be found in Indian and Asian markets or purchased through the internet. Look for the label "Green Jackfruit" or "Young Green Jackfruit" and be sure that it's packed in water or brine and not syrup. Cans of ripe jackfruit packed in syrup may be stocked nearby, but don't be tempted to substitute as the ripe fruit will be too sweet for this application.

Seaweed Infusion Ingredients

- ¼ cup (60 ml) boiling water
- 2 T (4 g) dried wakame flakes

Filet Ingredients

- ½ carton (6 oz/170 g) Mori-Nu™ extra-firm silken tofu, or similar
- 2 cans (17 to 20 oz each) green jackfruit in water or brine
- 2 T unmodified potato starch, cornstarch or arrowroot powder
- 1 T No-Eggy Mayo (pg. 202) or commercial egg-free mayonnaise
- 1 T seaweed infusion (details are provide in the preparation instructions)
- 1 tsp onion powder
- ¾ tsp sea salt or kosher salt
- ½ tsp garlic powder
- ¼ tsp ground white pepper

Additional Ingredients

- plain or seasoned dry breadcrumbs or finely crushed nuts
- cooking oil

Additional Items Needed

- baking sheet
- parchment paper or silicone baking mat

Preparation

Remove the silken tofu from the carton. Cut the block in half and reserve the one half for other uses (refrigerate in an airtight container). Slice the tofu into 2 slabs and place the slabs on a plate lined with several layers of paper towels or a lint-free kitchen towel to drain for a minimum of 30 minutes. Firmly blot the tofu with additional towels to remove as much moisture as possible. Set aside.

Create the seaweed infusion by steeping the wakame flakes in the boiling water in a heatproof cup. Let cool completely and then strain using the back of a spoon to press the seaweed. Reserve 1 tablespoon of the liquid; that's all that is needed for this recipe. Discard the remaining liquid and reserve the wakame for other recipes (miso soup perhaps?)

Drain the jackfruit, lightly rinse and drain again. If the jackfruit was canned in brine, rinse thoroughly and drain. Remove the tough core from each chunk of jackfruit with a sharp knife and discard. Break the chunks apart with your fingers and remove the soft seeds and discard. The remaining flaky pulp is the only portion you will want to use in the dish, so sort through the chunks carefully (there will be a significant amount of unusable material). Wrap the pulp in a lint-free kitchen towel and squeeze to remove excess water. The squeezed pulp should be barely moist.

Finely chop the jackfruit pulp and transfer to a mixing bowl; set aside.

Preheat the oven to 375°F/190°C. Line a baking sheet with parchment paper or a silicone baking mat; set aside.

Crumble the drained silken tofu into a food processor. Add the remaining filet ingredients including the 1 tablespoon of seaweed infusion and process until smooth. Stop as necessary to scrape down the sides of the processor bowl. Add the paste to the finely chopped jackfruit and mix well. Form filet shapes from the mixture no more than ½-inch thick.

Add 1 cup of plain or seasoned dry breadcrumbs or finely crushed nuts to a bowl or a plate. Gently press the filets into the coating and place the breaded filets on the parchment paper or baking mat. Bake for 30 minutes. Remove from the oven to cool for a minimum of 10 minutes before proceeding.

Finishing the Filets

To finish the filets, generously coat the bottom of a large non-stick skillet with cooking oil and place over medium heat. Fry the filets until golden brown on each side and transfer to a plate lined with a paper towel. If necessary, keep the filets warm in a low oven on a heat-proof plate until ready to serve.

Battered Tofysh Filets

Tender and flaky Tofysh filets are battered and fried and served with the condiments of your choice. This recipe yields 6 filets.

Filet Ingredients

- 10 to 12 oz (280 to 340 g) pressed extra-firm block tofu (see pg. 24 for instructions)
- ½ carton (6 oz/170g) Mori-Nu™ extra-firm silken tofu, or similar
- 2 T all-purpose flour (sorry, no substitutions)
- 1 T mild vegetable oil
- 1 tsp fine sea salt or kosher salt
- ½ tsp onion powder
- ¼ tsp garlic powder
- ¼ tsp ground white pepper

Seaweed Infusion Ingredients

- ¼ cup (60 ml) boiling water
- 2 T (4 g) dried wakame flakes

Dredging Ingredient

- ⅓ cup all-purpose flour (sorry, no substitutions)

Batter Ingredients

- ½ cup rice flour
- ¾ cup club soda or beer
- 2 tsp Old Bay™ or Chesapeake Bay™ seasoning
- 1 tsp baking powder (preferably aluminum-free)
- 1 tsp dried kelp powder

Additional Items Needed

- baking sheet
- parchment paper or silicone baking mat

Preparation

Press the block tofu thoroughly. The tofu should be barley damp. Crumble into a large mixing bowl, cover and set aside.

Remove the silken tofu from the carton. Cut the block in half and reserve the one half for other uses (refrigerate in an airtight container). Slice the tofu into 2 slabs and place the slabs on a plate lined with several layers of paper towels or a lint-free kitchen towel to drain for a minimum of 30 minutes. Firmly blot the tofu with additional towels to remove as much moisture as possible. Set aside.

Create the seaweed infusion by steeping the wakame flakes in the boiling water in a heatproof cup. Let cool completely and then strain using the back of a spoon to press the seaweed. Reserve 1 tablespoon of the liquid; that's all that is needed for this recipe. Discard the remaining liquid and reserve the wakame for other recipes (miso soup perhaps?)

Preheat the oven to 375°F/190°C. Line a baking sheet with parchment paper or a silicone baking mat; set aside.

Crumble the drained silken tofu into a food processor. Add the all-purpose flour, oil, salt, onion and garlic powder and white pepper. Add the 1 tablespoon of seaweed infusion and process the contents into a smooth paste. Stop as necessary to scrape down the sides of the processor bowl.

Add the tofu paste to the crumbled block tofu and fold to combine the ingredients with a sturdy silicone spatula until the mixture begins to hold together. Press the mixture evenly into the bottom of the bowl and divide into 6 roughly equal portions using the edge of the spatula.

Scatter the ⅓ cup of all-purpose flour on a plate and set aside. The flour will be used for dredging the filets.

With your hands, compress a portion of the tofu mixture into a ball. Flatten and shape the ball into a narrow patty about ½-inch thick. Carefully dredge the filet in the flour, press the flour into the filet, and place on the parchment paper or baking mat. Repeat with the remaining portions.

Bake uncovered on the middle rack of the oven for 30 minutes or until lightly golden and firm to the touch. Remove from the oven to cool for a minimum of 20 minutes to allow the filets to "set" before proceeding. Don't handle them until they have cooled a bit or they can break.

Battering and Frying the Filets

Whisk together the batter ingredients in a large bowl until smooth.

Dip the filets in the batter and fry in hot cooking oil until golden brown and crispy. They will brown quickly. Drain on paper towels. Serve while still hot with a wedge of lemon and cocktail sauce, Tartar sauce (pg. 195), or malt vinegar for dipping.

The fried filets are also ideal for soft tacos.

Shirataki Scallops

This is my own recipe for creating tender non-seafood scallops which bear a resemblance to their ocean counterparts in appearance, texture, aroma and flavor. After preparation, the scallops can be seasoned in any way you choose before pan-searing in the skillet but a simple finishing marinade is included in the recipe. Potentially, the scallops could be breaded and baked if you wish to experiment. If you are a scallop aficionado, please keep in mind that creating seafood textures with plant-based ingredients at home is challenging at best (without factory technology) and this analogue is not going to mimic scallops exactly.

Glucomannan, also known as konjac root powder, is the special ingredient in this recipe. Glucomannan is a pure soluble fiber derived from konjac root. It has no protein, no fat, no carbohydrates, and is gluten-free. As a food additive, it is used as an emulsifier and thickener. As a food ingredient, it is used commercially and at home for preparing Japanese shirataki noodles. Commercial shirataki noodles have a distinct "fishy" odor and those who have opened a package will be familiar with this scent. However, the aroma of freshly prepared konjac has a much milder seafood-like aroma. Glucomannan can sometimes be found in health food stores (where it is often sold as a diet aid) but can definitely be purchased through the internet (e.g., Amazon.com).

A small amount of pickling lime powder (an alkali) is used in this recipe to activate the glucomannan (this is not an extract from the lime citrus fruit). Without it, the glucomannan will not activate, so DO NOT omit! Pickling lime powder (calcium hydroxide) can be found in most supermarkets where products for home canning are located. This recipe yields 8 jumbo scallops.

Scallop Ingredients

- 1 cup water
- 1 T glucomannan powder
- 1 cup organic plain unsweetened soymilk
- 2 tsp organic sugar
- 1 tsp fine sea salt or kosher salt
- ¼ tsp pickling lime (calcium hydroxide) - DO NOT OMIT!

Marinade Ingredients

- ½ cup dry white wine such as Chardonnay or Sauvignon Blanc
  or ⅓ cup water plus the juice of 1 large lemon (about 2 T)
- 1 T tamari, soy sauce or Bragg Liquid Aminos™
- 1 tsp Old Bay™ or Chesapeake Bay™ seasoning,
  plus additional for seasoning the scallops after pan-searing if desired
- 2 cloves garlic, minced (2 tsp)

Pan-Searing Ingredients

- 1 T olive oil
- 1 T non-dairy butter or margarine

Additional Items Needed

- standard bread loaf pan

- wire whisk
- silicone spatula

Preparation

The scallops are very easy to make, but it is very important to follow the recipe and technique exactly as instructed for success.

Set aside the bread loaf pan, wire whisk and silicone spatula.

In a small dish, measure the glucomannan and set aside near your cooking area.

In a small saucepan, combine the soymilk, water, sugar, salt and pickling lime and whisk until dissolved. Place the saucepan over medium-low heat.

Begin sprinkling in the glucomannan powder while vigorously whisking the milk mixture. As soon as the mixture begins to thicken, set the whisk aside and begin stirring with a flexible silicone spatula. As the mixture continues to thicken, whip with the spatula and continue to cook until a stiff mashed potato consistency is achieved. If using a non-stick saucepan, the mixture will begin pulling away from the sides of the pan. This will take about 3 to 4 minutes.

Immediately remove the saucepan from the heat and transfer the mixture to the loaf pan with the spatula. The mixture will be very gooey and sticky. Pack the mixture into the pan and spread it as evenly as possible.

Let the mixture cool for about 15 minutes and then refrigerate uncovered for a minimum of 1 hour.

Now, invert the loaf pan onto a work surface to release the gel from the loaf pan. You may have to wiggle the gel a bit around the edges with your fingers to work it loose before inverting.

With a 1 and ½-inch to 1 and ¾-inch ring mold, cookie cutter or similar object, cut the gel into 8 rounds. The remaining gel can be discarded or it can be simmered with the scallops and later chopped, lightly sautéed and added to mock seafood soups. Handle the scallops carefully as they will be delicate and jelly-like at this stage.

Bring a large saucepan of lightly salted water to a simmer, place the scallops in the water and gently simmer for 10 minutes. Simmering will change the texture of the scallops and cook them all the way through.

Remove the scallops from the hot water with a spider or slotted spoon and place them on a plate lined with paper towels to drain and cool. When they are cool enough to handle, place them in a food storage bag and add the marinade. Press out the excess air, seal the bag and chill for a minimum of 30 minutes (longer marinating will increase the flavor).

Remove the scallops from the marinade and gently pat them dry.

Add the butter and oil to a skillet and place over medium heat. When the butter has melted, place the scallops in the skillet and cook until they are lightly browned on each side. Sprinkle with additional seasoning if desired. Transfer the scallops to serving plates and serve immediately.

A safe guideline for food storage shelf life would be about 1 week. I have no experience with freezing this particular analogue.

Mock Lobster

This is my own recipe for creating tender non-seafood lobster which bears a resemblance to rock lobster in appearance, texture, aroma and flavor. After preparation, the mock lobster meat can be used for Mock Lobster Rolls, and in such dishes as Mock Lobster Bisque, Thermidor and Newburg (the recipe for Newburg sauce follows this recipe). If you are a lobster aficionado, please keep in mind that creating seafood textures with plant-based ingredients at home is challenging at best (without factory technology) and this analogue is not going to mimic lobster exactly.

Glucomannan, also known as konjac root powder, is the special ingredient in this recipe. Glucomannan is a pure soluble fiber derived from konjac root. It has no protein, no fat, no carbohydrates, and is gluten-free. As a food additive, it is used as an emulsifier and thickener. As a food ingredient, it is used commercially and at home for preparing Japanese shirataki noodles. Commercial shirataki noodles have a distinct "fishy" odor and those who have opened a package will be familiar with this scent. However, the aroma of freshly prepared konjac has a much milder seafood-like aroma. Glucomannan can sometimes be found in health food stores (where it is often sold as a diet aid) but can definitely be purchased through the internet (e.g., Amazon.com).

A small amount of pickling lime powder (an alkali) is used in this recipe to activate the glucomannan (this is not an extract from the lime citrus fruit). Without it, the glucomannan will not activate, so DO NOT omit! Pickling lime powder (calcium hydroxide) can be found in most supermarkets where products for home canning are located. This recipe yields about ¾ lb. of mock lobster meat.

Blender Ingredients

- 1 and ¾ cup (420 ml) water
- 2.5 oz (70 g) pressed extra-firm block tofu (see pg. 24 for instructions)
- 1 T glucomannan powder
- 2 tsp organic sugar
- 1 tsp fine sea salt or kosher salt
- ¼ tsp pickling lime (calcium hydroxide) - DO NOT OMIT!

Additional Items Needed

- standard bread loaf pan
- wire whisk
- silicone spatula
- 2 tsp sweet paprika
- 1 tsp Old Bay™ or Chesapeake Bay™ seasoning

Preparation

Mock lobster is very easy to prepare, but it is very important to follow the recipe and technique exactly as instructed for success.

Combine the paprika and bay seasoning in a small dish. Sprinkle half of the mixture (1 and ½ tsp) over the bottom of the bread loaf pan; set aside. Reserve the remaining paprika/bay mixture for later. Place the wire whisk and silicone spatula near your cooking area.

In a small dish, measure the glucomannan and set aside near your cooking area.

Process the blender ingredients until completely liquefied and pour into a medium saucepan. Place the saucepan over medium-low heat.

Begin sprinkling in the glucomannan powder while vigorously whisking the tofu and water mixture. As soon as the mixture begins to thicken, set the whisk aside and begin stirring with the spatula. As the mixture continues to thicken, whip with the spatula and continue to cook until a very stiff and lumpy mashed potato consistency is achieved. The mixture should be quite difficult to stir at this point. If using a non-stick saucepan, the mixture will pull away from the sides of the pan. This will take about 3 to 4 minutes.

Remove the saucepan from the heat and immediately transfer the mixture to the loaf pan with the spatula. The mixture will be very gooey and sticky. Pack the mixture into the pan and spread it as evenly as possible. Sprinkle the remaining paprika/bay mixture over the gel and press firmly into the gel with the flat side of the spatula.

Let the mixture cool for about 15 minutes and then refrigerate uncovered for a minimum of 1 hour.

Now, invert the loaf pan onto a work surface to release the gel from the loaf pan. You may have to wiggle the gel a bit around the edges with your fingers to work it loose before inverting.

With the tines of a fork, pull the gel into small chunks. Pulling with the fork will create texture. The gel will be soft, gooey and sticky at this stage - this is normal. Bring a large saucepan of lightly salted water to a rapid simmer, place the chunks of gel into the water and simmer for 5 minutes. Simmering will change the texture of the mock lobster chunks and cook them all the way through.

Remove the mock lobster chunks from the hot water with a spider or slotted spoon and place them on a plate lined with paper towels to drain. Store the chunks in a food storage bag in the refrigerator until ready to use. A safe guideline for refrigerator shelf life would be about 1 week. I have no experience with freezing this particular analogue.

To reheat the mock lobster, mist a non-stick skillet with cooking oil spray and place over medium-low heat. Toss the chunks in the skillet until heated through. Use the chunks in your favorite recipe as desired. The chunks can also be sautéed in non-dairy butter or margarine with a bit of minced garlic and white wine for flavor if desired.

*   *   *

Newburg Sauce

Newburg sauce is a rich cream sauce flavored with dry sherry or Madeira and hints of nutmeg and cayenne pepper. It's superb for tossing with sautéed morsels of mock lobster and serving over toast or toasted English muffin halves. For seafood Newberg, add 6 ounces of mock lobster to the sauce and stir in 6 oz flaked Tunada just before serving. The sauce is also heavenly with sautéed mushrooms. Or try serving it over egg-free scramble for breakfast or brunch. This recipe yields about 1 cup of sauce.

Ingredients

- ¼ cup non-dairy butter or margarine
- 1 T all-purpose flour or rice flour
- 2 tsp nutritional yeast flakes
- 2 T dry sherry or Madeira
- ¾ cup plain unsweetened non-dairy milk (soymilk or almond milk works best)
- ½ tsp fine sea salt or kosher salt
- pinch of ground nutmeg
- pinch of cayenne pepper
- 2 T chopped fresh parsley for garnish (optional)

Preparation

In a small saucepan, melt the butter or margarine over medium-low heat. Add the flour and nutritional yeast and whisk until smooth. Cook for about 2 minutes. Do not brown the butter (lower the heat slightly if necessary).

Add the wine and whisk until smooth. Cook an additional 2 minutes. Slowly incorporate the milk while whisking the mixture until smooth. Add the salt and nutmeg and cayenne and bring to a low simmer. Cook the sauce for a few minutes until thickened, stirring frequently.

Add small morsels of mock lobster or a combination of mock lobster and flaked tunada. Continue to cook until heated through. Serve over toast or split and toasted English muffins. Garnish with chopped fresh parsley if desired.

Mock Lobster Rolls

Ingredients

- 1 recipe (12 oz) mock lobster, chopped
- ¼ cup Quick Greek-Style Yogurt (pg. 206) or commercial plain non-dairy yogurt
- 2 T No-Eggy Mayo (pg. 202) or commercial egg-free mayonnaise
- 1 rib celery, finely diced
- 1 T chopped green onion
- 1 T finely diced red onion
- 1 T fresh chopped parsley
- sea salt or kosher salt and coarse ground black pepper, to taste
- 4 bratwurst or hoagie buns
- 1 T olive oil
- sweet paprika for garnish (optional)

Preparation

In a lightly oiled non-stick skillet, briefly sauté the mock lobster to remove excess moisture; refrigerate in a covered container until chilled.

If using commercial non-dairy yogurt, place it in a strainer lined with paper towel and set the strainer over a bowl. Let the yogurt drain and thicken for 20 minutes.

In a mixing bowl, stir together the thickened or Greek-style yogurt, mayonnaise, celery and green onion. Fold in the mock lobster meat and season with salt and pepper to taste. Chill until ready to use. Just before serving, open the hot dog buns and brush the inside with olive oil.

Heat a grill pan over moderately high heat and grill the bread, cut side down, until toasted, about 3 minutes. Fill each with the mock lobster salad, dust with paprika if desired and serve immediately.

Gravies, Sauces and Glazes

Savory Onion Gravy

Ingredients

- 2 T mild olive oil
- 2 medium onions, peeled, halved and then thinly sliced
- 1 tsp organic sugar
- 2 T non-dairy butter or margarine
- ¼ cup all-purpose flour or rice flour
- 2 cups porq simmering broth (pg. 106) or any seasoned vegetable broth
- 1 tsp dark balsamic vinegar
- sea salt or kosher salt and coarse ground black pepper, to taste

Preparation

Add the olive oil to a saucepan and place over medium heat. Add the onions, sugar and a pinch of salt; sauté until very tender and golden brown in color. Add the butter or margarine and stir until melted.

Sprinkle in the flour and stir until a thick paste forms (roux). Cook the mixture until the flour is golden and emits a nutty aroma, about 2 minutes. The flour will stick to the bottom of the saucepan, but don't worry, as it will release when the broth is incorporated.

Incorporate the broth in increments, stirring well after each addition. Add the balsamic vinegar and bring the mixture to a boil, stirring frequently. Reduce the heat and simmer, about 5 minutes.

Ladle half of the mixture into a blender and put the lid in place. For safety, cover the lid with a dish towel, hold down firmly and start the blender on low-speed, gradually increasing speed. Return the blended gravy to the saucepan and season with salt and pepper to taste. Keep warm over low heat until ready to serve.

━━━━━━━━━━━━━━━━━━━━━━━━━━━━━━━━━━━

Hearty Brown Gravy

Preparation

Add the olive oil to a small saucepan and place over medium heat. Add the butter or margarine and stir until melted.

Whisk in the flour to create a thick paste (roux) and cook until the flour is golden and emits a nutty aroma, about 2 minutes. The flour will stick to the bottom of the saucepan, but don't worry, as it will release when the broth is incorporated.

Ingredients

- 2 cups beaf simmering broth (pg. 78)
- 2 T olive oil
- 2 T non-dairy butter or margarine
- ¼ cup all-purpose flour or rice flour
- Browning Liquid (pg. 26) or commercial equivalent
- sea salt or kosher salt and coarse ground black pepper, to taste

Incorporate the broth in increments while vigorously stirring. Add small amounts of browning liquid as needed for depth of color. Bring to a simmer and continue to stir until the mixture thickens. Add salt and pepper to taste. Reduce heat to low until ready to serve; stir occasionally.

'Jus'

Jus (pronounced "zhoo") is French for juice and "au jus" literally means "with (its own) juice". In American cuisine, the term generally refers to the broth itself, which may be served with the food or placed on the side for dipping.

Ingredients

- 1 T olive oil
- 1 shallot, minced or 2 T minced red onion
- 1 T all-purpose flour or rice flour
- 2 T dry sherry, optional
- 3 cups beaf simmering broth (pg. 78)

Preparation

Add the olive oil to a medium saucepan and place over medium heat. Add the shallot or red onion and sauté until tender. Reduce the heat to low and whisk in the flour until a smooth paste forms (roux). Cook until the flour emits a nutty aroma, about 1 minute.

Incorporate the broth in increments while vigorously whisking the mixture until smooth. Add the optional sherry and bring the sauce to a brief boil, stirring frequently. Reduce the heat to low until ready to serve.

Golden Gravy

Preparation

Add the olive oil to a small saucepan and place over medium heat. Add the butter or margarine and stir until melted.

Whisk in the flour to create a thick paste (roux) and cook until the flour is golden and emits a nutty aroma, about 2 minutes. The flour will stick to the bottom of the saucepan, but don't worry, as it will release when the broth is incorporated.

Incorporate the broth in increments while vigorously stirring. Bring to a simmer and continue to stir until the mixture thickens. Add salt and pepper to taste. Reduce heat to low until ready to serve; stir occasionally.

Ingredients

- 2 cups chikun simmering broth (pg. 42) or similar
- 2 T mild vegetable oil
- 2 T non-dairy butter or margarine
- ¼ cup all-purpose flour or rice flour
- sea salt or kosher salt and coarse ground black pepper, to taste

Tip: For velvety smooth gravy, process the entire contents in the blender.

Country Mushroom Gravy

Ingredients

- 2 T olive oil
- 8 oz mushrooms of your choice, sliced or chopped
- 2 T non-dairy butter or margarine
- ¼ cup all-purpose flour or rice flour
- 1 and ½ cup chikun simmering broth (pg. 42) or similar
- ½ tsp dried thyme leaves
- ½ cup plain unsweetened non-dairy milk
- sea salt or kosher salt and coarse ground black pepper, to taste

Preparation

Add the olive oil to a large saucepan and place over medium heat. Add the mushrooms and sauté until the liquid has evaporated and the mushrooms begin to brown. Stir in the butter until melted.

Sprinkle in the flour and stir until a thick paste forms (roux). Cook the mixture until the flour is golden and emits a nutty aroma, about 2 minutes. The flour will stick to the bottom of the saucepan, but don't worry, as it will release when the broth is incorporated.

Incorporate the broth in increments, stirring well after each addition. Add the thyme and bring the mixture to a boil, stirring frequently. Reduce the heat and simmer, about 5 minutes.

Add the milk and return to a gentle simmer. Season the gravy with salt and pepper to taste. Keep warm over low heat until ready to serve.

Queso Nacho Sauce

As the name implies, this Mexican-style cheese sauce is perfect for topping nachos. This recipe yields about 2 cups of sauce.

Preparation

Whisk the ingredients together in a small saucepan until smooth. Place over medium-low heat and stir slowly and continually with a flexible spatula until the mixture becomes bubbly, thickened, smooth and glossy.

Please note that the golden color will develop as the cheese sauce cooks.

Taste and add salt as desired and/or additional soymilk to lighten the consistency to your preference. Reduce the heat to low to keep warm until ready to serve, stirring occasionally.

Ingredients

- 1 and ¾ cup organic plain unsweetened soymilk
- ¼ cup nutritional yeast flakes
- ¼ cup tapioca starch
- ¼ cup vegetable oil
- 1 T mellow white miso paste
- 2 tsp raw apple cider vinegar
- 1 tsp fine sea salt or kosher salt
- 1 tsp ancho chili powder
- ½ tsp onion powder
- ¼ tsp ground red pepper or cayenne pepper

Queso Blanco Sauce

(Mexican White Cheese Sauce)

This Mexican-style white cheese sauce is flavored with mild green chilies and is wonderful for dipping warm tortillas or tortilla chips, or for pouring over your favorite Mexican or Tex-Mex foods. This recipe yields about 2 cups of sauce.

Ingredients

- 1 and ¾ cup organic plain unsweetened soymilk
- ¼ cup vegetable oil
- 3 T tapioca starch
- 1 T nutritional yeast flakes
- 2 tsp raw apple cider vinegar
- 1 tsp ground cumin
- 1 tsp fine sea salt or kosher salt
- 1 can (4 oz) diced mild green chilies
- 2 T finely minced onion
- garnish: 1 to 2 T chopped fresh cilantro (optional)

Preparation

Add all ingredients except for the chilies, minced onion and cilantro to a small saucepan and whisk until smooth.

Stir in the chilies, minced onion and cilantro and place over medium-low heat. Stir slowly and continually with a flexible spatula until the mixture becomes bubbly, thickened and glossy. Taste and add salt as desired and/or additional soymilk to lighten the consistency to your preference.

Reduce the heat to low to keep warm until ready to serve, stirring occasionally.

Golden Cheddar Sauce

This velvety cheese sauce has a mild cheddar flavor that will please the entire family. It's ideal for topping hot meatless meat sandwiches or for preparing macaroni and cheese and cheesy rice. Try pouring over freshly steamed vegetables or baked potatoes too. This recipe yields about 2 cups of sauce.

Ingredients

- 1 and ¾ cup organic plain unsweetened soymilk
- 5 T tapioca starch
- ¼ cup mild vegetable oil
- ¼ cup nutritional yeast flakes
- 2 T mellow white miso paste
- 1 T tomato paste or 1 and ½ tsp tomato powder
- 2 tsp raw apple cider vinegar
- ¾ tsp fine sea salt or kosher salt, or more to taste
- ½ tsp dry ground mustard
- ½ tsp onion powder

Tip: For a tangier sauce, add ½ tsp lactic acid powder or 2 teaspoons fresh lemon juice.

Preparation

Whisk the ingredients together in a small saucepan until smooth.

Place over medium-low heat and stir slowly and continually with a flexible spatula until the mixture becomes bubbly, thickened, smooth and glossy. Please note that the golden color will develop as the cheese sauce cooks.

Taste the sauce and season with additional salt as desired. Reduce the heat to low to keep warm until ready to serve, stirring occasionally.

Beurre Blanc

Beurre Blanc, literally translated from French as "white butter", is an elegant, rich non-dairy butter sauce made with a reduction of vinegar, white wine and shallots into which cold, non-dairy butter is blended until emulsified. The lecithin found in non-dairy butter forms the oil-in-water emulsion. Although similar to Hollandaise sauce in concept, it is not considered one of the classic French mother sauces. Beurre Blanc is delicious served over pan-grilled meatless meats and cooked vegetables.

Ingredients

- ¼ cup dry white wine
- ¼ cup white wine vinegar
- 2 T minced shallot
- ⅓ cup organic plain unsweetened soymilk
- ⅛ tsp ground white pepper, or to taste
- 1 cup non-dairy butter or margarine, cut into tablespoon-size pieces and chilled
- sea salt or kosher salt, to taste

Preparation

Boil the wine, vinegar, and shallot in a 2-quart saucepan over medium heat until the mixture has reduced to 2 to 3 tablespoons, about 5 minutes.

Add the soymilk and white pepper and simmer 1 minute.

Reduce heat to medium-low and add a few tablespoons butter, whisking constantly. Add the remaining butter, a few pieces at a time, whisking constantly and adding new pieces before previous ones have completely liquefied. The sauce should maintain the consistency of Hollandaise sauce, so lift the saucepan from heat occasionally while incorporating the butter so the mixture doesn't get too hot.

Remove from the heat, season to taste with salt and additional white pepper and pour the sauce through a fine-mesh sieve to remove the shallot; serve immediately.

Chef's Best Marinara Sauce

Ingredients

- 2 T olive oil
- 1 medium onion, diced
- 3 cloves minced garlic
- 1 can (28 oz.) crushed tomatoes
  or 2 lbs vine-ripened tomatoes, peeled* and crushed
- ¼ cup dry white wine (e.g., Chardonnay, Sauvignon Blanc)
- 2 T tomato paste
- 1 T organic sugar
- 1 tsp sea salt or kosher salt
- 1 tsp dried basil or 1 T fresh basil, finely minced
- 1 tsp dried oregano or 1 T fresh oregano, finely minced
- ¼ tsp coarse ground black pepper, or more to taste

To peel fresh tomatoes, blanch them by immersing them in boiling water for 1 minute. Immediately immerse them in an ice-water bath. The skins should slip off easily. Pulse the tomatoes a few times in a food processor to crush.

Preparation

In a large saucepan, sauté the onions in olive oil over medium heat until translucent. Add the garlic and sauté an additional 2 minutes.

Add the crushed tomatoes, tomato paste, white wine, sugar, salt, herbs and pepper. The sugar is important, as it tempers the acidity of the tomatoes, so do not omit unless you are diabetic. Bring to a simmer, cover and reduce the heat to just above low. Cook for about 45 minutes and season with additional salt and pepper as desired. The marinara sauce is now ready to use as desired.

Chef's Best Alfredo Sauce

Alfredo sauce is a creamy and rich white sauce traditionally served over fettuccini. Dairy parmesan cheese is a primary ingredient in traditional Alfredo sauce; however, non-dairy parmesan won't provide the same texture and richness; therefore non-dairy parmesan is reserved for garnishing the final dish. It's very easy to prepare and achieves the ideal nappe consistency for serving over pasta with chikun, tunada, and/or cooked vegetables. This recipe yields about 2 and ¼ cups.

Ingredients

- 2 cups organic plain unsweetened soymilk
- 1.5 oz (about ⅓ cup) whole raw cashews (pre-soaking unnecessary)
- ¼ cup mild olive oil
- 1 T nutritional yeast flakes
- 1 T mellow white miso paste
- 1 and ½ tsp onion powder
- 1 tsp garlic powder
- ¾ tsp fine sea salt or kosher salt, or more to taste
- ¼ tsp ground white pepper
- 2 T chopped fresh parsley
- non-dairy parmesan for garnish

Preparation

Process all ingredients except for the parsley and parmesan in a blender on high speed for 2 full minutes. Strain through a fine mesh sieve into a saucepan and cook over medium-low heat, stirring slowly and continually, until the mixture just comes to a simmer. Reduce the heat to low to keep warm until ready to serve; stir occasionally. Garnish with the parmesan and fresh parsley when serving.

Hollandaise Sauce

Hollandaise sauce is one of the classic French "mother" sauces. This buttery, lemony sauce is remarkably similar in texture and flavor to its egg-based counterpart; but unlike its counterpart, the emulsion will not curdle or break. Hollandaise is excellent served over pan-grilled meatless meats and cooked vegetables. This recipe yields about 1 cup.

Ingredients

- 1 T nutritional yeast flakes
- 1 and ½ tsp unmodified potato starch or cornstarch
- ¼ tsp sodium alginate, guar gum or xanthan gum (available from ModernistPantry.com)
- ½ tsp sea salt or kosher salt
- ⅛ tsp cayenne pepper
- ⅛ tsp ground turmeric
- ¼ cup (2 oz) non-dairy butter or margarine
- ¾ cup organic plain unsweetened soymilk or homemade almond milk
- 4 tsp fresh lemon juice

Preparation

Combine the nutritional yeast, starch, alginate or gum, salt, cayenne pepper and turmeric in a small dish.

In a small saucepan, melt the butter or margarine over low heat. Whisk in the seasoning blend and stir until smooth.

Whisk in the milk. Increase the heat to medium-low and cook, stirring frequently until the sauce comes to a low simmer. Do not boil! Whisk in the lemon juice and reduce the heat to low to keep warm until ready to serve, stirring occasionally.

Béarnaise Sauce

Tarragon and white wine adds a flavorful note to this elegant sauce. It's delicious served over pan-grilled meatless meats and cooked vegetables. This recipe yields about 1 and ¼ cup.

Ingredients

- 1 T nutritional yeast flakes
- 1 and ½ tsp unmodified potato starch or cornstarch
- ½ tsp fine sea salt or kosher salt
- ¼ tsp coarse ground black pepper
- ¼ tsp sodium alginate, guar gum or xanthan gum (available from ModernistPantry.com)
- ⅛ tsp sweet paprika
- ⅛ tsp ground turmeric
- 2 T minced shallot or red onion
- 2 tsp minced fresh tarragon or ¾ tsp dried
- ¼ cup dry white wine (e.g., Chardonnay, Sauvignon Blanc)
- 2 tsp white wine vinegar
- ¼ cup (4 T) non-dairy butter or margarine
- ¾ cup organic plain unsweetened soymilk

Preparation

Combine the nutritional yeast, starch, salt, pepper, alginate or gum, salt, paprika and turmeric in a small dish.

In a small saucepan over medium-low heat, simmer the shallot or red onion and the tarragon in the wine and vinegar until the wine is reduced by half, about 3 to 4 minutes. Reduce the heat to low. Add the butter or margarine and stir until melted. Whisk in the seasoning blend and stir until smooth.

Whisk in the milk. Increase the heat to medium and bring to a simmer. Stir continually until the sauce thickens. Reduce the heat to low to keep warm until ready to serve. Taste and add additional salt and pepper as desired. Stir occasionally.

Tartar Sauce

A classic condiment sauce for fried Clamz, breaded Jackfysh filets and battered Tofysh filets.

Ingredients

- ½ cup No-Eggy Mayo (pg. 202)
- 2 T finely diced cucumber dill pickle or prepared relish
- 1 T fresh lemon juice
- 1 T finely minced sweet onion
- ½ tsp Dijon mustard or coarse-grain mustard
- coarse sea salt or kosher salt, to taste
- coarse ground black pepper, to taste

Preparation

Whisk all ingredients together and chill to blend flavors for a minimum of 1 hour before using.

Creamy Horseradish Sauce

A classic sauce for beaf. This recipe yields about 1 cup.

Ingredients

- ¾ cup No-Eggy Mayo (pg. 202) or commercial egg-free mayonnaise
- ¼ cup Quick Sour Cream (pg. 204) or commercial non-dairy equivalent
- 2 T fresh lemon juice (about 1 lemon)
- 2 T prepared horseradish (not creamed), or more to taste
- sea salt or kosher salt, to taste

Preparation

Whisk together the ingredients in a small bowl until smooth and creamy. Transfer to a sealable container and refrigerate to blend the flavors and use within 1 week.

Chef's tip: To optimize the juice you get from a lemon or lime, roll it firmly under your palm on a work surface for a minute before juicing.

Chimichurri Sauce

(Chef's Favorite)

Chimichurri is an aromatic herb sauce that originated in Argentina and is traditionally used for grilled meat. In vegan gastronomy, it can be used as a sauce for a wide variety of meat alternatives such as grilled seitan, tofu, tempeh, portabella mushrooms or cauliflower "steak". It's also wonderful as a dip for crusty bread or for marinating cooked beans.

Ingredients

- ¼ cup water
- ¼ cup white wine vinegar or champagne vinegar
- 2 T red wine vinegar
- 2 cups chopped flat leaf parsley, loosely packed
- ½ cup roasted red pepper, skin removed plus additional for garnish if desired
- ¼ cup fresh chopped oregano, loosely packed or 4 tsp dried oregano
- 1 shallot, chopped
- 2 cloves garlic, chopped
- 1 tsp minced habanero or jalapeno pepper
- 1 tsp sea salt or kosher salt
- 1 tsp sweet paprika
- ¼ tsp ground cumin
- ½ cup extra-virgin olive oil

Preparation

Process all ingredients in a food processor but leave little bit of texture. Add salt as needed to taste. Store the sauce in an airtight container in the refrigerator until ready to use; shake well to re-emulsify before using.

Chef's Best BBQ Sauce

Rich, thick and tangy, this sauce is wonderful for brushing on meatless meats when grilling or broiling. This recipe yields about 2 cups.

Preparation

Melt the butter or margarine in a small saucepan over medium-low heat and sauté the garlic for 1 minute.

Whisk in the remaining ingredients and bring the mixture to a simmer. Reduce heat to low and cook uncovered, stirring occasionally, for about 1 hour until the sauce is thickened. Let cool and refrigerate to further thicken before using.

Jack D's BBQ Sauce Variation

Follow the recipe for the sauce but replace the water with a good quality whiskey or bourbon.

Ingredients

- ¼ cup non-dairy butter or margarine
- 6 cloves garlic, minced (2 T)
- 1 can (6 oz) tomato paste
- ½ cup dark brown sugar
- ½ cup water
- ¼ cup raw apple cider vinegar
- 1 T dried minced onion
- 1 T Worcestershire Sauce (pg. 25) or commercial vegan equivalent
- 1 T hickory liquid smoke
- 1 tsp fine sea salt or kosher salt
- 1 tsp prepared Dijon or spicy mustard
- ½ tsp hot red pepper sauce, or more to taste

Barbacoa Sauce

Barbacoa is a spicy Tex-Mex barbecue sauce that is superb when tossed with chunks or shreds of Stewing Beaf and served with tortillas, pico de gallo and guacamole. This recipe yields about 2 cups.

Ingredients

- 2 cups beef simmering broth (pg. 78)
- ¼ cup apple cider vinegar
- ¼ cup fresh lime juice
- 1 can (7 oz) chipotle peppers in adobo sauce (this ingredient packs a fiery heat, so reduce the amount for a milder sauce)
- 8 cloves garlic
- 1 T ground cumin
- 2 tsp dried oregano
- ½ tsp ground cloves
- sea salt or kosher salt, to taste

Preparation

Process all ingredients in a blender until smooth. Transfer the mixture to a medium saucepan and bring to a gentle simmer.

Cook uncovered for 45 minutes to reduce the mixture to about 2 cups before using.

Tamari Ginger Satay Dipping Sauce

This flavorful blend of ingredients makes a wonderful dipping sauce for beaf or chikun satay.

Ingredients

- 2 tsp cornstarch or arrowroot powder
- 2 T dark brown sugar
- ¼ cup tamari, soy sauce or Bragg Liquid Aminos™
- ¾ cup water
- 1 T fresh lime juice
- 2 tsp fresh grated ginger root
- 1 clove garlic, minced
- 2 T chopped green onions

Preparation

Create a slurry by mixing the starch with 1 tablespoon of water in a small dish until dissolved; set aside.

Combine the sugar, tamari and water in a small saucepan. Bring to a boil. Stir in the starch mixture. Reduce the heat to a simmer and add the garlic, ginger, lime juice and green onions. Continue to simmer, stirring frequently, for about 2 minutes to blend the flavors. Serve warm or cold.

——————————=)( )(=——————————

Spicy Indonesian Peanut Satay Sauce

Serve with satay, fried tofu, satay, Asian noodles or Asian greens.

Ingredients

- 2 T olive oil
- 3 scallions, chopped
- 3 cloves garlic, minced
- 1 T fresh grated ginger root
- 1 cup water
- 1 cup natural creamy or chunky peanut butter
- 2 T fresh lime juice
- 2 T tamari, soy sauce or Bragg Liquid Aminos™
- 2 T rice vinegar
- 1 T dark brown sugar
- 1 tsp Thai red chili paste, or more to taste

Preparation

Add the oil to a small saucepan and place over medium heat.

Sauté the scallions, garlic and ginger, stirring until fragrant, about 1 minute.

Stir in the remaining ingredients and bring to a simmer, stirring often until the mixture is smooth. Thin the consistency with small amounts of water as necessary.

Stir Fry Sauce

A sweet and moderately spicy stir fry sauce.

Ingredients

- 3 T tamari, soy sauce or Bragg Liquid Aminos™
- 2 T mirin (Japanese sweet rice wine)
- 1 T chili garlic sauce
- 1 T organic sugar or natural sweetener of your choice
- 2 tsp fresh grated ginger
- 2 tsp toasted sesame oil

Preparation

Whisk together the ingredients in a small bowl. Just before the stir fry is ready to serve, swirl the sauce around the sides of the wok and toss to glaze the meatless meat, vegetables and rice or noodles.

Hoisin Sauce

Hoisin is a thick, aromatic condiment sauce with a salty and sweet flavor. It is commonly used in Chinese cuisine. Use it as a grilling glaze for meat analogues; as an addition to stir fries; or as dipping sauce (try it with spring rolls). It is also used as a condiment for phở, the classic Vietnamese soup. My homemade variation contains no added sugar, starch, gums, starches, colors or preservatives, unlike most of its commercial counterparts, since the fruit naturally sweetens and thickens the sauce.

Ingredients

- 1 cup dark seedless raisins
- ⅔ cup water
- ⅓ cup tamari, soy sauce or Bragg Liquid Aminos™
- 2 T rice vinegar
- 1 clove garlic, chopped
- 2 tsp sesame oil
- ¼ tsp crushed red pepper
- ¼ tsp Chinese Five Spice powder

Preparation

Add all ingredients to a small saucepan and bring to brief boil. Remove from the heat and let the mixture cool. Add the mixture to a blender and process until smooth, about 1 minute. Press through a fine mesh sieve into the same saucepan to catch any stray particles. Transfer to a sealable container and store in the refrigerator until ready to use; the sauce will thicken as it chills. Due to its salt and vinegar content, the sauce should remain preserved and fresh for several weeks. This recipe yields about 1 and ½ cup.

Island Teriyaki Sauce and Glaze

This classic Asian and Pacific island-style sauce and glaze is superb for brushing on meatless meats when grilling or broiling. An Island Fire sauce variation is included. This recipe yields about 1 and ¼ cup.

Ingredients

- 2 tsp cornstarch, unmodified potato starch or arrowroot powder
- 1 T cooking oil
- 3 cloves garlic, minced
- 2 tsp fresh grated ginger root
- ⅔ cup unsweetened pineapple juice
- ⅓ cup light brown sugar
- ⅓ cup tamari, soy sauce or Bragg Liquid Aminos™

Preparation

In a small dish, dissolve the starch in 1 tablespoon of water to create a slurry and set aside. Heat the cooking oil in a small saucepan over medium-low heat. Don't get the oil too hot. Add the garlic and ginger to the pan and cook for 30 seconds.

Quickly add the pineapple juice before the garlic scorches. Add the starch slurry, brown sugar and tamari. Whisk well to combine. Increase the heat to medium and simmer the sauce, stirring constantly, for 2 to 3 minutes. Remove from the heat and set aside. The mixture will thicken into a syrupy glaze as it cools.

Island Fire Teriyaki Sauce and Glaze Variation

Follow the recipe for the glaze and stir 1 to 2 tablespoons Sriracha™ into the sauce while cooking.

Char Siu Glaze

This is my own recipe for creating an aromatic and delicious char siu glaze for Chinese-style spare ribz. Technically, char siu, which literally means "fork burn or roast" (char being "fork" and siu being "burn or roast"), refers to the traditional cooking method, rather than referring to the glaze itself. This recipe yields about 1 cup of glaze.

Ingredients

- ½ cup light brown sugar
- ¼ cup water
- ¼ cup tamari, soy sauce or Bragg Liquid Aminos™
- ¼ cup mirin (Japanese sweet rice wine)
- ¼ cup rice vinegar
- 1 T sesame oil
- 2 tsp fresh grated ginger
- 1 tsp onion powder
- 1 tsp garlic powder
- 1 tsp Chinese Five Spice Powder
- 1 tsp Sriracha™ or red pepper sauce, or more to taste
- 1 T beet powder or 1 small shredded beet

Preparation

Stir all ingredients together in a small saucepan, except for the beet powder or shredded beet, and bring to a gentle simmer. Cook uncovered for 20 minutes and remove from the heat. Let cool for 10 minutes and then stir in the beet powder or shredded beet and allow cooling for an additional 20 minutes. The mixture will thicken into a syrupy glaze as it cools.

Store the glaze in a sealable container in the refrigerator until ready to use. If shredded beet was used, strain the mixture into the container, using the back of a spoon to press and extract as much glaze as possible.

Brush the ribz generously with the glaze when grilling.

———————◦( )◦———————

Condiments

No-Eggy Mayo

This is my signature recipe for producing an egg-free mayonnaise that rivals real egg mayonnaise in both taste and texture. It's also much less expensive than commercial egg-free mayonnaise. The ingredients are readily available in most markets and an immersion blender or food processor makes this a nearly foolproof method of preparation.

The advantage of using a food processor is that the machine does most of the work for you. The advantage of using an immersion blender is that the mayonnaise will be thicker, yet requires less oil. The disadvantage of the immersion blender is that your hand and arm may become tired from controlling the blender. The immersion blender method also requires a little dexterity to manage blending with one hand and pouring the oil with the other hand.

I have personally used both methods many times and now favor the immersion blender method for producing the best quality mayonnaise. A standard blender is not recommended for preparing mayonnaise because once the mixture thickens, it's nearly impossible to keep it turning in the blades while adding the oil.

Sunflower, safflower, grapeseed, canola and soybean oil are the best oils for preparing this mayonnaise. Extra-virgin or virgin olive oil will add a bitter undertaste to the mayonnaise. If you wish to include olive oil, reduce the carrier oil by ½ cup and mix ½ cup olive oil into the carrier oil.

This is my own signature recipe and yields 2 cups of the finest egg-free mayonnaise.

Note: The recipe can be reduced by half for a 1 cup portion, but an immersion blender is required for preparation. The reduced amount of soymilk and oil will not provide sufficient volume for the food processor to blend and emulsify the mixture properly.

Ingredients

- ½ cup organic plain unsweetened soymilk, chilled
  (sorry, no substitutions; other plant milks will not emulsify properly)
- 1 T plus 1 tsp fresh lemon juice
- 1 tsp raw apple cider vinegar
- 2 tsp organic sugar
- 1 tsp dry ground mustard*
- ¾ to 1 tsp fine sea salt or kosher salt
- ¼ ground white pepper
- pinch of sweet paprika or cayenne pepper
- optional: pinch of kala namak (imparts an egg mayonnaise flavor)
- 1 and ½ cup vegetable oil if using an immersion blender; or
  1 and ¾ cup vegetable oil if using a food processor

*Do not omit this ingredient! Dry ground mustard not only adds flavor but is a natural emulsifier due to its high content of mucilage which coats the droplets of oil, and is therefore essential to the success of this recipe.

Preparation

Measure the oil into a liquid measuring cup (ideally it should have a "lip" for pouring). Set aside.

Immersion Blender Method

Place all of the ingredients EXCEPT for the oil into a 4-cup glass measuring cup or heavy glass/ceramic bowl. Insert the immersion blender and process the mixture for about 10 seconds.

Now with the immersion blender running on high speed, SLOWLY drizzle the oil into the blending cup or bowl. Move the blender up and down and side to side as you add the oil (you can stop blending to give your arm a rest as long as you stop pouring the oil; then resume when you're ready). Continue blending until all the oil is incorporated and the mixture is emulsified and very thick. Transfer to a glass jar or plastic container and refrigerate.

Note: Because immersion blenders are so efficient at high speed blending, adding the oil all at once may be tempting when using this method and it may produce an acceptable mayonnaise. However, it won't cut down on the blending time and the mayo will not have the same "fluffy" texture or stability as it would when incorporating the oil gradually or in increments. We're not seeking acceptable results here, we're seeking exceptional results. Please note that adding the oil all at once will definitely not work when using the food processor method described below.

Food Processor Method

Place all of the ingredients except for the oil into a food processor and process the mixture for about 10 seconds.

Turn the food processor on continuous run (if you have speed settings, run on high speed) and SLOWLY begin to drizzle the oil into the mixture through the food chute. The addition of the oil will take about 2 minutes, so be patient and don't rush. You should begin to note a change in the consistency of the mixture after about 1 and ¼ cup of oil has been added. Continue to slowly add the remainder of the oil. As soon as all of the oil has been incorporated, turn the processor off - the mayonnaise is finished. Transfer to a glass jar or plastic container and refrigerate.

Note: I cannot emphasize enough the importance of adding the oil slowly. If you add it too fast, the emulsion may break and revert back to a liquid.

Quick Sour Cream

Tofu-based sour cream has never appealed to me because of the chalky undertaste; and uncultured cashew-based sour cream doesn't work for me either because the natural sweetness of the cashews yields a product that is much too sweet for my liking (although it works in dessert applications). Cultured cashew-based sour cream, on the other hand, has a very accurate dairy sour cream flavor because the lacto-bacterial culture converts the natural sugar in the cashews into lactic acid, thus providing the authentic tanginess and eliminating the excessively sweet taste. However, preparing rejuvelac and culturing the cream takes several days and sometimes a quick alternative is appreciated.

It took some experimentation to achieve a texture and flavor that satisfied my taste, but I think this quick version makes an excellent alternative to its cultured counterpart. Please note that there is no alternative to using soymilk or lactic acid in this recipe. Thickening is dependent upon the curdling action of soymilk when lactic acid is introduced. Other plant milks will not react to the acid in the same manner. This recipe yields about 1 and ¾ cup sour cream.

Ingredients

- ¼ cup organic refined coconut oil (NOT virgin coconut oil)
- ½ cup (2.5 oz.) whole raw cashews (pre-soaking is not necessary)
- 1 and ¼ cup organic plain unsweetened soymilk (sorry, no substitutions)
- ¼ tsp fine sea salt or kosher salt
- 1 and ½ tsp lactic acid powder (available from ModernistPantry.com; sorry, no substitutions)

Preparation

Remove the lid from the coconut oil and place the jar or bottle into a microwave. Heat until melted (about 30 seconds to 1 minute depending upon the solidity of the coconut oil); avoid overheating the oil. Alternately, place the jar or bottle into a container filled with near boiling water and let stand until the oil melts. Measure the coconut oil and set aside.

Measure the lactic acid and set aside in a small dish.

Add the cashews, soymilk and salt to a high-powered blender, cover and process for 2 full minutes.

Remove the lid plug and with the blender running on high speed, add the coconut oil.

Reduce the speed to low and add the lactic acid powder. The cream will thicken instantly - turn the blender off. Do not continue to process once thickened.

Transfer the sour cream to an airtight container, seal and refrigerate until thoroughly chilled and thickened. Consume within 10 days of preparation.

Quick Crème Fraîche

Quick Crème Fraîche is an uncultured, soy-based soured cream with a lighter viscosity than American-style sour cream. It's quick and easy to prepare and naturally thickens on its own without added food starches, gums or gels.

Various chopped fresh herbs can be stirred in prior to serving if desired, to accommodate various ethnic cuisines (cilantro Crème Fraîche, for example, is an excellent topping for Tex-Mex Cuisine).This recipe yields about 1 cup.

Ingredients

- ¾ cup organic plain unsweetened soymilk (sorry, no substitutions)
- ¼ cup organic refined coconut oil (NOT virgin coconut oil)
- ⅛ tsp fine sea salt or kosher salt
- ¾ tsp lactic acid powder (available from ModernistPantry.com; sorry, no substitutions)

Preparation

Remove the lid from the coconut oil and place the jar or bottle into a microwave. Heat until melted (about 30 seconds to 1 minute depending upon the solidity of the coconut oil); avoid overheating the oil. Alternately, place the jar or bottle into a container filled with near boiling water and let stand until the oil melts. Measure the coconut oil and set aside.

Measure the lactic acid and set aside in a small dish.

Add the soymilk and salt to a high-powered blender and begin processing on high speed. Remove the lid insert and add the coconut oil.

Reduce the speed to low and add the lactic acid powder. The cream will thicken instantly - turn the blender off. Do not continue to process once thickened.

Transfer the Crème Fraîche to an airtight container, seal and refrigerate until thoroughly chilled and thickened. Consume within 10 days of preparation.

Quick Greek-Style Yogurt

(uncultured)

Non-dairy yogurt preparation typically involves introducing specific strains of lactobacillus bacteria into non-dairy milk. The yogurt culture then produces lactic acid which in turn thickens and acidifies the milk, thus creating the tangy yogurt. With this recipe and technique, the culturing step is bypassed and commercial lactic acid is added directly to the milk mixture, which creates a thick and tangy uncultured yogurt. While it lacks the probiotic benefits of cultured yogurt, Quick Greek-Style Yogurt offers convenience for culinary applications. No substitutions can be made for any ingredient in this recipe since each ingredient serves a specific function. This recipe yields about 2 and ¼ cup; should more be needed, simply double the recipe.

Ingredients

- 1.5 oz (about ⅓ cup) whole raw cashews (sorry, no substitutions)
- 2 cups organic plain unsweetened soymilk (sorry, no substitutions)
- 2 and ½ tsp lactic acid powder (available from Modernist Pantry.com; sorry, no substitutions)

Preparation

Rinse the cashews to remove any debris, drain and place them into a blender (they do not require pre-soaking). Add the soymilk and process for 2 full minutes.

Pour the mixture through a fine strainer into a small saucepan. This will capture any minute particles; a nut milk bag is not required.

Place the saucepan over medium-low heat. Stir slowly and continually until the mixture is hot and slightly thickened (just before coming to a simmer). Do not let the mixture boil. Remove the saucepan from the heat to cool for 30 minutes. Stir occasionally while cooling to discourage lumps from forming in the mixture and a "skin" from forming on the surface.

Whisk in the lactic acid powder until blended (the mixture will thicken instantly). Transfer to a sealable container and refrigerate until thoroughly chilled. Stir vigorously until smooth before using.

Greek Tzatziki

Greek Tzatziki is a cucumber sauce used as a condiment for Greek and other Mediterranean cuisine. This recipe is my own variation and yields about 2 and ½ cups.

Ingredients

- 1 English cucumber, peeled, split lengthwise and seeds removed
- 2 cups Quick Greek-Style Yogurt (pg. 206)
- 2 T extra-virgin olive oil
- 2 T minced sweet yellow onion
- 2 cloves minced garlic (2 tsp)
- 1 T red wine vinegar or raw apple cider vinegar
- 1 tsp fine sea salt or kosher salt, or more to taste
- ½ tsp coarse ground black pepper, or more to taste
- 2 tsp minced fresh dill

Preparation

Grate the cucumber on the largest holes of a box grater. Place the grated cucumber into a fine sieve and gently press with the back of a spoon to remove the excess water. Set aside.

In a bowl, whisk the olive oil into the yogurt until emulsified. Stir in the cucumber and remaining ingredients and season with additional salt and pepper to taste. Chill for a minimum of two hours to blend the flavors before serving.

Indian Raita

Raita is an Indian, Pakistani and Bangladeshi condiment used to temper the heat of Indian spices. This recipe is my own variation and yields about 2 and ½ cups.

Ingredients

- 1 English cucumber, peeled, split lengthwise and seeds removed
- 2 cups Quick Greek-Style Yogurt (pg. 206)
- 2 T minced green onion, including the green top
- 1 T fresh lemon juice
- 1 tsp fine sea salt or kosher salt, or more to taste
- ¾ tsp ground cumin
- ¼ tsp ground coriander
- 2 T chopped fresh mint

Preparation

Grate the cucumber on the largest holes of a box grater. Place the grated cucumber into a fine sieve, gently press with the back of a spoon to remove the excess water and then transfer to a bowl.

Add the remaining ingredients and stir until blended; season with additional salt as desired. Chill for a minimum of two hours to blend the flavors before serving.

Hari Chutney

(Cilantro Mint)

This bright green, tangy and refreshing Indian chutney is my absolute favorite condiment. Enjoy it with all plant-based Indian cuisine and as a spread or dip for samosa (deep-fried or baked pastry with savory filling), pakoras (Indian vegetable fritters), naan, papadum, roti and any and all other flatbreads and crackers. If you have a timid palate, start with ½ of the green chile and increase according to taste.

Try mixing the chutney with plain non-dairy yogurt for a uniquely different salad dressing. It also adds wonderful flavor to non-dairy Crème Fraîche, sour cream and even egg-free mayonnaise. The chutney will last about 1 week stored in the refrigerator; simply freeze any unused portion (try freezing in silicone molds or ice cube trays for easy use). This recipe yields about 1 and ¾ cup.

Chef's note: Cilantro is the predominant ingredient in this chutney and is essential to the flavor. If you're not a fan of cilantro, it's best to avoid this condiment since parsley or other herbs are not suitable substitutes for this particular recipe.

Ingredients

- 2 large bunches of cilantro (excess stems at bottom removed)
- 1 large handful of mint leaves (stems removed)
- 1 medium yellow onion, peeled and chopped
- 1 small green chile, seeded and chopped (or a large chile if you can take the heat)
- 1 clove garlic, peeled
- 2 T fresh lemon juice
- 1 tsp cumin seeds
- ¾ tsp sea salt or kosher salt, or more to taste

Preparation

Process all ingredients in a blender until smooth; season with additional salt to taste. Store the chutney in an airtight container in the refrigerator for up to 1 week.

Gourmet Dijon Mustard

A classic, zesty Dijon-style mustard flavored with white wine and my own special blend of seasonings. This recipe yields about 1 and ½ cup of prepared mustard.

Preparation

Place the shallot, garlic, bay leaf and tarragon in a small saucepan. Add the white wine and vinegar. Bring to a brief boil, cover and remove from the heat to cool to room temperature. Strain the infusion into a container and discard the solids. Transfer the infusion back to the saucepan and place over low heat.

Whisk the mustard powder, sugar and salt into the infusion and cook, stirring frequently until thickened, about 5 minutes. Avoid the fumes; they are powerful!

Ingredients

- 1 shallot, peeled and chopped
- 2 cloves garlic, crushed
- 1 bay leaf
- 1 tsp dried tarragon
- 1 cup dry white wine, preferably Chardonnay
- 2 T champagne vinegar or white wine vinegar
- ½ cup dry ground mustard
- 1 T organic sugar
- 1 tsp fine sea salt or kosher salt

Remove the saucepan from the heat, cover and let the mixture cool. The mixture will continue to thicken to the ideal consistency as it cools.

Transfer the prepared mustard to a sealable container and refrigerate. Once chilled, it can be used immediately, although the flavor will be rather pungent. Aging anywhere from 1 to 8 weeks will mellow the mustard. The flavor will continue to improve over time. Use within 6 months.

—————————————)( )(—————————————

Gourmet Ketchup

This recipe yields about 2 cups of thick and tangy, premium quality ketchup.

Preparation

Whisk all ingredients together in a small saucepan and bring to brief boil while stirring constantly. Reduce the heat to medium-low and cook uncovered for 30 minutes, stirring frequently.

Remove the saucepan from the heat and let the ketchup cool before transferring to a storage container with a lid. Stir occasionally as it cools. Cover and chill for at least 2 hours for the flavors to develop before using.

Ingredients

- 1 can (15 oz) tomato sauce
- 6 T tomato paste
- 1 cup light brown sugar
- ½ cup white wine vinegar or raw apple cider vinegar
- 2 tsp fine sea salt or kosher salt, or more to taste
- 1 tsp onion powder
- ½ tsp garlic powder
- ¼ tsp ground white pepper

Sweet and Smoky Tomato Jam

Although many people consider tomatoes to be a vegetable, they're actually a fruit; so why not make them into jam? Actually, tomato jam is more like a relish than a true jam. My partner Chef Mike and I created this blend one Sunday afternoon and we were thrilled with the lovely balance of sweet, tangy and smoky flavors. This jam is wonderful when used as an alternative to ketchup on veggie burgers and hot dogs. It's also excellent when served with cheese, such as non-dairy cream cheese on bagels or toast, or non-dairy chèvre on crostini or crackers. This recipe yields about 2 cups.

Preparation

Drain the excess liquid from the can of tomatoes and place the tomatoes into a food processor; do not process yet. If using fresh tomatoes, bring a large volume of water to a boil.

Core the tomatoes and place them into the boiling water for 1 minute. Immediately plunge them into an ice water bath. Once cooled, the skins should slip off easily. Place the tomatoes into the food processor; do not process yet.

In a medium saucepan, sweat the onion and garlic in the olive oil over medium-low heat, stirring occasionally.

Ingredients

- 1 can (28 oz) whole peeled plum tomatoes or 1 and ½ lb fresh plum tomatoes
- 1 T olive oil
- ½ cup diced sweet yellow onion
- 3 cloves garlic, minced
- ½ cup organic sugar
- ¼ cup sherry vinegar
- 2 T tomato paste
- 2 tsp smoked paprika
- 1 tsp fine sea salt or kosher salt
- ½ tsp ground white pepper

The goal is to soften and draw out the flavor of the onion and garlic without browning. When the onion becomes translucent, transfer the mixture to the food processor with the tomatoes and pulse a few times into a "salsa-like" consistency.

Transfer the tomato mixture back to the saucepan and stir in the remaining ingredients. Bring the mixture to a boil, reduce the heat to a gentle simmer and cook uncovered for 1 hour and 15 minutes, stirring occasionally. Let the jam cool and transfer to a sealable container. Refrigerate until well-chilled before serving. Keep in mind that this is a fresh jam, not a preserved jam, but the acidity and sugar will keep it fresh in the refrigerator for a few weeks.

———————————————<( )>———————————————

Cheese Melts Introduction

As the name implies, the cheese melts have the consistency of, well... melted cheese. Cheese melts are ideal for spreading on sandwiches before grilling, or for layering or stirring into any recipe where a uniformly melted cheese is desired, such as in mashed potatoes or casseroles (uniform melting is a common problem with many commercial non-dairy cheeses).

The cheese melts were formulated using organic plain unsweetened soymilk, therefore organic plain unsweetened soymilk is recommended for achieving the proper consistency and stability. If you choose to use commercial soymilk with additives or other non-dairy milks, expect variations in results. A small amount of food gum is added to increase viscosity and impart a slight stretch to the melt.

The melts can be prepared and used immediately for sandwiches or in recipes, or refrigerated for later use, which makes them very convenient. Any unused portions should be refrigerated in a food storage container with a lid. When chilled, the cheese melts become very thick and sticky but will re-melt instantly when heated.

>( )<

Colby Melt

Colby is a mellow, golden cheese which can best be described as having a very mild cheddar flavor. This recipe yields about 1 cup of melted cheese.

Ingredients

- ¾ cup organic plain unsweetened soymilk
- ¼ cup mild vegetable oil
- 3 T tapioca starch
- 2 T nutritional yeast flakes
- 1 T mellow white miso paste
- 1 T tomato paste or 1 and ½ tsp tomato powder
- ¼ tsp dry ground mustard
- ¼ tsp onion powder
- ¼ tsp fine sea salt or kosher salt
- ¼ tsp guar gum or xanthan gum

Preparation

In a small saucepan, vigorously whisk together the ingredients until smooth (a blender can also be used to efficiently combine the ingredients). Cook the mixture over medium-low heat, stirring slowly and continually with a flexible spatula. The golden color will develop as the mixture cooks.

As the mixture thickens and curdles (forms lumps), begin stirring vigorously until the curds disappear and the cheese becomes very thick, smooth and glossy. Keep warm over low heat, stirring occasionally, until ready to use. For a spreadable consistency, remove from the heat and allow the melt to thicken.

Jarlsberg Melt

Jarlsberg shares flavor similarities with Swiss cheese and can best be described as mild, buttery and nutty with a hint of sweetness. Do not omit the ground coriander, even though only a small amount is needed, as it is essential to the flavor of this melt. This recipe yields about 1 cup of melted cheese.

Ingredients

- ¾ cup organic plain unsweetened soymilk
- ¼ cup mild vegetable oil
- 3 T tapioca starch
- 1 T nutritional yeast flakes
- 1 T dry sherry or dry white wine*
- 2 tsp mellow white miso paste
- ½ T (1 and ½ tsp) sesame tahini
- ¼ tsp fine sea salt or kosher salt
- ⅛ tsp ground coriander
- ¼ tsp guar gum or xanthan gum

The sherry or wine can be omitted for health or ethical reasons, but this will alter the flavor profile.

Preparation

In a small saucepan, vigorously whisk together the ingredients until smooth (a blender can also be used to efficiently combine the ingredients). Cook the mixture over medium-low heat, stirring slowly and continually with a flexible spatula. The golden color will develop as the mixture cooks.

As the mixture thickens and curdles (forms lumps), begin stirring vigorously until the curds disappear and the cheese becomes very thick, smooth and glossy. Keep warm over low heat, stirring occasionally, until ready to use. For a spreadable consistency, remove from the heat and allow the melt to thicken.

Tangy Cheddar Melt

Tangy Cheddar Melt has a sharp bite which makes it a lively alternative to the milder Colby. This recipe yields about 1 cup of melted cheese.

Ingredients

- ¾ cup organic plain unsweetened soymilk
- ¼ cup mild vegetable oil
- 3 T tapioca starch
- 2 T nutritional yeast flakes
- 1 T mellow white miso paste
- 1 tsp tomato paste or ½ tsp tomato powder
- ½ T (1 and ½ tsp) raw apple cider vinegar
- ½ tsp onion powder
- ½ tsp lactic acid powder (available from ModernistPantry.com)
  or 2 tsp fresh lemon juice
- ¼ tsp dry ground mustard
- ¼ tsp guar gum or xanthan gum

Preparation

In a small saucepan, vigorously whisk together the ingredients until smooth (a blender can also be used to efficiently combine the ingredients). Cook the mixture over medium-low heat, stirring slowly and continually with a flexible spatula. The pale golden color will develop as the mixture cooks.

As the mixture thickens and curdles (forms lumps), begin stirring vigorously until the curds disappear and the cheese becomes very thick, smooth and glossy. Keep warm over low heat, stirring occasionally, until ready to use. For a spreadable consistency, remove from the heat and allow the melt to thicken.

For tangy, melted white cheddar, omit the tomato paste or powder.

Recipe Index

Printed in Great Britain
by Amazon